ENCYCLOPEDIA OF
DOGS

ENCYCLOPEDIA OF
DOGS

David Alderton

Bath · New York · Singapore · Hong Kong · Cologne · Delhi · Melbourne

First published by Parragon in 2008

Parragon
Queen Street House
4 Queen Street
Bath BA1 1HE, UK

Created and produced by

studio cactus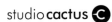

13 SOUTHGATE STREET WINCHESTER HAMPSHIRE SO23 9DZ

DESIGN Laura Watson, Sharon Rudd
EDITORIAL Jennifer Close

ISBN: 978-1-4075-2438-2

Printed in China

CONTENTS

ABOUT THIS BOOK

There is no universal system of breed classification for dogs but, generally, they are divided on the basis of their original function. Some categories such as the hound group are more natural than others, which may simply consist of breeds with diverse working ancestries. Not all breeds are recognized for show purposes, and recognition can vary between different organizations and countries.

BREED RECOGNITION
The divisions used in this book are linked to those employed by kennel clubs around the world, with acceptance by the U.K.'s Kennel Club (KC), the Fédération Cynologique Internationale (FCI), and the various American Kennel Clubs (AKCs) being listed under the individual entries.

This is not to say that judging standards are the same in each case, however, because these do vary between organizations, and in turn affect the judging process itself. In some instances, although dogs may exist in a wide range of colors, this does not mean that all varieties are universally accepted for show purposes.

COAT COLORS
The coat color swatches that accompany the individual entries give a guide to the colors and color combinations linked with particular breeds, but should not be interpreted literally in all cases. The cream swatch, as an example, describes breeds with very pale coats, whose coloration may range from white through to a dark shade of cream. More precise individual information about the colors associated with a particular breed can be found in the fact box accompanying the entry, although bear in mind that not all colors or coat variants are equally common within a breed. On the other hand, in some cases, as with the Golden Retriever, coat coloration can actually be a defining feature of the breed.

SYMBOLS IN THE BOOK
Aside from providing information about the size to which a dog of a particular breed will grow, its coat type, and its level of activity, these symbols can also assist in choosing a breed that will match your requirements. The height of most breeds is standard, but bear in mind that in the case of bigger breeds, bitches usually grow to a slightly smaller size than male dogs. Also, the level of exercise that an individual dog requires will be affected both by its age and its overall state of health.

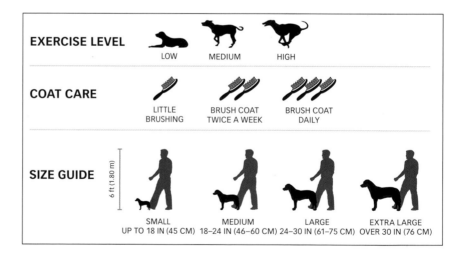

EXERCISE LEVEL	LOW	MEDIUM	HIGH
COAT CARE	LITTLE BRUSHING	BRUSH COAT TWICE A WEEK	BRUSH COAT DAILY
SIZE GUIDE	SMALL UP TO 18 IN (45 CM)	MEDIUM 18–24 IN (46–60 CM)	LARGE 24–30 IN (61–75 CM)	EXTRA LARGE OVER 30 IN (76 CM)

6 ft (1.80 m)

COAT COLORS

BLACK   CREAM   GRAY   BLUE   RED/TAN   GOLD   DARK BROWN

GOLD AND WHITE   BLACK AND WHITE   TAN AND WHITE   BLACK AND TAN   BLACK, WHITE, AND TAN   BLUE MOTTLED WITH TAN   BLACK BRINDLE

THE NATURE OF THE DOG

Dogs have been our closest animal companions since before the start of recorded history. They have traveled with us, fought with us, and saved countless lives. One of the great ironies, however, is the way in which people feel very close to dogs, and yet have despised, harried, and hunted their ancestor, the Gray Wolf. Wolves are now extinct in much of their former range, while the dog has spread worldwide, even down into South America and southern parts of Africa, which are areas where wolves never ventured. As society has changed over the course of millennia, so have dogs—a trend that is still apparent today, with dogs being kept increasingly for companionship rather than for working purposes.

FRIENDLY FACE The emphasis now is on developing dogs that look attractive and are very friendly by nature. A particularly boisterous and amiable breed, the Golden Retriever is one of today's most popular pets.

CANINE EVOLUTION

The earliest ancestors of today's wild dogs date back over 40 million years in the fossil record, to the late Eocene era. These early carnivores more closely resembled mongooses than contemporary dogs. They lived in North America, with the first example being called *Hesperocyon*—a slender, short-legged creature with a long snout and tail, growing to about 2.5 ft (0.8 m) overall. Little is known about its habits, but it probably fed on small mammals, scavenged, and ate some fruit. The first example of a canid that closely resembled a modern member of the family was the North American *Cynodesmus*.

FOSSIL EVIDENCE

Fossilized remains confirm that *Cynodesmus*, the first wild dog, occurred in the United States, in modern-day Nebraska, about 25 million years ago. It would have looked similar to a Coyote (*Canis latrans*). Already, the inner toe of each foot was becoming smaller in size, but these toes were still on the ground, rather than forming the dew claws that are a feature of both wild and domestic canids today.

While it is believed that *Cynodesmus* tended to ambush its prey, there was another group of canids, known as the borophagines, which are thought to have hunted in a similar way to contemporary wolves, living in packs. They split off from the *Hesperocyon* lineage about 30 million years ago, but ultimately played no part in the development of the family today, dying out about 1.5 million years ago.

The arrangement of the continents was very different during this era from that seen today. Most significantly, as far as the spread of the dog's ancestors was concerned, there was a land bridge connecting present-day Siberia with the western side of North America, occupying the

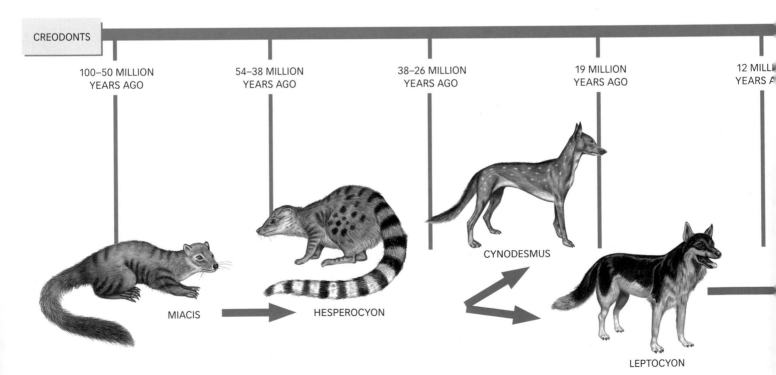

CREODONTS

100–50 MILLION YEARS AGO

54–38 MILLION YEARS AGO

38–26 MILLION YEARS AGO

19 MILLION YEARS AGO

12 MILL YEARS A

MIACIS

HESPEROCYON

CYNODESMUS

LEPTOCYON

area now filled by the Bering Sea. This enabled species to cross back and forth between the New and Old Worlds. The presence of the land bridge helps to explain why wolves occur throughout the northern hemisphere today. In fact, the earliest representatives of the *Canis* genus are believed to have originated in Eurasia. *Canis cipio* lived in Spain about 6 million years ago, during the late Miocene epoch, and probably evolved from the dog-like *Leptocyon*.

At this time, climate change was taking place, the world was becoming drier, and there were fewer areas of forest as a result. Instead, grasslands were becoming more widespread, which meant that there were fewer hiding places for herbivorous mammals. These mammals were altering in appearance, becoming lighter and more nimble. The early wild dogs were well suited to thriving in this type of landscape, and their pace meant they were able to hunt smaller prey such as antelope, whether on their own or collectively in packs.

Fossil evidence suggests that the ancestors of today's wolves crossed via the Bering land bridge into North America from Eurasia as recently as 700,000 years ago. Their ancestor was probably a Coyote-like wild dog, known as *Canis davisii*. Once back in North America, three different species developed: the Gray Wolf (*Canis lupus*) itself; the Red Wolf (*C. rufus*), which is now confined to a small area in the southeast of North America; and the Dire Wolf (*C. dirus*)—the largest and probably the most ferocious member of the group, which is now extinct. The Dire Wolf was probably too slow to adapt to chase down prey. The available evidence suggests that this species was a fearsome hunter, which preyed on large, slow-moving mammals such as mammoths. It was also a scavenger. Much has been learned about its habits from the discovery of over 2,000 bodies of these wolves at a site close to Los Angeles, on the western coast of North America. Here, at Rancho La Brea, were a series of tar pits that led unsuspecting animals—predators, prey, and scavengers alike—to their deaths.

BRAIN CHANGE

Studies of the skeletons of the early wild dogs provide much more than simply evidence about their size and shape. It can provide key information about how they lived. Based on the skull shapes of early canids, it is possible to determine that they did not start living in packs until about 1.5 million years ago. This is evident because a part of the frontal lobe of the brain, called the prorean gyrus, is enlarged in social canids such as the Gray Wolf, whereas no such change is apparent in wild dogs that live independently, such as foxes.

2 MILLION YEARS AGO

CANIDAE

WOLVES

FOXES

JACKALS

MODERN DOGS

WOLVES AND WILD DOGS

There are 33 living species in the family Canidae today, with representatives of the group occurring naturally on every inhabited continent, apart from Australia. Some species, such as the Gray Wolf (*Canis lupus*), range over a very wide area, whereas others, such as the Simien Jackal (*Canis simensis*), have a much more restricted range. Many species are currently under threat.

GRAY WOLF The Gray Wolf has been exterminated from much of its former range, especially in Europe. It had been wiped out in the British Isles by 1770, and is now extinct in two-thirds of mainland Europe.

RED FOX Red Foxes were taken to Australia back in the 1800s. This was partly in the hope that they would help to control the numbers of rabbits, which had also been introduced from Europe and had multiplied at a prodigious rate in the absence of any serious mammalian predators.

HUMAN INTERVENTION

People have had a significant impact on the present-day distribution of some members of the dog family. The early settlers of Australia brought dogs with them on their journey from southern Asia, and these were the forerunners of today's Dingo. The Dingo has since spread across the continent, reverting back to a free-living existence. It is therefore recognized as a feral dog, rather than a truly wild species. Dingoes actually show many characteristics of wild canids, however; for example, they have longer canine teeth than domestic dogs, and females will breed only once a year, rather than twice.

Another introduced species, both to Australia and North America, is the Red Fox (*Vulpes vulpes*). This occurred partly because of a desire among settlers to continue hunting, as they had in their native lands. Inevitably, however, some of these adaptable predators managed to outwit their pursuers and started breeding in the wild.

In the United States, the introduced Red Fox population has now spread from the east coast—where they were first introduced some 400 years ago—as far as Texas.

THE NORTH

Although wolves range into the far north, the Arctic Fox (*Alopex lagopus*) has a much wider distribution here, occurring right around the North Pole. It is superbly adapted to this environment. Its feet are completely covered with fur, its ears are reduced in size, and its coat is very dense, all of which protects it against the intense cold. There are two different color forms of the Arctic Fox, one of which is brownish while the other is bluish in the summer. In both cases, the color of their fur changes according to the season, turning either white or a very pale shade of blue-gray respectively, which helps them to merge into the snowy winter landscape more easily. This camouflage not only helps them to avoid detection by potential predators such as polar bears, but also makes it easier for the foxes themselves to obtain prey in an area where there is very little natural cover available. Rodents such as lemmings play a significant part in their diet, but birds and fish are also eaten readily. They even scavenge on carcasses of marine mammals, such as seals.

THREATS TO WILD DOGS

The greatest threat to the survival of wild canids in general is hunting by humans. This has led to the extermination of the Gray Wolf from much of its former range. This extermination has been triggered largely because of the way wolves will hunt domestic livestock, such as sheep, when wild prey is scarce. They actually represent little threat to people.

In addition, as domestic dogs themselves have spread throughout the world, so they have started to pose a threat to wolves in some areas, partly by the diseases that they can carry and transmit to wild canids. This is a problem as far as the survival of the endangered Simien Jackal is concerned. It is also possible for domestic dogs to crossbreed successfully with other *Canis* species, affecting their populations accordingly. This applies especially in areas where domestic dogs roam freely, and wild dogs have already been substantially reduced in numbers, making it harder for them to find mates among their own species.

UNDER THREAT African Wild Dogs face a number of serious threats, including habitat loss, human persecution (hunting and poisoning), and disease spread from domestic dogs.

ARCTIC WOLF A sub-species of the Gray Wolf, the spectacular Arctic Wolf still survives throughout its original range. Thriving in the Arctic, one of the world's harshest habitats, it rarely encounters human beings.

DOMESTICATION

The origins of the domestic dog were once believed to have been relatively recent, having begun some 15,000 years ago. But now, DNA studies have indicated that the association between people and dogs is much older, probably dating back over 100,000 years.

WOLVES AT THE DOOR

No one is certain as to where the domestication process first occurred. We do know, however, that all domestic dogs descended from the Gray Wolf (*Canis lupus*), and domestication took place at various localities within that wolf's range, which was much more extensive at that stage than it is today. The process probably started with wolf cubs being raised in human settlements, being kept as pets.

MASTIFF GROUP The Tibetan Mastiff was probably the original founder of the mastiff group of dogs, which has been highly valued through history as guardians and allies in war.

Before long, wolves would have accompanied people on hunting expeditions, and would have proved their value by helping to run down prey. As time passed, and these wolves bred, their offspring would have grown up in human company, and so gradually lost their fear of people.

Just as their character started to change, the appearance of these proto-dogs began to alter, too, reflecting in part the diversity in size and color that was present within different wolf populations. Other changes occurred, too, in terms of body shape and features such as ear shape and carriage. It was not just physical changes that took place either; the behavior of the early dogs started to diverge in some significant respects from that of wolves. While wolves communicate by means of howling, dogs have evolved the the ability to bark, and are generally much more vocal by nature. This is obviously of benefit to people, alerting their owners to the approach of strangers, and also potentially serving as an intimidatory gesture. Nevertheless, the tendency to howl is still seen in the more primitive breeds such as the Alaskan Malamute, which have also changed relatively little in appearance to their Gray Wolf ancestor.

VARIATIONS IN SIZE AND COLOR

While wolves are usually shades of gray, the variations seen in the color of dogs today are also apparent in the wild. The Arctic Wolf (*C. l. arctos*) is a pure white sub-species

PARIAH There are regions where dogs live in a semidomesticated state, on the edge of villages, hunting for their own food and scavenging within human settlements. The Dingo is the best-known example of a pariah dog.

of the Gray Wolf. Other populations of wolf, occurring in the arid surroundings of the Middle East, are reddish-fawn in color. Similarly, in terms of size, Gray Wolves in Alaska stand around 36 in (91 cm) tall at the shoulder, while the smallest sub-species was the Shamanu Wolf (*C. l. hodophilax*), occurring in Japan. It grew to just 14 in (36 cm), much smaller than many of today's breeds of dog.

DIVERSE ORIGINS

There is clear evidence to suggest that today's dog breeds developed in different parts of the world, at various times. This is reflected in the various types of dog that now exist. The mastiff lineage is one of the oldest, believed to

GREYHOUND The ancestral form of today's sighthound breeds is the Greyhound, whose appearance has altered little over the course of thousands of years, as is clearly seen from archeological evidence.

originate from Chinese wolves. They were subsequently taken westward into Europe, along the trade route known as the Old Silk Road, where mastiff stock gave rise to many of the breeds whose descendants are seen today.

Most larger breeds of dog of Old World origins, such as the Dogue de Bordeaux and Boxer, have mastiff blood. Subsequently, the mastiff influence spread to the New World thanks to European settlers, with breeds such as the Dogo Argentino being developed from such dogs.

Sighthounds, another ancient lineage, developed in the vicinity of Egypt, and were then used to develop similar breeds, initially in North Africa and the Middle East, including the Sloughi and the Saluki. Much later, they played a role in the ancestry of the scaled-down Italian Greyhound, which has proved to be a popular companion breed, and the Whippet, created for dog-racing purposes and dubbed "the poor man's racehorse."

THE ORIGINS OF BREEDS

The working ancestries of dogs helped to shape their appearance, with their physical characteristics in many cases reflecting the work that they undertook. Sighthounds are sleek, long-legged, deep-chested breeds built for speed, whereas mastiffs have sturdy legs, powerful bodies, and huge heads. Dogs are still often categorized for show purposes by the work that they used to undertake, even if today, this work has changed dramatically.

FORM AND FUNCTION
Hounds are the oldest lineage within the dog's family tree. Sighthounds were highly valued as hunting companions, and it is little coincidence that they developed primarily in the vicinity of the Middle East. Here, the countryside is relatively arid and open, with few trees to provide cover. It is an unrelenting landscape, where only the fittest can survive. Herbivores such as fast-running antelopes of various species occur in this type of terrain, and it is natural that early humans living here were keen to breed types of dog that could outpace these fleet-footed grazing animals.

Scenthounds were developed at a much later stage in history, with the St. Hubert Hound—which is basically the Bloodhound, a breed renowned for its tracking skills—being the ancestral form in this case. Its influence is especially apparent in French breeds, such as the Basset Artésien-Normand and the Grand Bleu de Gascogne, but extends over a much wider area of Europe, as reflected by Swiss breeds such as the Jura Laufhund.

SCALING DOWN
Hunting was an especially popular pursuit among the aristocracy in Europe from the medieval period onward,

SCENTHOUND Dogs' highly sensitive noses have been put to use for tracking purposes for centuries. Human and canine partnerships have been particularly effective in trailing escaped prisoners or missing persons.

but interest in dogs was not restricted to the men. The ladies of European courts desired dogs of their own, not to hunt with but simply to act as companions. This triggered not just the development of companion dogs, but also the miniaturization of existing breeds, a trend that has continued during the 20th century. The Italian Greyhound was one of the first breeds to be developed in this way, with breeders traveling to the royal courts of Europe in the hope of achieving sales. More recently, scaled-down versions of the Poodle, initially in a Miniature and then an even smaller Toy version have followed. Not all small dogs make great lap dogs however, as reflected by the industrious terrier breeds. Their bravery is such that many tiny breeds will venture within the lair of a much larger animal to drive it out for waiting hunters.

DIFFERING ROLES
Changes in human needs through the centuries have been mirrored in the types of dog being created. During the Middle Ages, the Bandogs had a reputation for their savagery, being used in combat, but they died out as

ITALIAN GREYHOUND Essentially a miniature Greyhound, similar to the Whippet, the Italian Greyhound was one of the earliest companion breeds, prized for its elegance and attractive temperament.

warfare changed and modern weapons developed. Shooting was ultimately to create a new group of dogs, which are now described as gundogs. They include the ever-popular Labrador Retriever. What makes retrievers and their relatives so suitable both as hunting companions and as pets is the fact that they were developed to work in close association with people on a one-to-one basis. They are highly responsive to training, and adaptable too, so that they can be used for a very wide variety of tasks, ranging from aiding the visually impaired to detecting explosives or drugs at airports.

The latest trend within dog breeding, reflecting the way in which dogs are kept increasingly as companions rather than for working purposes, is the creation of "designer dogs" such as the Labradoodle, a cross between a Labrador Retriever and a poodle. There is also a trend toward owning smaller companion breeds today, reflecting the fact that more people are living in cities, where space is at a premium.

LABRADOODLE The general aim with crosses of this type is to create a dog with a fairly individual appearance, while selecting for desirable qualities both in terms of appearance and behavior.

ENERGETIC Terriers are very energetic and highly inquisitive by nature, which helps them to track down and catch rodents. It also makes them playful and amusing companions.

ANATOMY

All dogs, irrespective of their size, have a very similar skeletal structure, with the greatest diversity between breeds tending to be in terms of their head shape or their limb bones. Dogs are able to run well and swim in most cases, as well as being able to dig or scratch, but they cannot use their limbs effectively to climb.

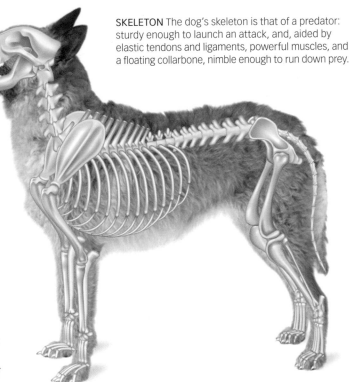

SKELETON The dog's skeleton is that of a predator: sturdy enough to launch an attack, and, aided by elastic tendons and ligaments, powerful muscles, and a floating collarbone, nimble enough to run down prey.

SKULL SHAPE

Skull length differs to some extent between individual wolves but, like many lupine characteristics, it has tended to become a more exaggerated point of distinction, as far as dog breeds are concerned. There are those, such as the German Shepherd, whose skull closely resembles that of a Gray Wolf (*Canis lupus*), but in other cases, the nasal area has become dramatically shortened, as in the case of breeds such as the Boxer or the Pug. Such skulls are described as being brachycephalic. Dogs do not have the ability to sweat effectively and so cool their bodies. They therefore rely heavily on panting and evaporation of moisture through the nasal chambers, but this ability is compromised in these brachycephalic breeds.

TEETH

The number and shape of the teeth are a consistent feature throughout the canid family, with forty-two in total. The small incisors are present at the front of the mouth, with the much larger and sharply pointed canine teeth at each corner. The key role of these teeth is to grab prey, with the gap behind the canines, called the diastema, allowing these large teeth to anchor tightly together when biting.

The cheek teeth, located further back in the mouth, comprise the premolars and the molars. Dogs have a special arrangement of these teeth that helps them to chew more efficiently. The last premolar in the lower jaw works in association with the first molar in the upper jaw, to shear through the food. Dogs generally bolt down their food, however, rather than pausing to chew. This reflects the habits of their wolf ancestors, where communal feeding means that they need to eat quickly.

ORIGINAL PROFILE With a tapering muzzle half the length of its head, the German Shepherd is visually very close to its wolf ancestors, although selective breeding has radically altered its behavior and temperament.

LOCOMOTION

Dogs are well equipped to move in a straight line, with some sighthounds being able to run at speeds equivalent to 30 mph (48 kph) or so over short distances. At the top of the front limbs, the collar bone has essentially

BUILT FOR SPEED A dog's legs are effectively fixed to give stability for running at high speeds rather than possessing the flexibility that we humans have in our wrists that enables us to climb.

disappeared, while the shoulder bone, called the scapula, has become flattened, serving to add to the stride length. Covering more distance by this means saves energy. The limbs themselves are elongated in the most athletic breeds, enabling them to move further at a single bound, making it easier for them to pursue athletic quarry such as antelopes or hares successfully. Dogs that are bred to stand and fight often have shorter, stockier limbs.

The shape of the chest of dogs actually gives a clear insight into their athletic prowess. Running at speed, even if simply sprinting over a short distance, demands oxygen, and the rib cages of hounds are relatively long; such dogs also have a deep-chested appearance when viewed in profile. It is not just the lungs that are significant for this purpose, but also the heart, which pumps the blood around the body. Conversely, dogs that are not athletically inclined, such as the diminutive French Bulldog, have much more of a barrel-shaped chest.

PANTING Brachycephalic dogs' breathing can be labored and noisy, and older individuals in particular will often snore loudly. Particular care is needed with such breeds when it comes to exercising in hot weather.

COAT TYPES

One of the obvious distinguishing characteristics of dogs is their particular coat type (its length and texture as opposed to its color). This feature also has a direct influence on the amount of care that an individual requires. Even if you are not particularly confident of being able to carry out the more difficult aspects of coat care yourself, however, you can obtain expert help from your local grooming parlor.

SHORTHAIRED BREEDS

Many dogs have a short, relatively smooth single coat, which provides a sleek covering over the body. In such cases, this will help to highlight whether your dog is in good condition (in which case the ribs will just be discernible) or decidedly overweight (in which case the ribs will be concealed

SHORTHAIR The Whippet is a classic example of a shorthaired breed. It is susceptible to cold and can often be seen sporting a special dog jacket.

WIREHAIRED Many terriers, such as this Jack Russell, and hunting dogs have wirehaired coats to protect them in dense undergrowth and brambles.

LONG HAIR Many spitz-type dogs, such as this Pomeranian, have long coats that help to keep them warm in the colder climates where they originated. Their luxurious coats can make them popular companion breeds.

COAT TYPES The hugely popular German Dachshund occurs in all three coat types: wirehaired, shorthaired, and longhaired.

beneath a layer of fat). Sleek-coated breeds include many of the hounds originating from the Mediterranean region, where the lack of a dense undercoat is beneficial in helping them to stay relatively cool. Such dogs are, however, more susceptible to feeling the cold in other parts of the world.

LONGHAIRED BREEDS

At the other extreme are the northern breeds, notably members of the spitz group, whose ancestors evolved in a bitterly cold environment. They have dense coats to protect them from the cold. This is achieved partly by having a double coat, with much thicker underfur, which helps to insulate the body from the cold by trapping warm air close to the skin. The longer outer hair also helps to prevent snow and rain from penetrating to this area of the fur. The appearance of dogs of this type typically alters somewhat through the year, because they develop a pronounced ruff of long hair around the neck in the winter, when their coat is more profuse.

The downside of this dense fur is that such dogs are at greater risk of heatstroke in summer, and may pant heavily at this stage, trying to cool themselves. From a practical standpoint, they also need more regular grooming than a sleek, smooth-coated breed, particularly when they are molting. They will shed their dense undercoat in the spring, and then molt again to a lesser extent during the autumn.

WIREHAIRED BREEDS

The third fur type that may be encountered in some dogs is a wiry coat. This is so called because of its texture, which feels rough to the touch. It also tends not to lie flat, but is raised slightly, standing away from the body. Just as in the other cases, this has a functional significance. It

helps to protect dogs that are working in undergrowth from suffering skin injuries arising from contact with thorns or sharp twigs, effectively serving as a barrier. Wire coats are commonly seen in gundogs and hounds, as well as terriers.

GROOMING NEEDS

As far as choosing a pet dog is concerned, a smooth-coated breed will be the easiest to look after in terms of its grooming requirements. It will simply require occasional brushing with a hound brush to remove loose hairs from the coat. Grooming wirehaired breeds is often more complex, particularly for show purposes. This is because they may not molt in a traditional way, and so they are likely to require their coats to be stripped by hand. Long-haired dogs are susceptible to tangles developing in their coats without daily grooming. Like wirehaired breeds, they are also more likely to pick up burrs and pieces of twigs in their hair when out walking in the countryside. Furthermore, the hair around the jaws may become soiled with food on occasions, when they are being fed "wet" food, and this area will need to be wiped.

HAIRLESS It might be thought that hairless breeds would be the easiest to look after but, in reality, their care needs are actually quite complex. They are susceptible to the cold in winter and heatstroke and sunburn in summer.

PERFECT PROTECTION Thick double coats protect their wearers from both cold and injury, and that of the Chow Chow was valued as a fur. A heavy coat like this needs a commitment to thorough, daily grooming all year.

COLORS AND MARKINGS

Dogs exist in a wide range of colors and shades, reflecting in part the variety of coloration seen in their Gray Wolf ancestor. In spite of their name, these wolves are not just gray in color. The Newfoundland race of Gray Wolf, now sadly extinct, used to have pure white fur, while desert-dwelling wolves tend to have a much more sandy-colored fur.

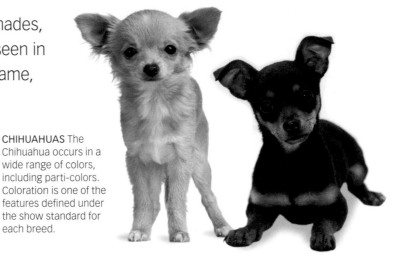

CHIHUAHUAS The Chihuahua occurs in a wide range of colors, including parti-colors. Coloration is one of the features defined under the show standard for each breed.

STANDARD COLORS

The range of colors seen in domestic dogs extends from pure white through shades of cream and red via gray to black, with so-called particolors such as black-and-white also being associated with some breeds. Pure coloration is actually quite scarce even in purebreds, with many such dogs actually displaying a small area of white fur on their chest, sometimes referred to as a star. Mutts in general will frequently display white areas on their bodies

RED SETTERS Certain breeds are defined in part on the basis of their coloration. The Irish Setter, which is often called the "Red Setter" because of its lustrous chestnut-red coloration, is a typical example.

and, in some cases, these patches can be quite extensive. It is also not uncommon for dogs to show white areas on their paws as well. There may also be a white area extending down between the eyes, which is referred to as a blaze.

The colors associated with individual breeds is something that predates the development of the show standard, and may reflect their working ancestries. The Komondor, for example, has a characteristic whitish color, which meant that these dogs blended in amongst the flocks of sheep that they protected against wolves.

In other cases, the coloration of breeds has been created from an aesthetic standpoint. This applies

HOUNDS Pack hounds tend to be bicolored or tricolored, usually in a combination of black, white, and tan.

particularly in the case of pack hounds, with selective breeding for coloration and markings ultimately helping to indicate the origins of a particular pack. Before the French Revolution of 1789, this was quite a common trait, but the overthrow of the aristocracy saw a decimation of the packs. Nevertheless, there are still some breeds, such as the Porcelaine, that survived this era.

CHANGING COLORS

Patterning can be influenced to some extent by age. For example, it is not unusual for Whippet puppies to develop darker markings on the bridge of the nose as they mature. This is the result of underlying changes in skin pigmentation becoming apparent where the fur is thin, however, rather than the fur itself darkening, even though this alters the dog's appearance.

In hairless breeds, their coloration results from their skin pigmentation, with the result that paler areas may take on

WHITE SHEPHERD White German Shepherds have formed the basis for a separate breed, often referred to as the White Shepherd, which is very popular in the United States, and defined on the basis of its coat color.

GRAYING WITH AGE In older dogs, a change in coloration may be observed, typically in the vicinity of the muzzle. This will be particularly apparent in dogs with dark coats.

a more pinkish hue when the dog is warm, because of the increase in blood flow to the skin at this stage. Individuals can differ quite widely in appearance.

Within a litter of puppies of a particolored breed, their patterning is likely to be highly individual. Even when the parents themselves are well matched, there is always the possibility that some of their offspring may display much more white (or indeed colored) areas within the coat than others. The patterning in such cases will be fixed throughout the dogs' lives.

There are some instances where deafness can be linked to coat coloration. This applies in the case of white Boxers, which are not recognized for show purposes. In the case of the German Shepherd, white-coated dogs were not accepted for many years under the breed standard, although the color was not linked to deafness.

EAR SHAPE AND SET

The shape of a dog's ears can vary quite considerably, as can their position or "set" on the sides of the head. This not only influences the overall appearance of the dog, but may also have a functional significance too, in the case of working breeds, helping to protect the ear itself from injury.

EAR TYPES

The Gray Wolf is characterized by its upright or pricked ears. The ear cartilage has some flexibility, helping the dog to pinpoint the source of the sound with great accuracy. The drawback of having prick ears is that it exposes the ear canal itself to injury, and this is a particular disadvantage for dogs that regularly run through undergrowth. Perhaps unsurprisingly therefore, drop ears, which hang down alongside the face, are most common

SPANIEL Drop ears help to guard against injury to the ear canal from thorns and branches, without significantly compromising the dog's hearing abilities.

HUSKY Pricked ears are a primitive trait that is still a feature associated with many breeds today, especially those that are most closely linked with the wolf itself, such as the spitz breeds from the far north.

in scenthounds, as well as gundogs, notably spaniels, which work in this type of terrain.

EAR INFECTIONS

However, the very heavy and well-furred ears of breeds such as the American Cocker Spaniel can predispose these dogs to infections. The way in which the ear canal is cut off from the outside environment means that bacteria, fungi, and ear mites can all flourish in these surroundings. The most common sign of a problem of this type will be the dog scratching one or both of its ears almost constantly, attempting to relieve the irritation.

A veterinary examination will be needed, so the precise cause or causes of the problem can be determined easily, and appropriate treatment given. It often helps if the long fur on the inside of the ear flaps is trimmed back slightly, aiding the circulation of air. Otherwise, this can predispose the animal to further infections, and lasting damage to the ear. Sometimes, by pawing repeatedly at its ear flap in the hope of being able to prevent the irritation, a dog can even cause the ear flap to start bleeding internally, with the resulting swelling being known as a hematoma.

FLIP FLOP The ears of German Shepherd Dog puppies always hang down by the sides of their face. Gradually, however, the ears become erect, although not necessarily both at the same time.

ANCESTRAL LINKS

The shape and size of a dog's ears can provide some insight into its ancestry. The ear flaps of breeds originally developed for fighting purposes, such as the Staffordshire Bull Terrier, are relatively small, compared with the size of the dog's head. This would afford them some protection in combat, since their small ears would be harder for an opponent to grasp.

CHANGING POSITION

The position of the ears can change between puppies and adult dogs. This is the case with German Shepherd Dogs, for example. For a period, such puppies may have one ear that sticks up while the other hangs down, although the final ear posture will be reached by the time they are six months old. In some individual cases, however, this change does not occur and the ears remain lying alongside the head throughout the dog's life.

In other breeds, the ears neither stick up nor hang down, but range somewhere in between the two extremities. Those typically displaying this characteristic include the Norfolk Terrier, with its semiprick ears that are folded some distance away from the head. There are also breeds with rose ears, notably the Whippet and Greyhound, which can alter to some degree in posture, depending on the dog's mood. This is not the only floral description in use either, with the upright, broad ears of the French Bulldog being described as tulip ears. The shape of the ear also helps to explain the description of button ears, as typified by the Shar Pei.

Ear cropping

In some countries, it is still permitted to alter the dog's appearance from an early age by surgery known as ear-cropping. This controversial practice is typically carried out with working breeds such as the Great Dane or Dobermann, in order to make them look fiercer. The cartilage of the ears then sticks up, rather than hanging down by the sides of the face as is normal. Just as with docking of the tail, however, this prevents a dog from communicating effectively, which it would normally do partly by alterations in its ear posture.

SENSES

Dogs see the world in a very different way from how we perceive it. This is a reflection of the fact that they are less reliant on sight than we are, with other senses, notably hearing and smell, being correspondingly more significant to them. This shift in emphasis reflects the fact that many wild dogs are naturally active at night, and so rely on hearing and smell to enable them to hunt successfully in the dark.

SIGHT AND SCENT

As domestication of the dog has proceeded, so a difference in reliance between the senses in various breeds has now emerged. The most obvious example of this type can be seen in the case of the hound group, whose members can be broadly split into sighthounds and scenthounds. A sighthound sees for about 270 degrees around the head, well above that of an average dog, which can see through an angle of approximately 180 degrees. Scenthounds like the Beagle have much broader nostrils than sighthounds, which allows them to detect scent molecules more efficiently. Their hunting styles differ, too, reflecting the fact that particular hunting attributes are better suited to some types of habitat than

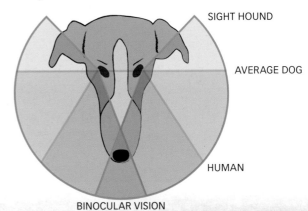

SIGHT HOUND

AVERAGE DOG

HUMAN

BINOCULAR VISION

FIELD OF VISION The average dog has a wider field of vision than humans' 120 degrees, at around 180 degrees, but there are noticeable differences between breeds. The Greyhound, with its sideways-pointing eyes, has the widest field, at 270 degrees, but a narrower overlap, or binocular field.

BORZOI Hounds need a broad field of vision to enable them to detect quarry. This is reflected by their head shape, with sighthounds, such as this Borzoi, characterized by long, narrow heads.

TASTE This is the least important sense for dogs and, compared to us, they have relatively few tastebuds and a poor sense of taste. The dog's highly developed sense of smell is far more important in identifying suitable food.

EAR SHAPE Wild dogs and wolves have pricked ears, but pendulous or semi-erect ears are a feature of many of our modern dog breeds, such as the Bernese Mountain Dog. Regardless of ear shape, dogs are much better at locating sounds than we are, using their independently mobile ears to pinpoint sound within six-hundredths of a second.

others. In order to hunt effectively, a sighthound must be able to locate its quarry easily, and clearly; its hunting skills will work best in open countryside rather than wooded terrain. It is here, however, that the ability of scenthounds to identify and follow invisible trails is invaluable.

The structure of a dog's eye is similar to ours, and dogs can see in color. This is because they possess cone cells that are responsible for color vision on the retina at the back of each eye where the image forms. Dogs and their relatives have far superior nighttime vision to us, which is crucial for desert-dwelling species, such as the Pale Fox (*Vulpes pallidus*), since their prey hides during the daytime.

The dog's nighttime vision is reinforced by the presence of a structure called the tapetum lucidum at the back of the retina, which acts like a mirror, reflecting light back through the retina, effectively increasing the light.

HEARING

Dogs have the ability to hear over a very wide frequency range, anywhere from between 16 and 100,000 Hz, whereas our upper limit is just 20,000 Hz. Their keen hearing enables them to detect ultrasound, which is inaudible to our ears. This ability is important for their

hunting skills. Rodents, which feature prominently in the diet of many small wild canids, communicate using very high frequencies.

The hearing abilities of domestic dogs probably differ somewhat from breed to breed, just as they appear to do in wild canids. However, those breeds with floppy ears do not appear unduly disadvantaged in terms of their hearing compared with the spitz breeds for example, with their erect, pointed ears.

TOUCH

A sense of touch is also important to dogs, and the whiskers around the face are used for this purpose. They are specialized hairs, modified for sensory purposes, which allow a dog to determine whether it can squeeze through a gap for example, without becoming stuck.

WHISKERS These long, touch-sensitive hairs on a dog's muzzle, chin, and eyebrows—also known as vibrissae—play a vital role in the dog's perception of the world through touch.

COMMUNICATION

Dogs rely heavily on their sense of smell, not just to locate potential quarry, but also to gain insight into the world around them. Scent is very important for communication purposes, allowing them to determine what other dogs have passed through a particular area, and to leave their own mark for other dogs that follow.

SCENTING The reason that male dogs cock their legs is that their scent is then deposited in a more prominent position, at a height where it will be easier for other dogs passing to detect it. Rain will tend to wash this away regularly, and hence the need to reinforce it.

SCENT MARKING

As a male dog attains maturity, typically around six months of age, he will stop squatting to urinate, like a bitch, and start cocking his leg at intervals when out for a walk. He is likely to choose prominent sites for this purpose to leave a mark that others passing the spot will not be able to ignore, with lampposts favored in suburban areas, where there may be a shortage of trees. A male dog urinates far more often than a bitch, establishing a claim to his territory. On a daily walk, your dog is likely to stop at the same localities to reinforce the scent.

Both sexes also communicate by means of their feces, using anal glands that transfer a musky secretion onto the feces, helping to identify the individual dog. Further scent

SMELLING OTHER DOGS Dogs can gain a good insight into which other dogs are resident in their area. Even if they do not meet face to face on a regular basis, they will be able to recognize each other instantly from their respective scents.

marking may be achieved by the dog scratching once or twice at the ground, having relieved itself. Apart from scratch marks, the dog will also leave traces of scent, using sweat glands located between the toes.

Scent helps to determine social ranking in a wolf pack, and this may explain why on walks some dogs insist on rolling in strong-smelling cow pats or fox excrement.

PHEROMONES

Just before a bitch is ready to mate, she releases chemical messages, called pheromones, in her urine. These scent molecules will be detected even in minute concentrations by males, thanks to a scent organ, known as Jacobson's organ, present in the roof of the mouth and connected to the part of the brain concerned with sexual behavior. Unneutered male dogs exposed to the pheromones will instinctively head off in search of the female.

BARKING

At first, puppies are virtually silent, and then they will start to bark briefly, often when excited, in a high-pitched tone, developing a deeper tone as they grow older. There are breed differences, too: the Basenji does not bark, uttering a yodeling call instead. Scenthounds, hunting as a pack, often in wooded areas, have a very distinctive baying call, enabling them to keep in touch with each other and indicate when they have picked up a trail.

BODY LANGUAGE

Dogs use their facial expressions, eye line, ear and tail position, and posture to communicate with other dogs and with humans. The position of eyes and tail are especially important in communicating dominance or submission.

CLEAR SIGNAL Everyone understands a wagging tail used to communicate pleasure, but there are further subtleties: This Golden Retriever's high-carried tail conveys dominance over the smaller dogs it is meeting.

BARKING Dogs bark for a variety of reasons. They may bark to give a warning at close quarters, to indicate distress (perhaps if tied up), or simply because they are overly excited.

BEHAVIOR

The dog's natural instinct, inherited from the Gray Wolf (*Canis lupus*), is to be a pack animal. This helps to explain why dogs make such good companions, simply because they will integrate closely with a family or even an individual. The key point, though, is that some breeds tend to have more dominant natures than others. These dogs are more likely to be difficult to manage, in the sense that they will not want a subservient role.

INTRODUCTIONS
When introducing two adult dogs for the first time, it is best done away from home, to minimize the risk of territorial aggression. When dogs meet initially, they tend to circle each other, sniffing cautiously. Body language is the best indicator at this stage as to whether or not they are likely to get along. They are likely to be wary at first, with their ears held slightly backward, and tails kept relatively horizontal.

After an initial period of contact, the dogs may seemingly lose interest in each other, wandering off and continuing to walk by themselves. However, you may notice signs of a challenge early on, if both are feeling very confident and neither wishes to adopt a more subservient role. The ears will be raised, as will the tail, and as the dogs approach cautiously, you may notice that

FIRST MEETING A puppy should integrate well into the family. It will also be much easier to introduce a puppy to a home alongside an older dog, simply because it will not be a rival to your established pet.

increasingly vocal, as both dogs draw back their lips, revealing more of their teeth, while their growling takes on more of a menacing tone. Ultimately, one dog will launch at the other, snarling fiercely and snapping at its rival, who may fight back. Such encounters are usually very short, however, with the loser rapidly running off, with its tail firmly tucked down between its legs in a sign of submission. The injuries in such cases are normally quite slight, given the relatively short period of contact. There is a danger of a much more savage encounter if the dogs are confined, which then prevents the loser from escaping.

WHAT TO DO ABOUT PROBLEM AGGRESSION

There are a number of steps that you can take to reduce displays of aggressive behavior, starting by muzzling your dog when out walking. In the longer term, arrange to have your dog neutered if he is male. This will result in a fall-off in his urge to be aggressive, which is driven partly by the male sex hormone testosterone. Seek the advice of a professional dog trainer, taking positive action to try to correct your pet's aggressive behavior. In the meantime, it is best to avoid popular dog-walking areas, or visit these at times when there are likely to be fewer dogs around.

MUZZLED Muzzles today are quite comfortable in terms of their design, and are a must if your dog is aggressive toward other dogs. However, they are not the ideal long-term solution for aggressive behavior.

they start growling. This sound will increase in intensity, and both are likely to raise their hackles too, which is the area of fur at the back of the neck.

Behaving in this way makes a dog appear slightly larger and potentially more intimidating to its rival. It may be that things are then resolved at this stage without any overt display of aggression. Sizing up its would-be opponent, one of the dogs breaks away from staring intently at the other, indicating that it does not wish to press ahead with a challenge. If not, however, then the brinkmanship continues. The dispute becomes

Inherent aggression

Certain breeds are more likely to behave aggressively, because of their origins. Those that were originally developed for dog-fighting purposes, such as the American Staffordshire Terrier (*below*), are likely to be more aggressive toward other dogs. Fighting is particularly likely to break out if two dogs of this type meet, simply because they will both have relatively assertive temperaments, and will be disinclined to back down. On the other hand, dogs that are most likely to be social when out walking will be breeds such as the Beagle, which have been bred over many generations to live as pack members.

STRANGE HABITS

There are a number of other behavioral traits seen in domestic dogs that they have inherited from their wild ancestors. Some of these can be hard to understand. As an example, the desire of some dogs to bury bones may seem puzzling, but it is absolutely normal. After making a kill, a pack of wolves will eat as much as they can, and then hope to return to the carcass to feed again later. The problem is that scavengers, ranging from birds to other mammals, are likely to be attracted to the scene of the kill, and so the wolves seek to conceal the remains of the carcass as effectively as possible, often by burying it.

Domestic dogs often display similar behavior when they are given a bone to chew, which effectively serves as a leftover part of a meal. A pet dog is unlikely to be hungry and so, having gnawed for some time on the bone, his innate instinct will be to conceal it.

SCRAPING A BED

Dogs may also use their feet when settling down to sleep, which can cause damage to cushion covers or similar

CURLING UP Sleeping in a curled-up position helps dogs to stay comfortable, reducing heat loss from their bodies by restricting the surface area exposed to the elements.

furnishings, as they scratch at the base of the chair or sofa. Such behavior mimics the way in which wolves dig at the ground, to remove any large, sharp stones that may otherwise cause discomfort when they lie down. Dogs circle round, curling their bodies as they ultimately settle down. Before long, however, especially in the home, a dog is likely to uncurl itself, tending to stretch

BURYING BONES Using his strong front legs, a dog digs a hole where he can bury his bone, scraping back the soil over the top again. In due course, he may return here to unearth it.

TEETHING PAINS Chewing is often linked to teething, which is completed at around six months of age. Puppies will chew as a means of relieving the irritation and pain caused by the teeth as they emerge through the gums.

out instead. The age of a dog also influences how it sleeps, because older dogs suffering with arthritis may find it painful to curl up in a ball.

CHEWING

Destructiveness is a characteristic of puppyhood, but the majority of dogs will grow out of behaving in this way, from about six months onward. Avoid leaving items that are likely to appeal to a puppy, such as shoes, within your pet's reach at this stage. Also, aim to deflect your dog's attention toward his own toys, and supervise his activities discreetly. This should minimize the risk of damage to furniture, or indeed the danger that your pet could gnaw through live electrical wiring, with deadly consequences.

BEING ALONE

One of the most common canine issues is separation anxiety, which appears to be on the increase, possibly because more dogs are left alone for longer periods.

While an old dog may sleep through much of the day, a puppy is very likely to become bored and frustrated under these circumstances. This may mean that when you go out, your dog develops a habit of whining and barking, to the extent that the first thing you know of the problem is when you receive complaints from your neighbors.

It is much better to be aware of this potential difficulty, and take steps to prevent it happening, rather than wait until a later stage, by which time it may be habitual and much harder to correct. In the first instance, you need to be sure that you have the time for a dog in your life. If you need to go out for long periods, consider choosing an older individual rather than a puppy, and be prepared to invest in employing a dog walker, who can exercise your pet in your absence.

WALKING THE DOG When you have to leave your dog alone for longer periods, give him a good walk beforehand, so that he should be tired and want to settle down and sleep, rather than becoming distressed.

LIFECYCLE

Breeding dogs is not something that should be undertaken without considerable thought. You could otherwise easily be adding to the countless number of unwanted puppies born each year. On the other hand, understanding the canid breeding cycle is important, not just to be able to control your dog's fertility, but also to be aware of the physiological changes that occur and the possible complications that may arise.

PROBLEM PUPS Certain breeds—notably those with large heads, such as Bull Terriers—are likely to encounter more difficulty giving birth, since the head of a pup can become stuck in the bitch's reproductive tract. Urgent veterinary attention is needed under these circumstances.

PREGNANT BITCH Only right at the end of the pregnancy is there a major growth spurt. This ensures that the bitch does not have to carry significant extra weight for longer than necessary.

MATURITY

Male dogs are likely to show signs of wanting to mate by the time they are six months old. In the case of bitches, however, it may not be until they are a year old that they have their first period of reproductive activity, which is referred to as being 'on heat'. There are also breed variances, with giant breeds, such as the Irish Wolfhound, being unlikely to be mature until they are at least two years old.

Male dogs can mate at any stage, whereas bitches are only fertile during their periods of heat. These usually occur twice a year, roughly at intervals of six months; however, a few breeds, such as the Basenji, come in to heat only once a year, like wild dogs.

THE BREEDING CYCLE

The initial stage of the bitch's reproductive cycle is known as preestrus. The earliest indications will be that the vulva starts to enlarge in size, and there may be a few flecks of blood evident here as well. Male dogs start to follow the bitch, but she deters all attempts at mating during this phase.

Mating will then take place during the subsequent estrus period. The male's penis contains a bone called the os penis, which helps to keep it rigid. Once penetration has taken place, the erectile tissue at the base of the penis swells, anchoring it in place in the bitch's vagina and creating what is described as a "tie." The male releases sperm soon afterward, and then the pair shift position, so that they are facing away from each other, with their hindquarters touching. It is at this stage that secretions from the prostate gland are released by the male, serving to aid the survival of the sperm and so assist fertilization.

The release of the bitch's eggs, called ovulation, takes place around the time of mating. They then move down through the oviducts, ultimately implanting after being fertilized in the horns of the uterus. The number of puppies is often quite variable, ranging from one to a dozen or more, depending partly on the breed of dog. Crossbreeding can sometimes result in smaller litters than if dogs of the same breed mate together.

The gestation period lasts approximately 63 days. The bitch needs to be provided with a suitable bed where she can give birth. Watch discreetly from a distance.

Assuming all goes well, the puppies will soon be suckling from the bitch. The puppies will start to take solid food from the age of about three weeks onward, and there are special weaning foods available for this purpose. Meanwhile, the bitch will be increasingly reluctant to suckle the pups, since this will start to become painful as their sharp teeth emerge. By the age of six weeks or so, the young puppies will be largely independent, but it is much better to wait until they are at least eight weeks old, and fully weaned, before separating the litter and taking a puppy to a new home.

FEEDING PUPS The first milk produced by the bitch contains protective antibodies that the young dogs absorb directly into their bodies, helping to protect them against infections.

Cryptorchidism

Sometimes, in male dogs of toy breeds, such as the Yorkshire Terrier, one or both testicles may fail to descend into the scrotum. This condition is known as cryptorchidism, and will need veterinary attention, because the retained testes can give rise to a sertoli cell tumor within the dog's body. Normally, both testicles should be present in the scrotum by the time that the dog is six months old.

CANE CORSO PUPS The number of puppies in a litter can vary enormously among breeds, from one to the high teens. These five Cane Corso pups are a typical number for this breed, whose average litter is between 4 and 6 pups.

DOG CARE

Looking after a dog is a real commitment, not just in financial terms, but also because this will take time every day. You will obviously need to feed, groom, and exercise your pet on a daily basis, and there are other important considerations that arise as well, such as making suitable arrangements for the care of your dog when you want to plan a vacation. It really is just like having another member of the family to consider, but in return you can be guaranteed a great companion who will be there for you at all times, complete with a wagging tail, throughout all of life's ups and downs.

AFFECTIONATE FRIEND Dogs are intelligent, sociable, and affectionate creatures. Their famed, unconditional loyalty to their human "family" deserves to be repaid with equally affectionate and consistent care.

CHOOSING A DOG

It is very important not to rush into choosing a dog, bearing in mind that all puppies look particularly cute! You need to carry out an assessment of your lifestyle to determine which type of dog would be most suitable, and, also, whether it really would be better to start with a puppy, or opt for an older dog that, through no fault of its own, may be in need of a good home.

A SUITABLE COMPANION

Perhaps the most important thing is not to be seduced simply by the appearance of a purebred dog; you must delve into its ancestry, which will give you an invaluable insight into its likely character and needs. If you live in a city apartment then, clearly, a lively gundog requiring

BIG RESPONSIBILITY For couples planning for a baby in the near future, a Great Dane puppy is probably not a sensible option: It will grow up into a large dog, easily capable of knocking over a toddler in the home.

plenty of exercise is not to be recommended. It would be better to select a companion breed, which are not just smaller in size, but also require far less exercise.

Large dogs are obviously more costly to keep than their smaller relatives, thanks to their bigger appetites. They are also likely to have a shorter lifespan, probably averaging about 10 years, compared with small dogs which are likely to live into their teens. They will also be stronger, and may not be as easy for elderly owners or younger children to control on a leash.

POINTS TO CONSIDER

The barking of a dog can an important consideration for those who live in an urban area. Here the size of the dog will not be a helpful indicator. Greyhounds, for example, rarely bark, whereas Chihuahuas are excitable, noisy dogs.

The gender of the dog can be significant, particularly if you are thinking in terms of buying a show dog. In this case, a bitch may be a better choice, because if she does well in the show ring, you can then use her for breeding purposes, keeping some of her puppies and developing your own show lineage.

For those who are simply seeking a pet dog, however, the emphasis may shift because it will be more costly to neuter a bitch than a male dog. Should you leave her intact, however, there is then a risk that she could slip away to

LITTLE TROUBLE Small dogs have small appetites and often require less exercise than larger dogs. They may be quite happy with a good daily walk, combined with an opportunity to explore off the leash in a local park.

find a partner while she is on heat and inadvertently end up pregnant. Over the longer period, there is a risk of a life-threatening infection of the uterus known as a pyometra developing in unneutered female dogs, as well as a greater possibility of mammary tumors too.

YOUR REQUIREMENTS

Training is obviously vital. When it comes to individual breeds, some are much easier to train than others. Chow Chows, for example, have a reputation for being unruly, whereas Whippets are quite amenable to training, often doing well in obedience classes at shows.

Consider your future. If you are planning for children, it might be wise to select a small, gentle breed such as a Cavalier King Charles Spaniel, which will have a tolerant nature, and is unlikely to be a problem, as opposed to a larger, more boisterous breed. However, certain small breeds, notably terriers, are likely to be more feisty and so are less suitable for a home with young children.

Another point to consider is the amount of grooming required. Long-coated or wire-coated dogs will require much more grooming than a smooth-coated breed.

ACTIVE TEENAGERS For families with older children, a breed that will match their energy levels is to be recommended—something responsive, genial, and playful. However, such dogs must have adequate exercise at all times.

AGILITY You may want a dog that you can enter for agility classes, in which case, a breed renowned for its energy and trainability is a good choice.

CROSSBREEDS

Not everyone wants to own a purebred dog, for a variety of reasons, and there are always a number of crossbred and mongrel dogs in need of homes. It may not be possible to gain as much insight into their origins as in the case of purebreds, but it should be possible to predict the likely adult size of puppies with some degree of certainty if their origins are known.

TYPES OF MUTT

Mutts can be divided into two groups, based on their origins. Crossbreeds, as their name suggests, are the result of crossing between two recognized breeds. Matings of this type, while tending to be frowned upon by dog organizations themselves, underlie the creation of so-called designer dogs such as the Labradoodle—a cross between a Labrador Retriever and Poodle (*see* pp. 102–103). Mongrels, on the other hand, are the result of random matings between dogs that do not have an immediate purebred ancestry.

One of the difficulties inherent in seeking a mongrel puppy is being able to estimate how large it will grow in due course. All puppies, even those of the giant breeds, are similar in size at birth, but then, the growth rate of

MONGREL Part of the appeal of mongrels is that they are very much "one-offs," set against the standardized appearance of purebred dogs. They are also less expensive to obtain.

PEDIGREE PUPPIES These Chihuahua puppies offer peace of mind in terms of a known size and temperament, but are likely to be a costlier option than randombreds.

CROSS BETWEEN TWO BREEDS Crossbreeds can throw up some distinctive-looking dogs, like this cross between a Border Collie and a Bouvier Bernois, but it is impossible to predict exactly which parental traits will be inherited.

Mutts and myths

One of the main reasons why people may prefer a mutt over a purebred dog is worry about the health problems that can afflict many breeds. On the other hand, some of the most common of these, such as hip dysplasia, which is a weakness of the hip joints, can also affect mutts. In fact, since screening for this ailment has become commonplace in purebred dogs, so its incidence has declined in such stock. This has been made possible because affected individuals are no longer playing any part in the breeding program, thus eliminating the defective genes. There is no such screening program used for mutts, leaving them still vulnerable to this condition.

There is also a widespread belief that mutts are healthier than their purebred cousins, but this is actually something of a myth. All dogs are equally susceptible to illnesses such as distemper, if they are not protected by vaccination. Furthermore, any dog—purebred or not—that has been reared with little concern for its welfare may be badly affected by fleas, internal parasites, and lice, not to mention ear infections, too.

bigger dogs starts to accelerate. As a meaningful guide, start by looking at a puppy's paws. If these appear relatively large compared with its body, then the likelihood is that it will grow into quite a big dog. A more accurate assessment can be made once the young dog is four months old, because by this stage, it will have reached approximately two-thirds of its ultimate adult height.

In the case of a crossbred, there is no guarantee that it will grow up to show a closer affinity to one parent than another. In fact, littermates may well differ in this respect, while in temperament too, they may be surprisingly variable. This, though, can be the appeal of the crossbred or mongrel: It will be different, with a character of its own. By nature, mongrels are well-adjusted dogs, and usually prove to be excellent family pets. They have adapted to this role over a number of generations, usually having been reared in urban surroundings, although their precise origins may well be obscure. If you are seeking a particular look, you can still find short or long-coated mongrels, as well as individuals with wiry coats or curly coats. They do tend to be of mixed coloration however, rather than pure-colored.

Most mongrels are straightforward to train, perhaps even being more receptive in some cases than certain purebreeds. Furthermore, they can compete against their purebred relatives at events such as flyball and agility, so there is no reason why you should miss out on some of the competitive fun associated with owning a dog by choosing a mongrel.

FLYING COLORS Mongrels, like this collie cross, can be the equal of many purebreds when it comes to the dexterity, intelligence, and the will to succeed necessary for agility courses.

THE RIGHT CHOICE It can be difficult to choose between two or more adorable puppies like these, so decide in advance exactly what you are looking for and listen to advice that you trust.

WHICH DOG?

When it comes to obtaining a puppy, you will have a number of options, which will be influenced partly by the type of dog that you are hoping to find. The most important aspect is to insure that the dog that you choose is healthy, and should settle well with you, so do not feel inclined to compromise on your decision.

You need to be patient, rather than rushing into a decision: A puppy should be part of your life for over a decade. If you are looking for a purebred puppy, you may be able to find one relatively near where you live. However, you may have to be prepared to travel internationally to find certain rarer breeds. Check the Internet for breeders near you. Reading the dog magazines can be helpful as well, because litters of puppies are frequently advertised here.

It is quite usual to view a litter when the puppies are perhaps just three weeks old, and choose one of the puppies at this stage, paying a deposit for it. An advantage of this is that you will be able to see the mother, if not the father, if a stud dog elsewhere has been used. Making a choice can be difficult, particularly if you are seeking a dog with exhibition potential, so be guided by the advice of the breeder, or take an experienced friend with you.

If you are choosing a puppy from a breeder as a pet, then you will simply need to assure yourself that the litter is healthy. Responsible breeders are increasingly taking advantage of screening programs, so ask to see any relevant certification relating to the breeding stock. Watch the puppies to insure that all appears well, and then, with the breeder's permission, pick up those that appeal to you.

RESCUE DOGS

There are many rescue organizations—both general and breed-specific—that will have both puppies and adult dogs in need of good homes. Contact your nearest shelter to see what is available, and if they would be prepared to home a puppy with you. You will need to make an appointment, and your home and yard may be inspected to insure they are suitable first.

WINNING WAYS If you are seeking a puppy with exhibition potential, follow the show results to see which breeders are winning regularly, and contact them to reserve a puppy if they do not have any currently available.

PET RESCUE Rescue centers can be a great source for wonderful pets, but be prepared to be patient with a rehomed dog. Older animals generally take longer to settle in new surroundings, compared with a puppy.

If you are seeking an adult dog, be prepared to allow the staff to assist in choosing the dog that in their opinion will be most suitable for you. They will have a good idea of the temperaments of the dogs in their care. It may be there is an individual that is only suitable for a home without children, or cannot be housed alongside a cat.

CAREFUL CHOICE When choosing to get a dog from a rescue center, be prepared to take it out several times before arriving at a final decision, allowing you to get to know each other and assess your compatibility.

Checking puppies

When choosing a puppy from a litter, check that none has a swelling in the umbilical area on the underside of the body, in front of the abdomen, indicating an umbilical hernia. Although this can be corrected by surgery, it will be a worry. Be alert to any signs of external parasites, such as lice sticking to hairs or flea dirt in the coat. A pot-bellied appearance may be indicative of a heavy build-up of parasitic worms in the upper part of the digestive tract. It is quite usual for a young puppy to appear sleepy at first when picked up, but it should soon wake up and will be alert, assuming that it is healthy. Check around the rear end, just in case there are any signs of staining here, indicating diarrhea, and the insides of the ears should appear clean.

ADORABLE PUPPIES This pair of cute pups will grow into feisty and fun Jack Russells, terriers rarely more than 12 in (26 cm) tall that can be more than a handful for their owners. Although small, they will need lots of exercise.

EQUIPMENT NEEDED

There are certain accessories that are essential for a dog; others are a matter of choice. It is a good idea to obtain the basic equipment before you acquire your new pet. This will give you a chance to hunt around to see what is available and will be most suitable for your pet. With a puppy, it is not a good idea to spend heavily on leashes and other accessories at first, because your puppy's needs will change as he grows older.

BEDS There are a wide variety of beds, but it is important to choose one that is suitable for the size and sleeping preferences of your dog. Some dogs prefer solid sides, while others like the freedom of a bean bag.

COLLARS

A collar complete with an identity tag attached is essential. A puppy at first should only be expected to wear a collar for relatively short periods of a few hours each day, until he becomes used to it. Choose a collar that affords space for your puppy's neck to grow. As a guide, there should be a gap of at least two fingers between the collar and throat, to insure that it is comfortable for the puppy. Check this regularly and be prepared to let out the collar as necessary, as the puppy grows.

SENSIBLE PRECAUTIONS

Although it will not be possible to allow your puppy out into public places until after he has completed his vaccinations at the age of three months, you will want to allow him to exercise in your yard and begin initial obedience training here in due course. Check right around the perimeter and use chicken wire to block any gaps through which your puppy might escape.

BEDS

It is important that a puppy has an area where he can sleep, but it is not really a good idea to provide a bed for this purpose until the teething phase has passed. As an interim measure, you can use a clean cardboard box, cutting down its sides carefully with scissors and lining the interior with an old cushion or pillow. An older dog can be trusted with a bed from the outset. The cushion lining the bed should be fully washable, to guard against any build-up of fleas, while a plastic bed can be washed out easily. Wicker beds are less satisfactory in this respect, and can also be easily damaged by chewing. Larger or older dogs may find a bean bag more comfortable. This will need to have a washable removable cover.

COLLAR AND NAME TAG Even if your dog has a microchip identification device (*see* p 71), he will still need a name tag on his collar so that, should he be lost, the person who finds him can contact you directly rather than a rescue center.

FEEDING

Choose heavyweight earthenware bowls, which cannot be tipped over, for both food and water. Stainless steel bowls may be tipped over, unless they are held in a supporting ring or on a stand. It is also a good idea to

CHECK FENCING If you are getting a puppy, bear in mind that they may be able to squeeze through comparatively small gaps. You may need to reinforce fencing until your puppy has grown larger.

BOWLS If you buy a bowl suited to the eventual size of your dog, make sure you do not overfeed your puppy.

acquire a doggy tooth-cleaning kit. Regular brushing from puppyhood should help to protect against dental problems later.

TOYS

Puppies are playful by nature. Bouncing balls and similar toys lend themselves to activity games, compared with either chew toys, which can be recommended during the teething phase, or tug toys of various types. Do not pull too hard with tug toys, as this might injure a puppy's teeth.

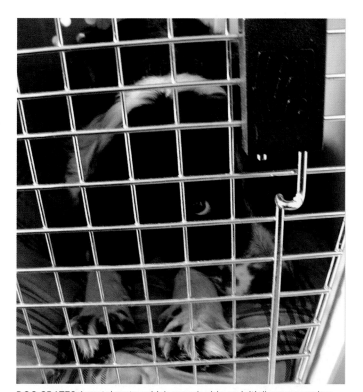

DOG CRATES A metal crate, which may double up initially as a carrying case for the puppy, can be very useful. By placing his bed within, you can close him in securely for short periods during the day when he is left alone.

TOYS A variety of well-chosen toys will save your puppy from boredom, and will hopefully save your belongings from being chewed during its teething phase!

SETTLING IN

Always arrange to bring your new dog home when you know you are going to be there for several days. This will give time to settle in your pet, and allow you to start to develop a routine together, in terms of care and feeding. At first, a dog, and particularly a puppy, may feel quite upset in strange surroundings but, with encouragement, it should not take too long for him to regain his confidence.

CAR TRAVEL A dog traveling in a car should be in a suitable location, such as this lined area, and properly secured. Never shut a dog in the trunk of a saloon car, as exhaust fumes could leak in with deadly consequences!

TRAVELING WITH YOUR DOG

When you set off to collect your puppy, take a suitable carrier with you for the trip, lined with a blanket. Position the carrier in an area of the vehicle where it cannot slide around. The safest location is probably on the floor of the vehicle, behind the passenger seat. With a mesh carrier, you will need to be sure that the puppy cannot reach the surrounding upholstery with his teeth or claws.

In the case of an adult dog, fitting a dog guard in the back of your vehicle is to be recommended. You will need to clear out this area, placing a blanket on the floor so your dog can sleep here, or at least sit comfortably on the trip home. Estate cars usually have rubber floor containers to protect the underlying upholstery from muddy paws.

Always take the most direct route home and, on a hot day, run the air-conditioning if you have this option, so your dog does not become distressed. Never park in a sunny spot and leave the dog in the vehicle on its own, even for a

NEW PLACES If you have a yard, give your new pet time to explore his new territory and relieve himself, but restrict his access to short periods.

TIRED OUT The new experiences and stress of moving to a new home can be exhausting for a puppy, so do not be surprised or concerned if your new arrival falls asleep almost immediately.

Introducing a new dog to existing pets

■ It will be much easier to introduce a puppy to an older dog, since it will tend to adopt a naturally submissive role. Even so, especially at first, do be certain to feed the dogs in separate parts of the home, as mealtimes are frequently a flash point for disputes.

■ Always make more fuss of the established dog, although your instincts may be to comfort the newcomer. This will serve to reinforce the existing order, lessening the likelihood of any displays of aggression between them.

■ A cat may choose to interact with the dog, or simply ignore him. It is very difficult to predict, but a young cat and dog that grow up together can sometimes become close companions. Never force the issue—allow them to meet on their own terms.

■ Be sure to keep rabbits and other small pets, which will be instinctively fearful of dogs, away from your new pet.

■ Take care with tortoises too—some puppies in particular will try to gnaw at their shells.

short time, because the temperature within the vehicle can climb to a fatal level for a dog within minutes, even if a window is left partially open.

You also need to bear in mind that it could easily be a puppy's first trip out, and even an adult dog may not be used to traveling in a car, so they may suffer from car sickness. This should only be a temporary problem however, which should soon pass once they have more experience of traveling in this way.

FIRST STEPS

When you arrive home, allow your new pet out into the yard, as he is likely to want to relieve himself after the

QUALITY TIME If necessary, take a few days off work when your new dog arrives and spend time helping him to settle in. This is an invaluable period for initiating sensible routines, and also for bonding with your new pet.

journey. Have everything ready on arrival, so that the dog can then have something to eat and drink, placing him outside again afterward. Then, almost certainly, following a brief period exploring his new home, he will fall asleep. Do not worry if he fails to make it to his bed—simply allow him to sleep on the ground at this stage if he prefers. Later, you can carry him to his bed, and, before long, he will sleep there on a regular basis.

FEEDING

It has never been easier to feed a dog, as is clearly apparent from the wide range of foods available not just from traditional pet store outlets, but increasingly from supermarkets and garden centers too. The pet food business is a highly competitive area, and the major companies involved have all invested heavily to develop foods that are not just nutritious but also highly palatable to canines.

DRIED AND CANNED FOODS Nutritionally, these foods are of equal value, but they are very different in texture and palatability.

EARLY DAYS

It is a good idea to find out what your dog was eating at his previous home and offer the same food to him for a few weeks. Especially in the case of a puppy, this reduces the risk of a serious digestive upset arising from a sudden change in diet. Switch over to the new food gradually.

Always read the feeding instructions on the packaging, because recommended quantities may differ.

APPROPRIATE FEEDING

Puppy diets are now widely used for young dogs, up to the age of six months or so, after which an adult maintenance diet is recommended. For older dogs, there are senior rations available, and there are an increasing number of breed-specific diets. While cans of dog food used to be very popular, these are now being supplanted on grounds of convenience by single-meal pouches. Dry-food diets are also very popular, offering a more concentrated source of nutrients, so that dogs require less to meet their nutritional needs than with wet food. It should therefore be weighed out carefully, to avoid unwanted weight gain. Dry food is not as appetizing as wet food, however.

If you are using cans, it is often better value to purchase large cans that may be used over the course of a day. Store the unused portion in a refrigerator, as in the case of open pouches. Dry food can be left in its bag, but insure that it stays dry.

HOW TO KEEP YOUR DOG IN TRIM

• Don't feed more than the recommended amount for your dog. Avoid offering treats regularly between meals.
• Insure that your dog cannot steal your cat's food, if you have a dog and a cat.
• Keep a check on your pet's weight (*see* p. 74).
• Give your dog regular exercise.

TAKING IT SLOWLY Make any changes to a puppy's diet gradually to minimize the risk of stomach upsets. Introduce the new food in stages and feed less and less of the old food over time.

EASY TO PLEASE Some small breeds, such as chihuahuas, are notoriously picky eaters, and are likely to turn their noses up at dry food. Others, such as this Jack Russell Terrier, are not at all fussy.

TREATS

A wide range of tempting canine treats are available, but they should always be used sparingly, since they are laden with calories and can easily contribute to your dog putting on weight. There are much healthier alternatives that you can use, such as pieces of carrot or dessert apple, which will be eaten just as readily by your dog.

Hygiene

Always wash your dog's food bowl after a meal, but do not do this with your own dishes. Having a clean bowl will insure that flies are not attracted into the home by the remaining traces of food. It also helps to safeguard your dog from eating from a food bowl that has been heavily contaminated by bacteria, which in turn could cause a digestive upset.

HOME COOKING

It can be difficult to insure the right balance of nutrients if you are cooking meat for your dog. In most cases, offal such as melts (spleen) and tripe (from the stomach) are used, but such foods are deficient in calcium, and a supplement will be needed. Discuss this with your vet.

Although there have been some quality issues concerning certain prepared dog food in recent years, it is generally much better, quite apart from being more convenient, to use food of this type, provided it is a recognized brand.

FEED APPLE AND CARROT Dogs are naturally omnivorous, and, in moderation, fresh fruit and vegetables can form a valuable part of a balanced canine diet, as well as being a healthy and appealing treat.

GROOMING

Most dogs shed their hair according to the season, with the heaviest molting period being in the early spring, when the thicker winter coat is lost. There is also likely to be a period in the early fall when you notice that your pet is shedding more than usual. If you groom your dog on a daily basis, then you will be able to remove most of the loose hair before it accumulates in the dog's environment.

CLIPPING AND TRIMMING

For the house-proud owner, there are a number of breeds that do not shed their coat in the traditional way. This group includes the poodles, as well as various terriers. Many owners have dogs of this type groomed professionally. Rather than rely on a fancy lion clip, however, you may simply want your pet poodle to be given a lamb clip, which keeps the coat short over the body. As well as having its coat trimmed, a dog will usually be given a bath at the same time at the grooming parlor. Regular visits every two months or so are necessary for such dogs, to insure that their coat looks smart.

EQUIPMENT

Once a dog is familiar with the grooming process, it is unlikely to resent it. Tease any knots apart carefully, so as

HAIR RETENTION Breeds like the poodle that do not molt may be a good choice for people who suffer from allergies to dog hair, as well as meaning that less vacuuming is needed to deal with shed hair.

DAILY RITUAL All dogs groom themselves, but giving your pet a little regular help will have wide-ranging benefits. It is a great way to strengthen the bond between pet and owner, and you may find it relaxes your dog.

not to hurt your pet by trying to comb them out of the coat. Invest in a comb that has rotating teeth, since these can be useful to break down knots without pulling on the hair.

A basic brush and comb will help to keep the coat in good condition, removing loose hair, with grooming itself having a tonic effect on the surface of the skin. Avoid brushes with nylon bristles, since they are likely to impart a static charge to the coat. There are various specialist pieces of grooming kit that may also be useful, depending on your dog's coat type. A hound glove, for example, will help to impart a glossy sheen to the sleek coat of many hounds, being used in the direction of the lie of the coat. A slicker brush is useful for removing dense undercoat when a dog is shedding its coat.

BATHING YOUR DOG

Regular baths every two to three months are recommended for most dogs, to control body odor. It helps to accustom a dog to being bathed from a relatively early age, so that your pet becomes used to this experience and will not struggle, since this will otherwise make the task much harder. Bathing can be done most easily outdoors in the yard, where it will not matter if the surrounding area becomes wet. It is not a good idea to use your own bath to wash your dog, on hygiene grounds, even if this is lined with a rubber mat to help the dog to stand and prevent any damage with its claws. A plastic baby bath or similar container will be required instead, and a special canine shampoo or, failing that, a mild children's shampoo. You will need a smaller container for bailing water over the dog, and an old towel to dry your pet afterward.

After bathing your dog, it is a good idea to keep it indoors until its coat has dried thoroughly. This is especially important in the case of small or elderly dogs, which may otherwise be vulnerable to chilling.

CLIPPING THE COAT It is perfectly possible to clip your pet yourself, using the correct equipment, but you should always learn from an expert. Some grooming parlors offer lessons to show you the correct technique.

Bathing

❶ Use your hands to slowly wet the coat, working up the legs and then over the back and underparts, while keeping the head dry. Work shampoo into the coat with your fingers.

❷ Rinse the suds out, refilling the bath with tepid water or simply using a gentle-pressure hose. Let your dog follow his instincts and shake his body vigorously, removing excess water.

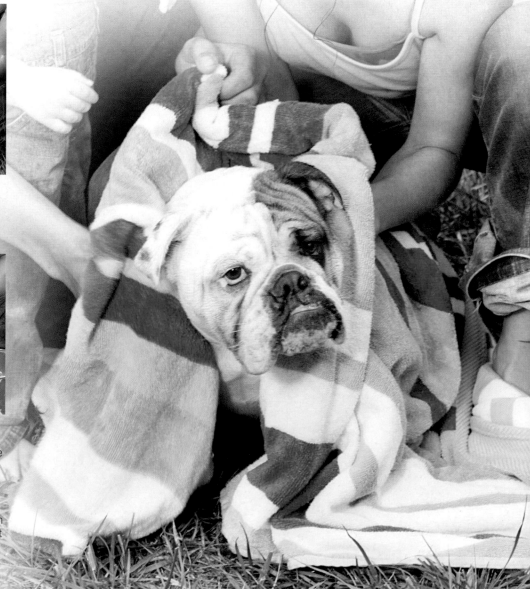

❸ Rub your pet's coat over with a towel, to dry it. You may want to use a hairdryer, although the resulting noise can easily upset a dog. Start on a low setting, with medium heat output.

BASIC TRAINING

There are certain basic instructions that your dog must learn, for its own safety and for the safety of others. Training should therefore begin at an early age with a puppy, to set out acceptable patterns of behavior. After toilet training has been dealt with, sitting and coming back on command are vital. Teaching your dog to accept a collar and leash is crucial in order to keep control during training.

TOILET TRAINING For the first four months or so of a dog's life he must be let outside every couple of hours during the day, and again last thing at night, in order to relieve himself.

TOILET TRAINING

One of the most important things that a puppy needs to learn is to be clean, and not to soil in the home. There are no shortcuts, and it is really a matter of being persistent and placing him outside every couple of hours or so during the day, and again last thing at night. Before long, he will appreciate what is required, and by four months or so, he will be asking to be let out, although it may be a further two months before he is completely house-broken. Training pads or even sheets of newspaper, which can be disposed of when soiled, can be used to cater for periods when you have to leave your pet on his own. Always clean up thoroughly, partly to insure that your puppy is not attracted back to this area by its scent.

SITTING

Teaching a dog to sit is reasonably straightforward since sitting is a natural posture. Start giving this instruction almost from the very outset, developing a routine when you feed your puppy. At first, he will not appreciate what is required, so keeping the food bowl in one hand, exert gentle pressure over the hindquarters to cause him to sit, albeit probably only momentarily at this stage. Very soon, you will find that your puppy is sitting, excitedly wagging his tail in anticipation of being given food.

Training to sit

❶ Always train your dog with a long leash attached to his collar, so that you are in control of his movements. Choose a quiet location so that he will not be distracted.

❷ Show your dog the food treat in your hand and give the command to "sit." If necessary, slowly raise the treat above his head so that he sits naturally in order to keep it in view.

❸ Immediately reward him with the food treat and praise, so that your dog associates sitting with a reward. Over time, you can phase out the treat as he learns to respond to verbal praise.

Training to lie down

❶ Once your dog is in a sitting position, show him the food treat in your hand, and bring it up in front of his nose.

❷ Move the hand holding the treat gradually down to the ground, so that the dog naturally follows it with his nose and lies down.

❸ Once he is completely prone, reward him immediately with the treat and verbal praise. However, it is important to maintain a calm tone of voice, because training will be less effective if he becomes overexcited.

the command "come" and start by keeping him on a long leash in your yard before attempting the exercise in a public place. When he returns on command you can try without the leash (again, in the yard initially).

The training process at home can be reinforced by signing up for a professional dog-training course. A major advantage of taking your puppy to such classes, once he is old enough, is that he can meet and socialize with other dogs, which should ultimately mean that he is less nervous.

The length of time taken to train a puppy successfully depends partly on how receptive your new pet is, and partly on how much time you devote to training and how clearly you communicate what you want your dog to do.

HAND SIGNAL It is a good idea to incorporate hand signals into your dog's training so that, ultimately, you will be able to communicate with your dog over a longer distance when you are out for a walk.

COLLARS AND LEASHES

It will take several days for your pet to become familiar with wearing a collar, but once this stage has passed, you can then start to teach him to walk on a leash. At first, he may resent being restrained, rolling about on the floor in an attempt to break free, but in a few days he will start walking reasonably well. Practice in your yard before going out into the street where there are more distractions. Getting your dog to return to you on command is obviously vital if you intend to let him off the leash in the park. Use

TREATS Use treats as a reward during early training sessions. Pats and praises will be adequate reward later on.

WALKING YOUR DOG

Dogs vary greatly in their exercise needs, thanks to their varying ancestries. Some breeds, such as the sled dogs, have tremendous stamina and need plenty of exercise, as do gundogs, which have been bred to work all day outdoors. On the other hand, companion breeds, such as the Pug, are usually far less active by nature. Age, too, plays a part, because a dog's energy level declines as it grows older.

MENTAL EXERCISE

Exercise for dogs is not just a physical need, it is important in providing mental stimulation too, helping to prevent them from becoming bored. It is important to accustom a young dog to going out for regular walks, once its course of vaccinations has been completed, partly to insure that it is well adjusted. Dogs reared in isolation tend to be more nervous by nature, and less social as far as other dogs are concerned. When letting your dog off the leash in a public space, make sure that you follow a few golden rules:
• Choose a quiet spot, away from farmstock and other dogs.
• Avoid anywhere close to a road.
• Remember to take some treats with you.
• Call your dog back to you before he goes any distance.
• Don't chase after your dog if he starts to run off. He will assume this is a game.

COMPANIONS Many small companion breeds, such as these Pugs, require relatively little exercise. However, this is not true of all small breeds; some terriers, for example, need a good daily run off the leash.

FURTHER AFIELD

The area where you walk your dog will depend partly on where you live. If you're lucky, there will be a local park, or open countryside. It may be worthwhile looking at a map for possible walks and talking with other dog owners, to see where they exercise their pets. A relatively short walk on a daily basis is much better than undertaking a single marathon walk on the weekend.

It may be that there is actually nowhere within walking distance of your home where you can let your pet safely off his leash, which means that you will need to drive further afield. Dogs often become excited when going out for a walk, and may start barking as soon as they get into the car. In order to prevent this problem arising, do not restrict your puppy's trips in the car to going for walks. Take your dog out for a drive when you need to visit a nearby store, for example, without actually giving him a walk on every occasion.

ROUTINE A dog needs a walk every day, not just on the weekends, so get into a healthy routine. Having a dog is a great excuse for getting a bit of exercise for yourself and your children.

THIRSTY WORK Your dog will get thirsty during a longer walk, so take him near to a clean water source or, alternatively, take along a special drinking bottle. There are designs available that do not require a separate bowl.

STAYING SAFE

Always watch where your dog is when he is off the leash, and call him back regularly to teach him not to stray too far. Take particular care if you encounter farm livestock when out walking, placing your dog on the leash at this stage. Cattle and horses may strike out at a dog, inflicting a serious or fatal injury, while dogs themselves can be unpredictable in the presence of sheep—a reflection of the hunting instincts of their wolf ancestor. They must be kept under control whenever they encounter sheep, particularly during the lambing period.

Weather protection

Many dogs are not deterred from going out for a walk in bad weather, but thin-coated breeds such as the Whippet will feel the cold, and should be given a suitable coat. There is a wide choice available today, ranging from lightweight rainproof coats for summer use through to heavier winter coats. It will also be worthwhile keeping an old towel in the car, which you can use to clean your dog's paws when they are muddy.

MEETING OTHER DOGS A walk in the park is a good opportunity for your dog to socialize with other dogs. Meeting other friendly dogs will make your pet less nervous. What's more, it's a chance for a bit of fun.

TOYS AND GAMES

Puppies in particular have a very evident playful streak to the natures, which actually helps them to understand more about the world around them, but even older dogs can be eager to have a game. Playing with your pet in this way helps to build and reinforce the bond between you, and can also be useful for training purposes. The right choice of toy depends to some extent on the type of dog that you have.

BALL GAMES Only use balls that are large enough not to be swallowed. Small balls may cause your dog to choke or lead to an obstruction in the digestive tract.

WHICH TYPE OF TOY?

Solid, terrier-like dogs, such as the Bull Terrier, often appreciate a tug toy, which enables them to test their strength with you. Do not pull too hard, however, since this may injure your dog's mouth. Dogs such as Labradors whose instincts are to retrieve will be more likely to favor flying disks, which they may even catch in mid-air on occasions. If you are playing with a friend as well, though, do not simply throw the disk back and forth, expecting your dog to run between you. He will soon become bored and is likely to lose interest in the game and will then wander off. Terriers often appreciate ball games, being instinctively inclined to chase after a ball in the same way that they would pursue live prey, such as a rat. And throwing a ball saves you walking too far!

BONES Most dogs enjoy gnawing bones, but give only sturdy limb bones from cattle. Never allow a dog to have chicken bones that will splinter and may cause choking.

BORN TO CHEW Young dogs are particularly likely to appreciate chew toys when they are teething, but they can be beneficial for older dogs, too. There is evidence to suggest that they may help to keep the teeth clean.

PLACES TO PLAY

If you have a yard, you should be able to play safely with your dog there, particularly with a tug toy, although obviously you are likely to be more restricted than in a park. Alternatively, if you take a toy when you go out on a walk with your dog, choose the locality carefully. Avoid areas where other dogs are being exercised, because they may decide that they want to join in the game, too, and this can lead to fighting. An area of open country is ideal, but keep an eye on where the toy lands, even though your dog may well be able to locate a missing ball if encouraged to do so. Should you not be able to throw a ball any distance, perhaps because of a shoulder problem, there are now sling-type units available that can project balls great distances with minimal effort.

TRAINING AND TOYS

If your dog appears reluctant to play with one particular type of toy, try another; dogs are quite individual in terms of having a favorite toy. With an older, rescued dog, it may simply be that he has never had any toys in the past, and is unsure what to do. Nevertheless, do persist in persuading him to play. Before long, you should find that he is actively looking forward to playing, bringing a toy to you as a way of asking for a game.

Toys can provide a good way of teaching a young dog to drop an item when told to do so. If you need to take a toy (or any item) away from your dog, place your left hand on either side of the top jaw, and then prise down the lower jaw. This should cause the object to fall out of the dog's mouth. A dog will soon learn to drop a ball of its own accord for you, so that you can throw the toy again. If your dog gets into the habit of destroying household objects, chew toys can be used to deflect a dog's attention.

CHEW TOY Chew toys are more hygienic to have around the home than bones. Some are designed to squeak to add to the fun.

FRISBEE Flying disks are great toys for highly active dogs and retrievers. Only use frisbees designed especially for dogs.

TUG TOY In games of tug, it is important that you can win! If your dog keeps winning, he may start to think that he should be the boss!

PLAYING Some toys are designed to be retrieved from water, often with a section of rope that allows the object to be thrown further with less effort. Always check that your dog is able to get out easily from a body of water.

DOGS AND VACATIONS

There will be times when you will need to decide on the best course of action, as far as your dog is concerned, when you want to take a vacation. In some cases you may be able to take your pet with you, although it is more likely that you will have to arrange alternative care. Possible options range from using a boarding kennel through to hiring the services of a professional dogsitter.

STAYING HOME Older dogs might be better off staying home. Reputable companies specializing in dogsitting advertise in homestyle magazines or through the Internet. Always check references carefully however.

TRAVELING WITH YOUR DOG

If you are intending to take a touring vacation, then it may be feasible to make arrangements for your dog to accompany you. This depends, however, on how you are traveling and what you hope to do on the trip. If, for example, you are going to be driving yourself, and have a motorhome, you will have tremendous flexibility. On the other hand, if you have to rely on hotels, you will need to plan your route carefully so you can stay at "dog-friendly" venues.

POSSIBLE DANGERS AWAY FROM HOME

If you do take your dog with you when traveling long distances, be prepared to stop regularly to give your pet a comfort break and a drink. Also, be aware of potential dangers that your dog may not have encountered before. There may be venomous snakes in the area or dangerous

IS YOUR VACATION SUITABLE? Your dog will no doubt prefer to spend the time with you rather than with strangers, but if you do choose to take him with you, make sure that your activites are suitable for a canine companion.

compare the facilities on offer, and talk with the staff, before reaching a decision.

PET-SITTING

Dogs generally settle well in kennels, and there is no worry that your pet will forget you while you are away, but, particularly if your dog is very elderly, you may need to consider other options. Pet-sitting services are now becoming increasingly popular. This entails having an experienced pet-keeper staying in your home while you are away, not only looking after your dog, but also any other pets that you may have, as well as taking care of other household tasks, such as watering houseplants.

An additional benefit of having a pet-sitter is that someone will be in your home while you are away, so it will be more secure. You will probably need to notify your home insurance company that they will be staying while you are away, so as not to invalidate your policy.

Boarding kennel checklist

■ Be sure that your dog's vaccinations are up-to-date, including a kennel cough vaccine.
■ Remember to take your pet's vaccination certificate.
■ Take your dog in a day early, to save a last-minute panic.
■ Leave your contact details, plus those of your vet.
■ Remember to take any medication that your dog is receiving.
■ Take one of your pet's favorite toys with you for his kennel.

PARASITES Ticks that can spread a number of serious infections, such as Lyme Disease, are rife in some areas, so you will need to check your pet for signs of these parasites if you have been out hiking for the day.

cliffs. Certain breeds are more at risk in dangerous situations than others. Retrievers, for example, will almost instinctively venture into water and yet plunging into the sea off a breakwater could be very dangerous, partly as there could be hidden obstructions. Currents can be hazardous, too, even though such dogs are generally strong swimmers. If in doubt, keep your dog on a leash. Be aware, too, of local laws that may actually prohibit dogs from a beach during the vacation season.

KENNELS

There are times when it will not be possible to take your dog with you, and then you will have to make alternative arrangements. The most obvious solution is to reserve space at a boarding kennel, but you will need to arrange this at the earliest opportunity to insure that there is a vacancy, especially during peak vacation periods.

If you have not used kennels in your area before, you may be able to obtain advice from your vet or dog owning friends. Alternatively, you could try phoning two or three at random, and arranging a time to visit. You can then

VETERINARY CARE

Routine health care is especially important in the case of puppies. Vaccines will protect them against the major infectious illnesses, such as distemper. These are otherwise likely to be deadly or may affect the dog for the rest of its life, assuming that it can be nursed through the initial infection. Regular deworming is vital, too. Once again, it is younger dogs that are especially at risk from these parasites.

CHOOSING A VET

An important consideration when choosing a veterinary practice is its proximity to where you live, should you need to take your dog in an emergency. Hopefully though, you should be visiting only to have your puppy neutered in due course, and for annual check-ups and booster vaccinations. With an older dog, however, more frequent visits are likely to be needed. These will allow for early diagnosis of any problems, which are more likely to arise at this stage, helping to insure they can be addressed more successfully.

All veterinarians are trained to the same standard, but you may be happier seeing one person throughout, so check whether this is possible. Insure that opening times fit in with your work schedule. Also, you need to be aware of whether there is an appointments system, or if it is a matter of turning up and being seen, which may take longer.

When deciding on a practice, you can ask friends who have dogs themselves for advice, or simply contact a couple of practices near you, and decide which you prefer. There may be differences in the cost of basic services like vaccinations, so you can ask about these too.

EARLY DAYS

It is always a good idea to take your puppy or dog to have a veterinary checkup as soon as possible after acquiring your new pet. Your vet can then check your puppy over thoroughly, listening to his heart for example, to insure that there is no abnormality here that could become a significant problem later in life. In the rare event that a problem is identified, you can discuss this with the breeder straight away and then decide what to do.

INSURANCE

The cost of veterinary care can be high, reflecting the advances in medicine and surgery that have occurred over recent years. Veterinary insurance can be especially helpful for unexpected bills, such as an accidental injury.

Check the cover matches what you require and read the small print carefully. Be aware of how much you will have to pay in the event of a claim, and also look for exclusions. In particular, if your pet already has a preexisting medical condition, the likelihood is that this will not be covered.

MICROCHIPPING

A means of permanently marking your dog with a microchip is now offered by many veterinary practices. The chip

ANNUAL BOOSTER AND CHECK-UP Regular yearly visits to the vet are a good opportunity to pick up on the early warning signs that can indicate health problems in your pet, as well as being a time to renew vaccinations.

contains a code that can be read by a special scanner passed over the area, which energizes the chip and detects the information (which is also stored separately in a central database). Should your dog stray and pass into the care of an animal rescue organization, they will be able to trace you by this means.

Microchipping provides a back-up to an information disk or capsule attaching to the collar. The system is accurate, and it is possible to insure that the chip is working at the time of insertion, although, on rare occasions, it may shift position within the body, making it harder to detect.

DEWORMING

Deworming is particularly important in young puppies, since they may have a heavy burden of *Toxocara* roundworms acquired from their mother. These, in turn, can pose a threat to human health, through their eggs. Eliminating parasitic worms is relatively easy if you deworm your dog regularly, following your vet's instructions.

MICROCHIP This identification device is about the size of a grain of rice and is located within a capsule, which is injected under the skin. Once in place, it should cause no discomfort or inconvenience to the dog.

VULNERABLE Since your puppy will not initially be fully protected against infections, don't let him associate with other dogs when you first visit the vet's office. Keep him confined either in a carrier, or sitting on your lap.

FIRST AID

Puppies, in particular, can end up in a variety of situations where they may require emergency first aid, and the aim should always be to obtain veterinary treatment as quickly as possible. If feasible, call your practice to check on the best course of action in an individual case, before taking your pet to the vet.

ROAD TRAFFIC ACCIDENTS

If you find a dog that has been hit by a vehicle, try to move it to the kerbside before checking its condition. If a dog is able to walk, use a temporary leash, but do not put yourself and others at risk by attempting to catch a dog in moving traffic after an accident. Remember, too, that the dog will be in pain and shock and is likely to bite, if restrained.

When moving an unconscious dog, try to keep its body level, picking it up from beneath rather than tipping it, as this might worsen any internal injuries. There could be internal complications that may not be immediately apparent in the case of a dog that seems not to be badly injured. A veterinary check-up is important in all cases.

HIDDEN DANGER Shock is a risk with all kinds of injury, and can be a killer. If you suspect the onset, wrap your dog in a blanket to keep him warm and elevate his hindquarters to increase the blood flow to the brain.

ROAD ACCIDENT The first priority is usually to move an injured dog from a dangerous location. If you a have a blanket or coat to hand, a makeshift stretcher will help you move the animal without exacerbating any injuries.

DANGEROUS GAMES Be especially vigiliant with puppies, as their exploits and curiosity can lead them into trouble.

BROKEN LIMBS The treatment for fractures in canines is essentially the same as in humans. Check the tightness of any bandages regularly for signs of swelling beneath.

Traumatic skin injuries from collisions may need grafts, while fractures can be stabilized in a variety of ways, with wires, pins, and casts, just as in human medicine.

PUPPY PROBLEMS

A puppy's natural curiosity means that it is more likely to end up requiring first aid that an older dog. It will snap at flying insects such as bees ad wasps, and may end up being stung inside its mouth. You may not be aware of what has actually happened, but always suspect a sting if, having been outside, your puppy starts pawing repeatedly at its mouth and is distressed. The consequences of a sting can be very serious if this occurs at the back of the throat, because the resulting swelling may block off the windpipe, impairing the dog's ability to breathe.

PADS

Although a dog's pads look quite tough, they can be sliced quite easily by pieces of sharp metal or glass on the ground and are then likely to bleed profusely. Use whatever you have available that is clean as a temporary bandage to put pressure on the wound, helping to stop the bleeding. You should then seek veterinary advice.

POISONING

Symptoms in this case can vary widely, depending on the poison: Give your vet as much information as possible. In some instances, giving an emetic to make the dog sick is recommended, but this is contra-indicated in other cases.

BURNS

If your pet does become burnt for any reason, cool the area as much as possible using cold running water, and again, consult your vet without delay.

WARNING SIGNS Listlessness may be the first sign of poisoning—other symptoms will depend on the agent. If your dog shows signs of weakness, lack of coordination, vomiting, or unconsciousness, contact a vet urgently.

OLD DOGS

On average, old dogs are now living longer than ever before, thanks to a combination of factors, including better diets and veterinary care. Modern treatments for illnesses associated with old age, such as cancers, have advanced significantly, to the extent that even large dogs should live for at least a decade. The record for canine longevity is held by Bluey, a working Australian Cattle Dog who lived to 26 years old.

OVERWEIGHT DOG It is important to weigh your pet regularly and check the results against the recommended weight range for the breed.

WHAT YOU CAN DO

While there is a genetic component that affects the lifespan of dogs, dictating that smaller breeds will live, on average, longer than their giant cousins, you can play your part in insuring that your pet enjoys a long, healthy life. One of the most important things is to give your dog regular exercise, and also not to overfeed him. Obesity is becoming a serious problem in dogs, exposing them to a range of ailments from diabetes to heart disease that are likely to end their lives prematurely. You can assess whether your dog is overweight by running your hands over his ribcage. You should be able to feel these bones, but if they are hard to locate then your dog is overweight. With determination, it will be possible to slim your pet down. Many veterinary practices now offer weight-watch clinics for dogs, where you can obtain help and advice.

Weight gain is likely to occur after neutering, becoming more of an issue from about five years onward, as a dog's level of activity will naturally start to slow down. You will need to adjust the quantity of food that you are offering, and cut out treats, replacing these instead with healthy tidbits like a slice of carrot. Your vet may recommend using a special weight loss diet as well, which contains fewer calories, as a way of speeding the weight loss process.

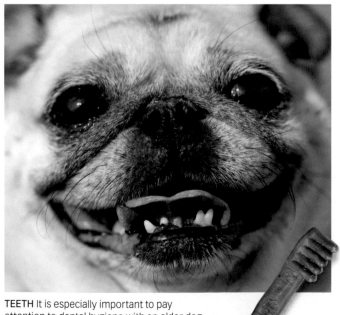

TEETH It is especially important to pay attention to dental hygiene with an older dog. Teeth-cleaning chews may help in addition to regular tooth-brushing.

The older dog

What to expect with an older dog:
- Some graying of the fur around the muzzle.
- Whitish cataracts may form in the eyes.
- Your dog's hearing may not be as acute.
- May show signs of stiffness first thing in the morning.
- May start to develop small warts.

Changes requiring veterinary investigation:
- Significantly increased thirst.
- Breakdown in toilet training.
- Loss of appetite.
- Abnormal swellings on the body.
- Breathlessness.
- A reluctance to walk.
- Difficulty in seeing.

ADDRESSING THE AGING PROCESS

Older dogs may suffer from a wide range of age-related health problems. Ongoing monitoring of your dog's health will help to pick up such problems and allow treatment to be given to stabilize his condition. Blood tests can check things such as renal function, which will deteriorate to a variable degree with age. Supplements can be of help, too, in addressing the problems of aging, for ailments ranging from kidney disease to arthritis.

SLOWING DOWN It is normal for ageing dogs to slow down and exercise less, and their diet may need to be adjusted to prevent weight gain. However, check for any health problems that may be causing a drop off in activity.

DENTAL PROBLEMS

Bad breath is not uncommon in older dogs, and this can be linked to dental disease. Dogs frequently suffer from a build-up of tartar on the teeth. Over time, this hardens and results in inflammation of the adjacent gum line, which becomes eroded around the base of the tooth. The tooth then become weakened, and bacteria can gain access to the root, which will result in a very painful abscess and can lead on to a more serious generalized infection. Keep your dog's teeth as healthy as possible by brushing them regularly using a special canine dental kit. Dogs can generally adapt well to losing teeth, but you may need to switch your pet over to a diet based on wet food.

A DOG'S LIFE

Dogs today are being kept increasingly as companions, rather than for their working abilities. Over the course of little more than a century, their role has altered dramatically, with this change being triggered initially by a growing interest in competitive showing. The original working abilities of breeds have not been neglected though, and there are still field trials where dogs are assessed on these traits rather than on their appearance, which is the case in the show ring. Some dogs compete with equal success in both areas but, increasingly, there has been a divergence in appearance or "type" between working and show dogs of the same breed.

SHETLAND SHEEPDOG Some herding and gundog breeds have separated into down-to-earth working lines and show dogs with features like fuller coats. But many a show Sheltie still combines brains and beauty, scoring well in trials.

THE CHANGING ROLE OF THE DOG

What sets the dog apart from all other domestic animals is the way it has adapted, in terms of its association with us. Dogs have performed a very wide range of roles through history, mirroring the changes that have taken place in human society down through the millennia. This is still an on-going process, as reflected by the growing number of so-called designer dogs now being created.

PUGGLE The increasingly popular Puggle is a designer crossbreed created by crossing the Pug and the Beagle. The result is a good-natured, active, and playful companion breed with a distinctive and endearing expression.

HUNTERS AND GUARDIANS

At the outset, dogs were kept as hunting companions, helping to provide food, in addition to acting as guardians around settlements. Then, once agriculture started to develop, dogs were soon being used to herd and guard livestock. Their role as hunting companions subsequently continued to diversify, to the extent that when shooting became a fashionable pastime in the 1800s, breeds of dog were created specially as gundogs. It is the

HERDING DOGS The Border Collie is one of those breeds that is still kept in many countries as a herding dog but is also a hugely popular pet. They retain strong herding instincts and need a great deal of exercise.

ROTTWEILER The Rottweiler is a hugely popular breed that has been around since the time of the Romans. They need careful handling.

adaptability of the dog that has seen their skills being used in a wide range of different activities. Some of these, such as truffle hunting, are both localized and very specialized activities.

The most significant change to date started in the late 1800s, however, reflecting a more general trend that was becoming evident in society. The increasing mechanization that was taking place in Europe and North America gave many people more leisure time and greater wealth, as reflected by a growing middle class. This was a time of evolutionary theory, and people were embarking on selective breeding of a wide range of plants and animals, which became known as "fancying." The results of their endeavors were seen at shows and, in this respect, dogs were no different from other domestic species.

THE SHOW SCENE

Up until this stage, there had been no breeds as such but, rather, dogs had developed recognizable characteristics linked to their work. The breed concept of today arose in conjunction with the show scene. In Britain, an entrepreneur called Charles Cruft spotted the huge opportunity presented by the public's growing interest in dogs. His involvement in this area began when he set up a business selling stale biscuits (brought back by ships) as dog food, on behalf of an entrepreneur called James Spratt. Up until this time, there had been no commercially produced foods for dogs. While Spratt was destined to set up one of the first dog food companies, Cruft's name has become indelibly linked with the most famous dog show in the world.

Cruft started by seeking support from wealthy patrons. His first show was an event just for terriers, but it proved very popular. This led him to organize a much larger spectacle in 1893, where he confidently proclaimed that every breed in the world could be seen. Cruft was a great showman, and even managed to persuade Queen Victoria to exhibit at this event, significantly increasing its profile. Before long, he was running special trains from around the country to this event.

Family member

Dogs in general are becoming much more central to people's lives, with the tendency being to treat them increasingly as a member of the family. There is no doubt that today many dogs are pampered to a greater extent than ever before, although, sadly, a minority still face lives of uncertainty and neglect.

Crufts revolutionized people's view of dogs, and had an impact far beyond the United Kingdom. Similar events were soon being run in other European cities and further afield, in North America, for example, where the Westminster Show held in New York also became an annual event. Cruft was also responsible for introducing a number of today's popular breeds, such as the Boxer.

SHOWING Today, dog shows are hugely popular all around the world, from small local shows held outdoors to international shows held in massive indoor arenas.

BREED STANDARDS

The way in which dogs are categorized at shows may not be immediately evident to an onlooker, but there is a very clear format. In the first instance, the breeds are divided up into different groups, such as hounds, that reflect their origins, known as their breed group. Then within each actual breed division, there will be various "classes" depending on the size of the show and its popularity.

COMPARING TO THE STANDARD In spite of the impression that is given at shows, each dog is judged against the perceived ideal example of the breed, rather than the other members of that particular class.

SETTING THE STANDARD

The ideal example of each breed is encapsulated in the breed standard, which is laid down by the registration body, such as the Kennel Club in the United Kingdom, or the *Fedération Cynologique Internationale* (*FCI*) in mainland Europe. The situation is more confused in the United States since there are a number of separate registration bodies, of which the best known is the American Kennel Club.

Recognition of breeds for show purposes is the prerogative of the individual kennel club. Most operate a system that takes account of a breed's popularity. Once this reaches a certain level, the breed is added to a provisional register, and an interim standard will be drawn up. In the case of a foreign breed, this standard is likely to be based on the requirements in its country of origin. Assuming the breed's popularity then continues to grow, it will ultimately progress to obtain full recognition.

SHOWING THE SAME BREED Depending on the size of the show, there will be various classes within each actual breed division, such as classes for puppies, or for older, "veteran," dogs.

WINNING GAITS As a sighthound, the Afghan is expected to have a flowing movement, whereas the stocky English Bulldog will display more of a rolling gait when being trotted by its handler.

Handling in the show ring

Although in many cases, the handler is also the dog's owner, this may not apply at the major events. Increasingly, professional handlers are being used to show leading examples of the breed at their best, with a view to impressing the judge. Sometimes, however, a dog may show better when being handled by someone familiar, rather than a virtual stranger.

FINDING A WINNER

The same judging principles apply as one moves up through the rankings. Class winners compete for the best of breed title, and each of these then progress to best in group. Finally, these winners then compete for the best in show award, again being adjudged against their individual breed standard. It can be difficult in some cases to predict with a puppy just how well it will do in the show ring. Some dogs seem to blossom, and develop what can be described as a winning personality, helping them to perform well and catch the judge's eyes.

The standard is an attempt to portray in words a description of what the breed should look like, in all respects, including coloration. But the information included under different breed standards does vary—they are not set out in the same way for all breeds. The majority of standards will specify the dog's height, including any variance between males and bitches, but will not necessarily state the breed's preferred weight. The color is usually an important factor and a dog can lose marks for flaws in this area. A judge needs to be intimately acquainted with the requirements of the standard when assessing a class.

It is not just the physical features, but also how these combine to contribute to the dog's movement. Different breeds move in different ways, depending on their particular body shape, which will have a direct influence on their so-called gait. Sighthounds, for example, tend to have a flowing movement, reflecting their athletic nature, whereas those of dogs with a stocky appearance, such as the English Bulldog, will be quite different, displaying more of a rolling gait when being trotted by their handler in the show ring.

SHAR PEI A number of highly distinctive breeds such as the Shar Pei have been brought back successfully from the edge of extinction.

COMPANION DOGS

As the name suggests, this group of dogs has not been developed for any specific task other than to act as companions for humans. Small dogs have been kept for this purpose for millennia, with such individuals being cherished pets of the Romans, and among the ancient civilizations of Central and South America, as well as in Asia.

ITALIAN GREYHOUND The Italian Greyhound was bred from the standard Greyhound kept for hunting purposes. Many companions were created this way.

ORIGINS

There is no clear ancestral lineage in the case of companion breeds, in contrast to the situation with hounds. Such dogs have occurred on all continents, with the only link between them being their small size, which is why they are also often referred to as toy breeds. In a number of cases, companion dogs were effectively smaller examples of larger breeds. They lived around the homes of the wealthy, being fashionable companions then, just as members of this group still are with media celebrities today.

In the 1600s, Charles II of England popularized the toy spaniel that still bears his name, often being seen taking these dogs out walking along Birdcage Walk in London. Subsequently, it was the Pug, a breed of likely Oriental origins, which became linked with William of Orange. In China, itself, small dogs were highly prized.

In South America, too, there were small dogs such as the Peruvian Inca Orchid being kept as companions. This and other hairless breeds were also valued as bedwarmers, helping to keep their owners warm during the bitterly cold nights experienced in the Andean mountains. Today, unfortunately, only a relatively few of these ancient dogs survive, but it is a breed from Central America, named after the Mexican province where it originated, that now ranks as an archetypal companion breed. The Chihuahua has become one of the best known of all toy dogs worldwide, although its precise origins are unknown.

The Bichon Frisé is now the most widely kept

PRECIOUS PEKINGESE In China, toy breeds were very highly prized. Indeed, in the case of the Pekingese, attempting to steal one from the Emperor's court was punishable by death.

BICHON It is possible to track the Bichon lineage back thousands of years, with these small companion dogs all being distinguished by their white, fluffy coats. They are today's most popular companion breed.

example of the group, although the Bolognese is possibly the ancestral form, originally bred in Italy with a history believed to extend as far back as A.D 1000. Bichon stock was subsequently taken to French colonies off the coast of Africa. In Madagascar, the breed evolved into the Coton de Tuléar, with a similar, but now extinct, variety created on the nearby island of Réunion.

MODERN MINIATURIZATION

Not all attempts at miniaturization have been successful, however. There used to be a strain of miniature Beagles, called Pocket Beagles on account of their size, which were popular as far back as the reign of Queen Elizabeth I of England in the 16th century, but they finally died out during the 1930s. In recent times, new toy breeds have been created, most notably in the case of the Poodle. Unfortunately, however, such reductions in size are often accompanied by a decline in the breed's soundness.

Having been bred over the course of centuries to act as companions, the toy breeds are ideally suited to domestic living. They are generally very intelligent and responsive by nature, making them easier to train than larger dogs created for working purposes. Their exercise needs are modest and so they are ideally suited to modern-day urban life. They are a good choice for older owners, because their size means they are easy to pick up when necessary. Their lifespan is also likely to be longer than that of larger breeds.

TOY POODLE Not content with what is now called the Miniature variety, bred down in size from the Standard Poodle, breeders then developed an even smaller Toy form.

CHIHUAHUA Many small dogs have a powerful bark, considerably louder than their size may suggest, and prove to be alert watchdogs. This may be a cause of friction with near neighbors.

COMPACT COMPANIONS Recent years have seen a fad for "handbag dogs" tiny enough to ride in their owners' designer bags. While the image is appealing, welfare organizations are worried by pets being treated as fashion accessories.

TERRIERS

Dogs have always had a natural tendency to hunt, and this instinct remains strong in the case of the terrier breeds. The British Isles is the area of the world where the majority of today's terrier breeds were created. They were created essentially as industrious, hardy farm dogs, and still display great stamina even today. Some are still kept on farms for their working abilities.

PATTERDALE There are a number of terriers of more recent origins, such as the Lucas and Patterdale Terriers, which remain localized in their area of origin and are still unrecognized for show purposes.

SMALL BUT TOUGH

The short-legged appearance of many terriers was significant, because it meant that they could venture underground with relative ease, down into a fox's lair for example. This demanded considerable bravery, because the terrier would be expected to drive out the fox, which would then have to seek sanctuary elsewhere, being pursued by a waiting pack of hounds once it emerged above ground. The terrier's short legs, however, were such that it would often have difficulty keeping up with the hounds, and so these dogs might be carried in a pannier by one of the huntsmen on horseback.

Most terriers are versatile hunters, so they are capable of ambushing unwary rabbits, although being employed more commonly to hunt down and kill rodents around the farm. This ability then developed into an urban pastime during the early Victorian era, which saw the establishment of rat pits in taverns.

PIT DOGS

Ratting contests attracted large audiences, who wagered on the outcome. The terriers were set against rats obtained from rat catchers, to see how many they could kill in a set period of time, or how long it took the dog to dispatch all the rats in the pit. One of the best-known

ACTIVE It is important not to be fooled by their size, because terriers generally need plenty of exercise, possessing great stamina. They can also prove to be rather obstinate by nature, and need sound training.

terriers of this era was a Manchester Terrier called Billy. He managed to kill 100 rats in just six minutes and 13 seconds. The outcome did not always favor the dog, however, because in an era before inoculations against leptospirosis, terriers were particularly vulnerable to this rat-borne disease.

Other even more macabre forms of entertainment, were developed in the growing industrial cities. Dog fighting became popular, with the tenacity and bravery of terriers putting them in the front line of such contests. Breeds that were developed for this purpose include the Staffordshire Bull Terrier. Terriers, generally, prove to be rather obstinate by nature, and need sound training from puppyhood. This is also important to reduce their innate tendency not to be very friendly toward other dogs, particularly in the case of those originally developed for fighting purposes.

IN DECLINE

As there has been less need for working terriers over recent years, their numbers have fallen to the extent that some breeds now face an uncertain future. Others, notably those that have been miniaturized even further, such as the Yorkshire Terrier, often tend to be considered more as companion dogs today.

Terriers are loyal, intelligent companions. They are also very hardy, long-lived dogs, which thrive in a rural environment. Terriers are generally small in size, which means they will not take up much space in the home, and their lively personalities mean they make good companions, especially for older owners. They will also prove alert guardians around the home.

As far as keen gardeners are concerned, the way in which many terriers will dig in flower-beds as well as on the lawn will not be perceived as a particularly endearing trait. Also, their rather impatient and often dominant natures mean they are probably not the ideal choice for a home alongside young children.

PIT BULL Breeds that were developed for fighting include the notorious American Pit Bull Terrier, which is banned in a number of countries.

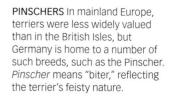

PINSCHERS In mainland Europe, terriers were less widely valued than in the British Isles, but Germany is home to a number of such breeds, such as the Pinscher. *Pinscher* means "biter," reflecting the terrier's feisty nature.

HOUNDS

Hounds represent the oldest group of dogs, having been developed primarily for hunting purposes. They are broadly divided today into sighthounds and scenthounds, reflecting the way in which they pursue their quarry. Most countries have their own breeds of hound, although some of these, such as the Lithuanian Hound, for example, still remain very localized in their distribution.

ANCIENT BREEDS

Lightly built sighthounds were among the early types to develop, principally in North Africa and the Middle East. Breeds from these areas, such as the Sloughi and Saluki, are among the most ancient, while breeds from the Mediterranean islands, such as the Ibizan Hound and Cirneco dell'Etna, show similar influences.

RACERS Greyhounds are popular today as racing dogs, but they are an ancient type and images of dogs bearing an unmistakable similarity to Greyhounds have been discovered among the artefacts of ancient Egypt.

AFGHAN HOUND Grooming hounds is relatively easy since the majority have short coats that require very little care. There are, however, one or two notable exceptions to this rule.

Sighthounds have a narrow nose, with their eyes being well positioned toward the sides of the head to give a good view of the world around them. This helps them to identify movement in their vicinity and detect their quarry. The body of a sighthound is built for speed, with its broad, deep chest affording good lung capacity, while the muscular hindquarters provide rapid acceleration and pace. Most sighthounds tend to hunt individually, or in couples, pursuing their quarry through open countryside where they can maintain visual contact.

SCENTHOUNDS

Sighthounds excel in the semidesert areas of North Africa and the Middle East, but a different hunting strategy is required in wooded areas of northern Europe. Here, the ability to track quarry by scent becomes significant.

The development of scenthounds reached its greatest diversity in France, prior to the French Revolution of 1789, when most of the country's châteaux had their own packs of these hounds. A further change occurred with the emergence of the basset forms of many of these breeds. This name originates from the French word *bas*, meaning "low," reflecting the stature of such dogs with their characteristic short-legged appearance.

Unlike the situation with other groups of dog, the development of hounds has not progressed significantly over recent years. A number of breeds, such as the Otterhound, are now regarded as being endangered, since they are no longer kept for their traditional purpose. As the case of the Irish Wolfhound confirms, however, such breeds can build up a significant following in the show ring and among pet owners sensitive to the needs

HUNTING HOUNDS Coloration is relatively standardized in pack hounds, being either bi- or tricolored, enabling individual packs to be distinguished from a distance by their markings.

of these dogs. There are still various breeds of hound that are unlikely to be seen at major shows.

CHARACTERISTICS

Hounds are lively, friendly, and responsive dogs by nature. They are ideal for a home with children in view of their playful natures. Thanks to their predominantly smooth coats, hounds need very little grooming, even when molting, and coat care for those breeds that exist in a wirecoated form is also quite straightforward. The social nature of most hounds, particularly scenthounds, means that they tend to agree well together if you want to keep more than one dog at home. Not all hounds require long walks—Greyhounds, for example, need little more than an opportunity to run in an open field or park for a relatively short time.

Training hounds not to run off when out walking is often relatively difficult, particularly in the case of scenthounds, since they will be instinctively inclined to set off on a trail. Scenthounds also tend to have rather greedy natures, which can predispose them to obesity unless their food intake is adequately controlled and balanced with the amount of exercise they are being given.

BLOODHOUND The St. Hubert Hound, or its modern descendant in the guise of the Bloodhound, represents the oldest of the scenthounds. Its influence can be seen in virtually all of today's breeds of this type.

HOUNDS Scenthounds will pursue quarry across many miles of countryside if required, coping with some serious obstacles along the way. Hunting with hounds is still popular in many countries, although it was recently banned in the United Kingdom.

GUNDOGS

The ancestry of contemporary gundogs can be traced back to the dogs that were used as hunting companions when bows and arrows were still being employed to kill game. The emergence of modern gundog breeds began as a result of the rise of shooting that began in Great Britain in the 1800s. Bred to work on a one-to-one basis with their handler, it is not surprising that this group of dogs has also become so popular among pet seekers.

RETRIEVERS

The Labrador Retriever and the Golden Retriever, which are the most popular breeds by far in the world today, are both members of this group. As their names suggest, the original purpose of these gundogs was to retrieve shot game, working effectively in a wide range of terrain, and not being afraid to enter water to obtain shot waterfowl.

POINTERS AND SETTERS

Whereas retrievers as a group are relative newcomers, whose origins can be linked directly to the rise of interest in shooting, pointer breeds have been in existence for perhaps 500 years or more. They are very versatile shooting companions, being able to indicate the presence of quarry at the outset by adopting their characteristic pointing stance, leaning forward with one of their front legs raised slightly off the ground. Subsequently, they can retrieve the shot game.

Setters represent another older division within the gundog category, with their name deriving from the old English verb "set," meaning "to sit" They, quite simply, sit down or crouch low when they detect game.

SPANIEL Extremely versatile and generally very friendly, working spaniels track down prey and flush it out for the waiting hunters. They then use scent to find the fallen quarry and retrieve it.

GORDON SETTER The Gordon Setter is a lively and intelligent gundog with a distinctive black-and-tan coat color. He has not yet achieved the level of popularity enjoyed by many other gundogs.

SPANIELS

The other major group of breeds that are classified as gundogs are the spaniels. They will effectively locate and flush quarry, particularly birds, for the waiting guns, picking up scents readily and making able retrievers too.

The physique of various spaniels does differ significantly, however, with the Clumber Spaniel as an example, being a slower, more deliberate worker than the lively Cocker Spaniel, which has been further evolved in the United States to hunt quail. In addition, there is often a divergence now in type between working gundogs and those seen in the show ring.

Some gundogs have acquired unparalleled levels of popularity, whereas others are still localized in various parts of Europe and elsewhere.

CHARACTERISTICS

Gundogs as a group are intelligent, affectionate, and responsive companions, settling well in the domestic environment, although their level of activity is such that they really need the opportunity to exercise in a rural area on a daily basis. Training is normally quite straightforward, especially if begun at an early age. The coloration of some of these breeds, such as the Irish

Setter with its chestnut-red coat, is striking. Grooming is not particularly arduous, especially if you allow mud in the coat to dry so it can then be simply brushed out. There is a good range in size among gundogs, providing scope in terms of choosing a domestic pet. Retrievers in particular are generally well disposed to younger members of a family. If you enjoy going on long walks, then this type of dog may be suitable for you.

While Labradors especially can suffer from hip dysplasia, spaniels are susceptible to ear infections because of the shape and positioning of their ears (*see* p. 28). It is also an unfortunate fact that Labrador Retrievers are prone to obesity, particularly after being neutered, and their weight should be monitored to prevent unwanted weight gain. Gundogs frequently enter water without any warning, which can be very dangerous in certain situations. This behavior can also create difficulties when you are faced with a very wet dog who needs to be taken home in your car.

CHOCOLATE LABRADOR Labradors should have "soft" mouths, meaning that they are able to retrieve shot game, such as the duck seen here, without breaking the skin.

HERDING DOGS

One of the features that has cemented the relationship between dogs and people is the way they have adapted to changes in human lifestyles. Once people gave up a nomadic lifestyle dependent on hunting and started to farm, new types of dog were developed. Dogs assisted humans in controlling the movements of goats, sheep, and other livestock, as well as guarding these animals from predators.

COMPETITIONS

Breeds of herding dog have been developed in most parts of the world, and their appearance is influenced to a large extent by the terrain in which they have evolved, usually over the course of centuries. In many instances, they have a dense and often quite long water-resistant coat, as typified by that of the Bearded Collie, which serves to protect them from the worst of the weather.

The dogs in this group are actually quite variable in size, which tends to be a reflection of their function. Perhaps surprisingly, cattle dogs in general tend to be small in size, as typified by the Welsh Corgis. This is because they had to be nimble, darting in among herds of cattle, being able to persuade reluctant individuals to move by nipping at the backs of their feet. The dog could then slip away easily if the cow decided to lash out.

ANATOLIAN SHEPHERD Various regional forms of the Anatolian Shepherd Dog have been identified in Turkey. They are not essentially herding dogs, however, but are devoted flock guardians.

SHEEPDOG TRIAL A sheepdog trial taking place as part of the Rydale Country Show in Cumbria, England. Dogs are expected to control and pen the sheep, with their handlers staying in the background.

GUARDIANS

In areas where wolves used to represent a real danger to livestock, herd guardians were developed. Such breeds include the Anatolian Shepherd Dog, which originated in Turkey. Not all areas of the world could support a number of different breeds to work with farmstock. This resulted in the development of dogs that could not only herd but also undertake other tasks around the farm. The Norwegian Buhund is a typical example, even adapting to the role of hunting companion, although its herding instinct is so ingrained that it will even round up farmyard poultry.

COMPETITIONS

A number of herding dogs are still largely unknown outside their area of origin, and are characterized essentially by their working ability rather than their type. Sheepdog trials provide an opportunity for handlers to

HERDING DEER Dogs will herd a wide variety of animals including deer and even geese. A dog's herding instinct derives from its wolf ancestor, which drives its prey toward other pack members during the hunt.

Country dogs

Herding breeds are not suitable as companions for everyone, and are better suited to a rural rather than urban lifestyle. They vary widely in size and temperament. Some herding breeds have longer coats than others, and this will impact on the amount of time that you will need to devote to grooming. Herding dogs generally are very responsive, and learn fast. It is no surprise that in areas such as doggy dancing, where owner and dog must work together in harmony, collies and similar breeds excel. They make excellent companions, being used to forming a very close bond with people, and can prove alert guardians around the home.

test the skills of their dogs in a competitive environment. Classes are usually held at agricultural shows, rather than in a typical dog show environment. The dogs control the movements of the sheep using their body posture and positioning. Their skill is largely instinctive, having been passed down through many generations.

WORKING DOGS

In some respects, the description of working dogs is really a catch-all, because with the exception of the companion dogs, all of today's breeds were originally created to undertake specific tasks. What helps to separate dogs in this group is the diversity of tasks that they have undertaken.

PULLING MILK CHURNS Dog were once used to pull heavy carts laden with churns of milk from farms to the cheese manufacturers, before taking the finished products on to market.

POWERFUL BREEDS

Many working breeds are large, powerful dogs, and some share common ancestries, so that there are several sub-groups within this division. The far north, for example, is home to sled breeds such as the Alaskan Malamute, which had a vital role in moving supplies and people between the remote isolated communities in this part of the world before the advent of mechanized transportation.

GUARD DOGS

Many members of the working group actually owe their origins to mastiff-type stock—formidable animals with huge heads and powerful jaws that are the ultimate guard

BERNESE MOUNTAIN DOG In Switzerland, Bernese Mountain Dogs would work in pairs to pull heavy carts, harnessed carefully with leather straps. Today, this attractive breed is popular in the show ring.

CHARACTERISTICS

Loyal and affectionate, working dogs can be trusted guardians. They are friendly and affectionate by nature toward those who are part of their family circle, and usually prove amenable to training. Bear in mind, however, that male dogs of these larger breeds often grow considerably larger than bitches and can be rather more assertive by nature as well. Aside from exhibiting your dog, depending on the breed you choose you may even be able to take part in sled-racing competitions with your pet, helping to keep both of you fit. Sled dogs do need thorough grooming, but a number of the other working breeds are shorthaired, so that coat care in such cases is relatively straightforward.

It is very important to investigate the individual origins of a particular breed of interest, since members of this group can be quite diverse in terms of their ancestries and temperament. The large size and strength of many working breeds means that controlling them on a leash may be difficult. They also have correspondingly large appetites, making them relatively costly to keep, and cleaning up after them can be a considerably more daunting task than poop-scooping after a terrier, for example. Also, as is usual for large dogs generally, their maximum lifespan is likely to be shorter than that of smaller breeds, rarely exceeding ten years.

MASTIFF Recognizable by their large size, stocky bodies, and a wide head with powerful jaws, Mastiffs have an overhang of skin around the lips, known as jowls, while the skin on the forehead is wrinkled.

dogs. Although the description of "mastiff" denotes a breed, it is also indicative of an ancient bloodline that is thought to have begun in the vicinity of China thousands of years ago. The ancestral form, the Tibetan Mastiff, is not just believed to represent one of the oldest canine bloodlines, but it is also one of the biggest breeds in existence even today, weighing in at a maximum weight of about 180 lb (82 kg). In the past, much heavier examples existed, weighing nearly twice this figure.

Mastiff stock is believed to have reached Europe from Asia along the Old Silk Road, which was the major trade route. The Neapolitan Mastiff is a descendant of this early period in history, with its ancestry extending back to the days of ancient Rome. These early mastiffs soon spread widely through Europe, often being used in battle. Before long, they were being bred in a number of different countries, with the result that today, the United Kingdom, Spain, France, and Italy are just some of the countries with native mastiff breeds. The overall impression of all the mastiff breeds is one of tremendous strength.

DALMATIAN Bred to run alongside carriages to deter highwaymen, Dalmatians have tremendous stamina and require a great deal of exercise.

SEEKING EMPLOYMENT Although technically a herder, the German Shepherd Dog has proved itself competent in a host of working roles. Working dogs are intelligent, motivated breeds that thrive on a structured, busy life.

DESIGNER DOGS

There is a new trend apparent among dog owners that has led to the rise in popularity of what are now being called "designer dogs." It is a phenomenon that is growing in pace, partly as a result of fashion, but also because of the undeniable appeal of such dogs. They represent the result of crosses between existing purebreds with the aim of capturing the most desirable traits of both parents.

PUGGLE The extremely flattened face of the Pug, which can be off-putting to some, is modified in the Pug-Beagle cross. The Puggle, as he is known, has a particularly endearing expression.

NEW ROLES

Designer dogs do not represent a new breed category for show purposes as yet, although there are already signs that this might occur in the future. Currently, there is still variability in inherited features, which is part of their charm.

Although this type of breeding has acquired a novelty value, with designer dogs attracting widespread media interest, it is simply a continuation of the same trend that has taken place since the very start of the domestication of the dog. The dog's popularity has always been due in part to the way in which it has adapted to our lifestyles, and today's designer dogs are no different in this respect.

Almost all the breeds that exist today originally undertook specific tasks. As a result, this means that they retain aspects of their personalities that reflect their origins. Breeders creating true designer dogs (as distinct from wolf-dog hybrids) are usually aiming to refine the personalities and characteristics of these dogs to make them better companions, which is the main role of the dog today.

It was the transformation of the dog from workmate to showdog and household pet that actually created the standardization apparent in breeds today. Now, another major shift is occurring, with people seeking to develop types of dog that fit in well with their lifestyles, rather than simply choosing a dog on the grounds of its appearance. Quiet, cute, small, and trainable are just some of the characteristics that are usually favored in designer dogs.

THE ORIGINS OF DESIGNER DOGS

In spite of media coverage suggesting that designer dogs are a 21st-century phenomenon, serious interest in them is not new, as it began in the 1950s. Perhaps ironically, there is even an early example of the designer-dog phenomenon from this era in a portrait that has pride of place in the august headquarters of the Kennel Club in London. It shows HM Queen Elizabeth II with a Dorgi—

a cross between her sister's Dachshund and one of her Pembroke Welsh Corgis—and it is the only portrayal of a nonpedigree dog in the entire building!

WHY POODLES?

Poodles have played the most significant role so far in the ancestry of designer dogs, partly because they do not shed their fur. This characteristic means that they are not as messy around the home as most breeds, again reflecting our lifestyle preferences. Perhaps just as significantly, however, they generally seem to be less likely to trigger an allergic reaction in people who are sensitive and might otherwise not be able to have a dog. This hypoallergenic aspect associated with designer dogs can be critical especially for disabled people, who may otherwise be deprived of canine assistance. In fact, Labradoodles—currently the best known of the designer dogs—were originally created for this reason to aid those with impaired sight.

Poodles have also been widely used in breeding designer dogs because they are intelligent and responsive by nature, proving good companions. The fact that they occur in several sizes increases the potential for matings with other breeds.

COCK-A-POO Cock-a-poo (a cross between a Cocker Spaniel and a Poodle) Toy crossbreeds are particularly popular, and smaller Poodles have been used to create, among others, Cock-a-poos, Yorkiepoos, Pekepoos, and Shih-poos. While owners are often very happy with these charming crosses, some breeders are exploiting the trend with little regard to welfare.

CONTINUATION OF A TREND

The range of designer dogs continues to increase, with over 75 such crosses having been named to date. The trend is now firmly established to combine parts of the name of both ancestral breeds in that of the designer dog. Hence Labradoodle, reflecting a cross between a Labrador Retriever and a Poodle, or a Cock-a-poo, which is the result of a Cocker Spaniel-Poodle ancestry.

Although to an extent the breeders of such dogs are simply following what has been occurring over the course of centuries, there is another aspect underlying the designer dogs phenomenon. They reflect a growing quest for individuality, since purebred dogs have become almost indiscernible from each other in terms of type if not coloration today, when seen in the show ring. Designer dogs are essentially "one-offs"—they stem from purebred lineages, and yet littermates often vary quite widely in terms of their overall appearance. This exclusivity is further emphasized by the relatively high prices that such dogs can command, because they are often more costly than either of their purebred ancestors.

A further feature of designer dogs is that they are often promoted as being potentially healthier than their pure-bred counterparts. This reflects the fact that top show lineages of pedigrees are often closely related, and may be at risk from a host of breed-specific health problems.

Nevertheless, there is no absolute guarantee that designer dogs will suffer less from hereditary or

SCHNOODLE A Schnauzer and Poodle cross, the Schnoodle combines the guarding instincts of the Schnauzer with the intelligence and playfulness of the Poodle.

Top 20 designer dog breeds

Puggle: Pug x Beagle
Goldendoodle: Golden Retriever x Poodle
Labradoodle: Labrador Retriever x Poodle
Cock-a-poo: Cocker Spaniel x Poodle
Cavachon: Cavalier King Charles Spaniel x Bichon Frisé
Yorkie-poo: Yorkshire Terrier x Poodle
Zuchon: Shih Tzu x Bichon Frisé
Schnoodle: Miniature Schnauzer x Poodle
Shih Poo: Shih Tzu x Poodle
Malkie: Maltese x Yorkshire Terrier

Malt-a-poo: Maltese x Poodle
Poochon: Poodle x Bichon Frisé
Yo-chon: Yorkshire Terrier x Bichon Frisé
Cockalier: Cocker Spaniel x Cavalier King Charles Spaniel
Silkshire Terrier: Silky Terrier x Yorkshire Terrier
Maltichon: Maltese x Bichon Frisé
Shiffon: Shih Tzu x Brussels Griffon
Shih Apso: Shih Tzu x Lhasa Apso
Lhasa Poo: Lhasa Apso x Poodle
Shorkie Tzu: Shih Tzu x Yorkshire Terrier

GOLDENDOODLE Along with the Labrador, the Golden Retriever is the world's most popular breed. Crossing this breed with a Poodle to form a miniature Golden Retriever was always going to be a hit.

LABRADOODLE Far and away the most famous of the modern designer dogs, the Labradoodle is a cross between the Labrador Retriever and a Poodle. Very cute, and available in black, cream ("gold"), or chocolate.

congenital health ailments. They can be vulnerable to hip dysplasia, for example, since this is a relatively common condition affecting a range of larger dogs. More unusual metabolic problems, however, such as a copper storage disease, which is seen largely in the Bedlington Terrier, are probably less likely to arise.

Just as significantly, however, the responsiveness of designer dogs is frequently better than that of their pure-bred counterparts, as far as training is concerned. As an example, Beagles are lively, good-natured companions, but being scenthounds, they are hard to train, often

running off on their own, and they need plenty of exercise. If crossed with the Pug, however, creating so-called Puggles, you have a type of dog that is less demanding in terms of its hunting desires and yet is also likely to prove more responsive, as a result of the fact that Pugs have been kept as pets for centuries. The extreme flattened face of the Pug, which can be off-putting to some would-be owners, is effectively modified too, creating dogs that are less vulnerable to eye injuries.

While initially there can be a wide divergence in appearance between littermates from such crosses, breeding such dogs to each other (taking care to avoid mating closely related individuals together) then results in the development of characteristic traits.

YORKIE-POO The combination of Yorkshire Terrier and Poodle aims to maximize the cute factor. The results of such crosses are still highly variable, however.

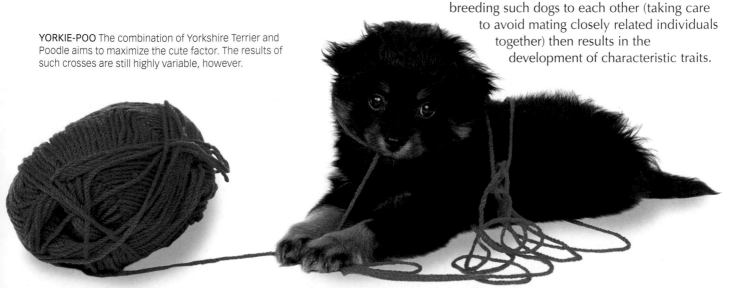

COMPANION DOGS

Today, many breeds created for a working purpose are kept simply as companions, but for thousands of years humans have bred dogs purely for that role, from Pekes in China to Bichons in Europe and hairless breeds that acted as living hot water bottles in South America. Usually miniatures with the same proportions as full-sized dogs, these are still some of the best companions. They have been bred for submissive docility and affection, while aggression, hunting instincts, and other "awkward" traits have been quietly sidelined. Today, there is a growth area in cute crossbreeds—often created, it seems, for the sake of a quirky name.

CHIHUAHUA (*see* p. 110) This is the breed that has graced a thousand handbags, beloved of celebrity blondes. One of the earliest companion breeds, the Pekingese (*see* p. 128), was bred to fit in the sleeve of a robe.

American Eskimo (Miniature and Toy)

ORIGIN United States
HEIGHT 9–15 in (23–38 cm)
WEIGHT 6–20 lb (2.5–9.0 kg)
EXERCISE LEVEL
COAT CARE
REGISTERED AKCs
COLORS White

These are the smaller editions of the Eskimo Dog (*see* p. 314), for those who like the perky spitz looks and personality in a compact package. While the larger version is a plausible working breed, the smaller classes have no purpose beyond companionship.

BREED ORIGINS

This looks very much like a miniature Samoyed (*see* p. 361), and white was always the most popular color for that breed in the United States. The Siberian dog may well have been involved in the development of the "Eskie," along with white Keeshond, but it seems most likely that the main ancestors were white German Spitzes brought by European settlers.

The first dogs were registered in 1913, and took the name of their breeders' kennels, American Eskimo, for political reasons. The breed in all its sizes spread across the continent with Barnum and Bailey's circus, performing all sorts of tricks including being the first dog to walk a tightrope. Today, these busy little dogs make wonderful family pets, still eager to learn tricks and perform.

SNOWY DOG The breed still has the classic features that help a dog in the snow: a thick, dense coat, lavishly plumed tail, and dark skin around the eyes to reduce the effects of glare.

NOT A SOFT TOY These little dogs have a big appetite for activity. They enjoy a long daily walk, and need it too, because this is a breed that can gain weight easily if inactive.

Australian Shepherd (Miniature)

ORIGIN United States
HEIGHT 13–18 in (33–45 cm)
WEIGHT 15–30 lb (6.8–13.6 kg)
EXERCISE LEVEL
COAT CARE
REGISTERED None
COLORS Blue or red merle, black, red, may have white and tan markings

Among variations on this breed's name, are the North American Miniature Australian Shepherd, once the North American Shepherd, reflecting the fact that its name and its nationality are at odds.

 BLACK

 RED/TAN

 BLUE MOTTLED WITH TAN

BREED ORIGINS

This breed is descended from the Australian Shepherd, a breed created entirely in the United States using dogs from Australia and New Zealand. That breed was noted for its friendly personality, and so creating a smaller breed that would fit in better with urban lifestyles was a natural step. The smallest of the big breed were selected as breeding stock, and the aim is to produce a perfect miniature in all physical respects, with the same lively and engaging character as the parent. Intelligent and trainable, this is a wonderful dog for an active family, and will relish being allowed to show off in trials.

CITY SLICKER This breed's size means it can be kept comfortably in urban confines, its trainability means it can be well behaved, and it has a low inclination to bark.

Australian Silky Terrier

ORIGIN Australia
HEIGHT 10–11 in (25–28 cm)
WEIGHT 12–14 lb (5.5–6.3 kg)
EXERCISE LEVEL
COAT CARE
REGISTERED KC, FCI, AKCs
COLORS Blue and tan

As much terrier as toy, this breed is similar in appearance to the Yorkshire Terrier, but not quite so diminutive. Although created as a companion breed, it is more than capable of despatching small vermin, and quite feisty when it comes to declaring and defending its interests.

BREED ORIGINS

Although the Australian Silky Terrier only appeared at the turn of the 20th century, its origins are not clearly known. It is probably a cross of the Australian Terrier and the Yorkshire Terrier, possibly with some Skye Terrier thrown in. It can be territorial and independent, so early socialization and obedience training are essential. Given these, this lively and inquisitive breed makes a cheering companion.

STRICTLY DECORATIVE The long coat is fine and silky, and matts easily, so does require daily grooming. Despite its length, it is not insulating, because it lacks an undercoat, so this is a warm-weather breed.

Bichon Frisé

ORIGIN Tenerife
HEIGHT 9–12 in (23–30 cm)
WEIGHT 10–16 lb (4.5–7.2 kg)
EXERCISE LEVEL
COAT CARE
REGISTERED KC, FCI, AKCs
COLORS White

These playful dogs have been popular companions for centuries, and make excellent family pets. The breed's fluffy appearance stems from its distinctive double-layered silky coat.

BREED ORIGINS

It is thought that the Bichon Frisé is descended from the ancient European water spaniel called the Barbet. This is reflected by its name, which is an abbreviated form of Barbichon, translating as "Little Barbet." The breed is also called the Tenerife Dog, and the Bichon Tenerife, reflecting the fact that its development took place on this island, part of the Canaries group off the northwest coast of

Africa. Its ancestors were probably introduced there from Spain over 500 years ago. They became highly sought-after pets at the royal courts of Europe, before gradually falling out of favor and ending up as circus performers. The breed's name is pronounced "Beeshon Freezay."

SNOW WHITE The coat of this breed is naturally curly. It is trimmed back on the face, and this serves to emphasize the round, dark eyes.

Bolognese

ORIGIN Italy
HEIGHT 10–12 in (25–30 cm)
WEIGHT 6–9 lb (2.5–4.1 kg)
EXERCISE LEVEL
COAT CARE
REGISTERED FCI
COLORS White

Although closely related to the Bichon Frisé, the Bolognese differs significantly because its coat is not double layered, although it does stick up rather than lying flat. This is described as "flocking," and gives the breed its fluffy appearance.

BREED ORIGINS

The precise ancestry of the Bolognese is something of a mystery. Its closest relative within the Bichon group is the Maltese, but it is unclear whether the Maltese is its direct ancestor or descendant. The Bolognese's origins date back to around A.D. 1000, with the breed then evolving in the Italian city of Bologna, from which its name is derived. The Medici family in Italy

gave these dogs as gifts to obtain favors and many European rulers fell under its charm.

Part of the Bolognese's undoubted appeal, aside from its attractive appearance, is the very strong bond that these dogs form with their owners.

ONLY WHITE While today, only white examples of the Bolognese are known, both black and piebald examples were recorded at an earlier stage in its history.

Cavalier King Charles Spaniel

ORIGIN United Kingdom
HEIGHT 12 in (30 cm)
WEIGHT 12–18 lb (5.5–8.0 kg)
EXERCISE LEVEL
COAT CARE
REGISTERED KC, FCI, AKCs
COLORS Black and tan, Blenheim, ruby, tricolor

This breed has an attractive appearance and pleasant disposition. They are not particularly energetic dogs, so they are suited to city life, and ideal for a home with children.

RED/TAN

TAN AND WHITE

BLACK AND TAN

BLACK, WHITE, AND TAN

BREED ORIGINS

Small spaniel-type dogs became very fashionable in Britain during the late 1600s, being favorites of King Charles II, as is clear from contemporary paintings. Subsequently, however, their appearance began to change. The modern breed owes its existence to a rich American called Roswell Eldridge. During the 1920s, he put up substantial prize money at Crufts for examples of the King Charles Spaniel or English Toy Spaniel (*see* p. 121), which resembled the original 17th-century type. Over the five years of Roswell's involvement with the show, the number of such dogs being exhibited increased, and gradually, this type of spaniel became more popular. It was then recognized as the Cavalier King Charles Spaniel, to separate it from its now relatively scarce close relative. The most evident distinguishing feature between the breeds is the longer nose displayed by the Cavalier.

TRICOLOR Black and white is predominant in this coloring, with these colors being evenly distributed. Tan markings show above the eyes, on the cheeks, and in the ears.

BLENHEIM This coloring is the most popular variety, having been originally created on and named after the Duke of Marlborough's estate. Rich chestnut coloring is separated by individual white markings, with a white central area usually evident on the center of the head.

BLACK AND TAN These puppies display their raven-black coloring, offset with tan markings. The other variety is ruby—a rich red shade.

Chihuahua

ORIGIN Mexico
HEIGHT 6–9 in (15–23 cm)
WEIGHT 2–6 lb (1.0–2.75 kg)
EXERCISE LEVEL
COAT CARE (sh) (lh)
REGISTERED KC, FCI, AKCs
COLORS No restrictions on color or patterning

The smallest breed in the world, the distinctive-looking Chihuahua possesses the character and bark of a much larger dog. They are noisy by nature, and have a fearless temperament.

 BLACK CREAM GRAY BLUE RED/TAN

BREED ORIGINS

The Chihuahua is named after the province in Mexico where it originated, but its ancestry remains mysterious. It may be a descendant of a range of companion breeds which were kept throughout the Americas in the pre-Colombian era. Others suggest that its ancestors might have been brought from Spain by the early settlers, and may have

SMOOTH-COATED This is the traditional form of the breed, which is characterized by a domed, apple-shaped head. Its large ears are positioned at an angle of about 45 degrees to the head.

interbred with local dogs to create the breed of today. Chihuahuas first started to attract attention outside Mexico during the 1850s, when they became fashionable companions for wealthy U.S. women, and even today, the breed enjoys celebrity status.

LONGCOATED The coat is soft, with the hair forming a very evident plume on the tail. Longer fur is evident too on the sides of the face, and on the underparts of the body, with feathering on the legs. The coat itself lies flat.

Chinese Crested Dog

ORIGIN China
HEIGHT 11–13 in (28–33 cm)
WEIGHT 5–10 lb (2.3–4.5 kg)
EXERCISE LEVEL
COAT CARE
REGISTERED KC, FCI, AKCs
COLORS No restrictions on color or patterning

These unusual dogs occur in two different forms: mainly hairless, or with a normal covering of hair. If at least one of the parents is hairless, both types can occur in the same litter.

BLACK

DARK BROWN

BREED ORIGINS

The mutation that has given rise to the various hairless breeds that now exist has occurred in different parts of the world, with the Chinese Crested representing an Asiatic example of this phenomenon. These dogs were known in the West by 1686, based on a contemporary illustration in an English publication, but they remained scarce. The breed was largely unknown in North America until the 1920s, but then attracted a loyal following, with detailed stud books being maintained. Among the

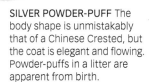
SILVER POWDER-PUFF The body shape is unmistakably that of a Chinese Crested, but the coat is elegant and flowing. Powder-puffs in a litter are apparent from birth.

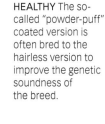
HEALTHY The so-called "powder-puff" coated version is often bred to the hairless version to improve the genetic soundness of the breed.

more famous owners of the Chinese Crested of that period, appropriately, was the striptease artist Gypsy Rose Lee. In its Chinese homeland, these dogs were highly valued not just as companions but also as guardians around the home, being alert to the approach of strangers. They are equally useful for this role today.

The care of the hairless Chinese Crested may initially appear less demanding than for the coated, powder-puff version, and certainly these dogs do not require as much grooming, but care needs to be taken to protect them not just from the cold but the risk of sunburn as well. Like other hairless breeds, Chinese Crested do not always have a full complement of teeth, although this rarely affects their eating ability.

SHOW TALK The hair on the head is the crest, with that on the tail being called the plume. The areas of hair on the lower legs are called socks, with the hair's overall texture being soft and silky.

CHIHUAHUA (*see* p. 110) Surrounded by colorful and
probably misleading legends, this is the ultimate toy dog.
Less snappy and yappy than it once was, it has seen a
phenomenal growth in popularity in recent years.

Coton de Tuléar

ORIGIN Madagascar
HEIGHT 10–12 in (25–30 cm)
WEIGHT 12–15 lb (5.5–6.8 kg)
EXERCISE LEVEL
COAT CARE
REGISTERED FCI
COLORS White

This breed is one of relatively few to have originated from Africa, and has grown rapidly in popularity over recent years, both in North America and Europe. It is another member of the Bichon group, as reflected partly by its white coat.

BREED ORIGINS

Almost certainly, the ancestors of this breed were brought from Europe to the Madagascan port of Tuléar, as commemorated by its name. This probably occurred as early as the 1600s, and these small dogs soon became status symbols for wealthy people living on this island, which lies off the east coast of the continent. Being bred here in isolation over the course of hundreds of generations, these dogs gradually diverged somewhat in appearance from their ancestors. It was prohibited for all but the nobility to own them, and they remained unknown elsewhere, right up until the 1950s. A small number were then permitted to leave the island and taken to Europe, while in the United States, they were not seen until the mid-1970s.

WET DOG! Although traditionally the coat falls forward over the face, the wet coat reveals the unmistakable Bichon profile. A similar but now extinct breed existed on the island of Réunion.

COAT The rather fluffy, cottony texture of the Coton de Tuléar's coat is a distinctive feature of these dogs. Although white is the traditional color for the breed, individuals with cream or black patches occasionally occur.

French Bulldog

ORIGIN France
HEIGHT 11–12 in (28–30 cm)
WEIGHT 20–28 lb (9.1–12.7 kg)
EXERCISE LEVEL
COAT CARE
REGISTERED KC, FCI, AKCs
COLORS Cream, gold, liver, black and white, black brindle

The bat-like ears and stocky build of the French Bulldog are very distinctive. Its short coat means that grooming is minimal, but it can be prone to snoring, because of its compact facial shape.

CREAM

GOLD

GOLD AND WHITE

BLACK AND WHITE

BLACK BRINDLE

BREED ORIGINS

There used to be a Toy Bulldog breed which was widely kept by lacemakers in the English city of Nottingham. Forced out by increased mechanization, during the 1850s many of these skilled craftspeople emigrated to northern France. Not unsurprisingly, they took their pets with them, and some crossbreeding with local dogs occurred. Crosses with terriers may have resulted in the raised ears that are so characteristic

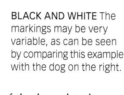

BLACK AND WHITE The markings may be very variable, as can be seen by comparing this example with the dog on the right.

of the breed today. Word of these bulldogs spread to the city of Paris, and soon they became fashionable pets in the capital. They became popular too in other parts of Europe and especially the United States, but in Britain, the breed proved controversial when it was first introduced during the 1890s.

GOOD COMPANION
The French Bulldog is a lively, friendly breed with relatively modest exercise needs.

BRINDLE Mixing of light and dark hairs in the coat is not uncommon in French Bulldogs, as is a white patch on the chest.

German Spitz

ORIGIN Germany
HEIGHT 8–16 in (20–41 cm)
WEIGHT 7–40 lb (3.2–18.0 kg)
EXERCISE LEVEL
COAT CARE
REGISTERED KC, FCI, AKCs
COLORS Range of solid colors; bicolors allowed in Miniature and Toy

The family of German Spitz breeds can be separated by size, with the Giant being the largest. There is also a Standard variety, as well as Miniature and Toy forms. They are all similar in temperament.

BLACK

CREAM

GRAY

GOLD

DARK BROWN

BREED ORIGINS

The origins of the German Spitz date back at least to 1450, and since then, as in the case of other breeds, there has been a tendency to scale these dogs down in size creating companion breeds. There is also frequently confusion between the German Toy Spitz and the Pomeranian (*see* p 130), because they share a common ancestry and are very similar in appearance. The German breed was created first, with the Pomeranian

FULL COAT The ruff of fur around the neck is more pronounced in the winter, when the coat is at its most profuse. This contrasts with the short hair on the lower part of the legs.

subsequently being developed on separate lines in the United Kingdom, from imported German stock, to the extent that they have now existed as separate bloodlines for over a century. There are some differences in the recognition of the different Spitz breeds as far as coloration is concerned. The Giant variety exists in solid colors only, while bicolors are also seen in the case of the Miniature and Toy variants.

FACIAL APPEARANCE The German Spitz breeds are described as being vulpine, or fox-like, as a result of their facial appearance. A white blaze between the eyes is often a feature of bicolors.

Havanese

ORIGIN Cuba
HEIGHT 8–14 in (20–36 cm)
WEIGHT 7–13 lb (3.2–5.9 kg)
EXERCISE LEVEL
COAT CARE
REGISTERED FCI
COLORS Black, white, blue, gold, dark brown

Lively by nature but easy to train, the Havanese has established a following that extends far beyond Cuba where it developed. They are versatile companions, watchdogs, and even poultry herders.

 BLACK
 CREAM
 BLUE
 GOLD
 DARK BROWN

BREED ORIGINS

The Havanese is of Bichon stock, with its ancestors probably having been introduced to Cuba quite early during the settlement of the New World, when the island was a significant stopping-off point for ships from Europe. The breed is named after Havana, Cuba's capital city. They thrived on the island for centuries, but became much rarer after the Communist takeover in 1959. Many of those who fled to the United States took their Havanese with them, and this actually boosted the breed's popularity in North America. Today, they are seen at shows around the world.

COAT The Havanese's coat has a soft texture, and as with other Bichons, tends to be white in color. The muzzle of these dogs is long and tapered.

STYLING The longer hair on the head reflects the breed's origins in a hot climate, protecting the eyes from the sun. It is traditionally tied up into a topknot.

Inca Hairless Dog

ORIGIN Peru
HEIGHT 10–28 in (25–71 cm)
WEIGHT 9–55 lb (4.0–25.0 kg)
EXERCISE LEVEL
COAT CARE
REGISTERED FCI
COLORS Black or dark brown

Hairless dogs were quite common in parts of Central and South America in pre-Columbian times. The Inca Hairless is now one of the rarer surviving examples, better known in North America than Europe.

BREED ORIGINS

These dogs were originally bred by the Huanca people of South America, as a source of food. Then, when the Incas conquered them in 1460, they took to looking after the dogs instead, using them as bed warmers. Two different strains were recognized, based on their appearance. The dark strain was known as the daytime dog, in contrast to the Peruvian Inca Orchid (see p. 129) with its pinkish, mottled skin. The latter dogs were only allowed out at night, to avoid sunburn, being kept in rooms decorated with orchids during the day. Their descendants still survive in small numbers in Peru through to the present day.

Although hairless individuals predominate in litters, occasional puppies are born with a full covering of hair.

CONSISTENCY IN APPEARANCE Relatively even, dark pigmentation over the entire body is a characteristic feature of the Inca Hairless Dog.

INCA HAIRLESS The breed's relatively large, flexible ears are held up when the dog is alert, and hang back down along the sides of the head when it is relaxed.

HAIR These dogs are not entirely hairless, with traces of fur most likely to be seen on the head, tail, and lower legs.

Italian Greyhound

ORIGIN Italy
HEIGHT 13–15 in (33–38 cm)
WEIGHT 10–15 lb (4.5–6.8 kg)
EXERCISE LEVEL
COAT CARE
REGISTERED KC, FCI, AKCs
COLORS Cream, gray, blue, red and tan, gold and white, blue and white

A miniaturized version of the Greyhound itself (*see* p. 195), this breed will prove to be an excellent family pet, but it is usually shy with strangers, unless adequately socialized from an early age.

CREAM   GRAY   BLUE   RED/TAN   GOLD AND WHITE

BREED ORIGINS

Small examples of greyhounds have been documented right back to the days of the ancient Egyptians, but it was in Italy that the breed came to prominence from the 1400s onward. Italian Greyhounds were sought-after pets, particularly in royal circles, as is clear from their inclusion in paintings by Jan van Eyck and others. Unfortunately, by the end of the 1800s, the desire to create ever smaller individuals had resulted in the breed becoming seriously weakened. It took careful breeding in the early part of the 20th century to restore its vigor, and increase its numbers. Nevertheless, even today, Italian Greyhounds are expensive to purchase, reflecting their relative scarcity. Just like their larger cousin, they do not need a large amount of exercise but prefer to engage in brief, fast-paced runs. One very evident point of distinction is the high-stepping gait of these small greyhounds, however, a trait that sets them apart from the Greyhound itself.

BLUE AND WHITE Bicolored Italian Greyhounds usually have a white blaze extending between the eyes, broadening out over the jaws and down to cover the upper chest.

COAT AND EARS A sleek, fine, and glossy coat is characteristic of the Italian Greyhound. The ears are held out sideways as shown here, when the dog is alert, being kept folded alongside the skull at other times.

Japanese Chin

ORIGIN Japan
HEIGHT 8–14 in (20–36 cm)
WEIGHT 4–7 lb (1.8–3.2 kg)
EXERCISE LEVEL
COAT CARE
REGISTERED KC, FCI, AKCs
COLORS Black and white, tan and white

These small dogs can prove very determined by nature, with a temperament that has been likened to that of a cat in some respects. They lack a dense undercoat, so grooming is not arduous.

BLACK AND WHITE

TAN AND WHITE

BREED ORIGINS

The forerunners of the Japanese Chin were probably brought from China, possibly as long ago as A.D. 500. Even today, the breed bears some similarity to the Pekingese, with which it probably shares a common ancestry. Since Japan was closed to Westerners for centuries, it was not until the second half of the 1800s that the Japanese Chin started to become widely known. It soon became very popular in royal circles in the West, just as it had been a favored companion of the ruling class in its homeland.

COLORATION Black and white coloration is often seen in the Japanese Chin. These dogs are surprisingly quiet by nature, and adapt well to city life.

Japanese Spitz

ORIGIN Japan
HEIGHT 15–16 in (38–40 cm)
WEIGHT 13 lb (5.9 kg)
EXERCISE LEVEL
COAT CARE
REGISTERED KC, FCI
COLORS White

These beautiful small dogs resemble spitz breeds, with pricked ears, a pointed muzzle, and a tail that curves over the back, but are much smaller. They are lively and intelligent.

BREED ORIGINS

The striking similarity to the Samoyed breed (*see* p. 361) is not coincidental, because it was probably small examples of this breed that laid the foundations for the development of the Japanese Spitz. Crossings followed during the first half of the 20th century with a variety of other small spitz breeds, and finally, in 1948, the Japan Kennel Club officially recognized the Japanese Spitz.

APPEARANCE The fluffy white coat of the Japanese Spitz is a characteristic feature of the breed. It also has a very evident ruff of longer fur under the chin, as seen here.

King Charles Spaniel

ORIGIN United Kingdom
HEIGHT 10–11 in (25–27 cm)
WEIGHT 8–14 lb (3.5–6.5 kg)
EXERCISE LEVEL
COAT CARE
REGISTERED KC, FCI, AKCs
COLORS Solid tan, black and tan, white and tan, tricolor

Despite its spaniel name, this has never been a gundog, but was a royal toy. Diarist Samuel Pepys noted of King Charles "the silliness of the King, playing with his dog all the while."

RED/TAN

BLACK, WHITE, AND TAN

BREED ORIGINS

When spaniels were first developed, larger pups were chosen for working dogs, but smaller ones eventually became toy companion breeds. Early examples had a longer muzzle, like the Cavalier King Charles today, but crossing with snub-nosed oriental breeds in the 18th century gave it a new look.

An affectionate dog that fits well into urban life, the King Charles

Spaniel's drawback is that it is prone to health problems and shorter lived than many small dogs.

ROYAL COLORS This breed's colors have regal names. Tan is called ruby and tan and white Blenheim, and in the United States tricolor is Prince Charles and black and tan is King Charles.

Kromfohrländer

ORIGIN Germany
HEIGHT 15–18 in (38–46 cm)
WEIGHT 20 lb (9.0 kg)
EXERCISE LEVEL
COAT CARE
REGISTERED FCI
COLORS Tan and white

This is a relatively new addition to the list of German dog breeds, with the distinction of being created as a companion breed. The majority of today's Kromfohrländers are still kept in Germany itself.

BREED ORIGINS

In the aftermath of World War II, American troops took a brown-and-white wirehaired terrier that they found in France along with them, as they pushed into Germany. When they were nearing Frankfurt, their dog reverted to a civilian life, and mated with a terrier-type mongrel. The resulting breed was recognized by the German Kennel Club in 1953, and named for the Krumme Furche

area where it began. These are easily trainable, affable dogs that suit a family lifestyle. There are two coat varieties: wirehaired, or rough, and the rather rarer smooth-coated type.

ROUGH COAT This is the most common and popular form of the Kromfohrländer. The long, straight front legs are characteristic of the breed.

Kyi Leo

ORIGIN United States

HEIGHT 9–11 in (23–28 cm)

WEIGHT 13–15 lb (5.9–6.8 kg)

EXERCISE LEVEL 🐕

COAT CARE ✂️✂️

REGISTERED None

COLORS Cream, gold, gold and white, black and white, tan and white

The result of a deliberate crossing between two other companion breeds, the Kyi Leo is still quite scarce, and yet to make any impact in Europe. Most of these dogs are black and white in color.

CREAM   GOLD   GOLD AND WHITE   BLACK AND WHITE   TAN AND WHITE

BREED ORIGINS
This breed is the first designer dog to be recognized as a specific breed. It was created from crossings between a Lhasa Apso and a Maltese in the San Francisco region of

BREED DETAILS The Kyi Leo is rather like a scaled-down Lhasa Apso, but with a longer nose and coat. It relates very well to people.

California that began during the 1940s, although progress was slow at first. Gradually their popularity rose and their numbers increased, growing from 60 individuals in 1972 up to 190 by 1986. The breed's name comes from the Tibetan description of "kyi," translating as "dog," reflecting the Lhasa Apso's contribution, and "leo" meaning "lion." Dogs of apparently identical origins are also listed under the name of American Lamalese by some registration bodies.

Lhaso Apso

ORIGIN Tibet

HEIGHT 10–11 in (25–28 cm)

WEIGHT 13–15 lb (5.9–6.8 kg)

EXERCISE LEVEL 🐕

COAT CARE ✂️✂️✂️

REGISTERED KC, FCI, AKCs

COLORS Range of colors from black to cream; black and white

The long, flowing coat of the Lhasa Apso is very elegant, but its condition can only be maintained with daily grooming sessions. Occasionally, a smooth-coated individual crops up in a litter.

BLACK   CREAM   GRAY   GOLD   BLACK AND WHITE

BREED ORIGINS
These small dogs were considered sacred by the Tibetan monks who kept them in their monasteries. They were believed to be a repository for the souls of dead monks. Unsurprisingly, therefore, Lhasa Apsos were not sold to outsiders. Occasionally, however, the Dalai Lama who ruled Tibet would give a pair as a gift to the Chinese Emperor. It was probably

not until the late 19th or early 20th century that the breed first reached the West, and it was not until after World War I that it started to become established in Britain. This proved to be a protracted process, with these striking dogs not becoming well known until the 1960s.

COAT The Lhasa's hair is very dense, and offers excellent protection against the elements.

Löwchen

ORIGIN France
HEIGHT 10–13 in (25–33 cm)
WEIGHT 10–18 lb (4.5–8.1 kg)
EXERCISE LEVEL
COAT CARE
REGISTERED KC, FCI
COLORS No restrictions on color or patterning

When its coat is trimmed, the Löwchen looks rather like a lion, justifying its alternative description of Little Lion Dog. Its name is pronounced as "lerv-chun," and it is a very ancient breed.

 BLACK CREAM RED/TAN DARK BROWN TAN AND WHITE

BREED ORIGINS

It is believed that the breed was widely known across Europe as long ago as the 1500s and, in spite of its Germanic name, the Löwchen's origins are believed to lie in France. The coat was trimmed into the lion-cut, which removes hair from the lower body and upper legs, so that they could act as bed warmers for the nobility, while the resulting leonine appearance was believed to convey strength. In 1973, numbers of the breed had plummeted to the extent that it was estimated that there were fewer than 70 still alive in the world. Thanks to publicity surrounding their plight, breeders have successfully taken up the challenge of preserving this breed.

UNTRIMMED In the Löwchen's untrimmed state, its Bichon family resemblance is clear.

Maltese

ORIGIN Malta
HEIGHT 9–10 in (23–25 cm)
WEIGHT 4–13 lb (1.8–5.9 kg)
EXERCISE LEVEL
COAT CARE
REGISTERED KC, FCI, AKCs
COLORS White

Although it was once called the Maltese Terrier, there has never been anything of the terrier about this breed; it has also been called, more understandably, the Bichon Maltais. It is an engaging little dog, seemingly without fear or awareness of its diminuitive size.

BREED ORIGINS

This breed has been kept as a companion since Phoenicians brought the ancient Melita breed to Malta 2000 years ago. A pure line of descent from that dog is unlikely, and today's Maltese probably has both miniature spaniels and the Miniature Poodle in its heritage. It is active and playful, but with maturity adapts to a more sedentary lifestyle and city life. It is good with children or other dogs.

PERFECTLY COIFFED The long silky coat lacks an undercoat and mats easily. The demands of daily grooming are the biggest commitment with this breed.

MALTESE This is another example of the Bichon group, which originated on the island of Malta in the Mediterranean. Its dark eyes, eyelids, lips, and nose make an attractive contrast with its white coat.

Mexican Hairless

ORIGIN Mexico
HEIGHT 11–22 in (28–55 cm)
WEIGHT 9–31 lb (4.1–14.1 kg)
EXERCISE LEVEL
COAT CARE
REGISTERED FCI, AKCs
COLORS Any color or combination; solid dark colors preferred

This breed's original Nahuatl name is Xoloitzcuintle, which is affectionately shortened to Xolo, pronounced "show low." It also has a coated variety, which was known as "itzcuintle."

BLACK

BLUE

DARK BROWN

BREED ORIGINS

This primitive-looking breed has a long history, and was present before the Spanish arrived in the region. Its name comes from the god Xolotl, who made the dog from a sliver of the Bone of Life and gave it as a guide to humans. The less romantic side of this religious role is that until quite recently the dog was eaten for its healing qualities or at ritual ceremonies. Today, it enjoys a longer if less exalted life as a quiet but intelligent and highly athletic companion, bonding strongly to its owners.

FLUFFY TOY Dogs have varying degrees of hairlessness. The coated variety is used in breeding to avoid a rare fatal disorder that affects some dogs carrying two genes for hairlessness.

STANDARD HAIRLESS The dominant gene that causes the hairlessness also affects the teeth. Many hairless dogs will have rotated teeth or even lack some teeth.

Papillon

ORIGIN France
HEIGHT 8–11 in (20–28 cm)
WEIGHT 9–10 lb (4.0–4.5 kg)
EXERCISE LEVEL
COAT CARE
REGISTERED KC, FCI, AKCs
COLORS White with a range of colors

It may look like a stuffed toy, have a name meaning butterfly in French, and have been a favorite prop for romantic portraits, but this breed is no brainless lapdog: The fluff is all on the outside.

GOLD AND WHITE   BLACK AND WHITE   TAN AND WHITE   BLACK, WHITE, AND TAN

BREED ORIGINS

These small companions date back to the Renaissance under the name Continental Spaniel, and are still called Continental Toy Spaniels. They may be descended from the Spanish Dwarf Spaniel of the 16th century, crossed with northern spitz types for a more delicate face. While its history is not well recorded in writing, it was a favorite in works of art, depicted in frescoes and oil paintings from Titian's *Venus of Urbino* to Largillière's portrait of Louis XIV and his family. In many of these, the structure of the dogs' ears is unclear, and it seems that

DOGS WITH WINGS
At first, calling a dog "butterfly" might not seem descriptive, but a glance at the ears and facial markings makes it clear how apt the name is.

the Papillon appeared in the 16th century, with the original drop-eared type being given the name of Phalène (*see* p. 129) sometime later to distinguish them.

BREED QUALITIES

With their fine, silky coat, plumed tail, and extraordinary ears, it is not hard to see why this breed became popular. The coat, which lacks an undercoat, needs less attention than might be expected to keep it looking picture perfect. Papillons can be possessive of their owners and territory, but given an outlet for their energy make engaging companions.

QUICK LEARNER The Papillon loves outdoor exercise, and given a little training, its playful nature and surprising speed and athleticism make it adept at obedience trials, performing tricks, and in agility classes for small dogs.

Pekingese

ORIGIN China
HEIGHT 6–9 in (15–23 cm)
WEIGHT 7–12 lb (3.0–5.5 kg)
EXERCISE LEVEL
COAT CARE
REGISTERED KC, FCI, AKCs
COLORS Any color

According to legend, this breed is the result of a mating between a lion and a monkey. The tale does an equally good job of explaining its appearance or describing its personality.

BLACK   RED/TAN   GOLD   TAN AND WHITE

BREED ORIGINS

The origins of the Peke are far too distant to be known: It was recently confirmed as one of the world's most ancient breeds by DNA analysis, showing just how long-standing the desire to keep dogs as companions is. It was kept at the Chinese imperial court in the Forbidden City, and brought back to the United Kingdom in the 1860s, having been taken from the court in the Opium Wars. Today, it is the parent of many crossbreeds with names like "Peke-A-Pom."

BREED QUALITIES

This breed behaves as if it is well aware of its royal past. They can be very obstinate, and it is surprising just how heavy such a small dog becomes when it does not wish to go somewhere. Pekingese tend tobe loyal to their owners, wary of strangers, and inclined to bark like little watchdogs.

ROYAL RULES This breed is still true to the standard written by Dowager Empress Tzu Hsi, with hairy paws for silence, a color to match every robe, a ruff for dignity, and bow legs to prevent it wandering.

Peruvian Hairless/Peruvian Inca Orchid

ORIGIN Peru
HEIGHT 15–20 in (38–50 cm)
WEIGHT 20–28 lb (9.0–12.7 kg)
EXERCISE LEVEL
COAT CARE
REGISTERED FCI, AKCs
COLORS All solid colors, can have pink points

Known in FCI as the Perro Sin Pelo del Perú or Peruvian Hairless, this is also called the Peruvian Inca Orchid and Inca Hairless Dog, as well as Flower Dog and Moonflower Dog.

BLACK BLUE DARK BROWN

BREED ORIGINS

Nobody knows quite where these hairless dogs originally came from. Images of such dogs appear in ceramic art around A.D. 750, but in the Peruvian coastal cultures of Chimú, Moche, and Vicus rather than the high-mountain Inca cities. Their Quechan name is Calato, meaning naked, and their warmth was valued for supposed curative properties, but the *conquistadores* also reported that they were eaten. Outside its homeland the breed has a dangerously small gene pool, with scarcely any new imports. Like many primitive dogs, they are wary of strangers, but usually good with children and other dogs.

NAKED TRUTH The skin needs care to avoid acne and dry patches, and bicolor dogs are discouraged because the pink skin is prone to sunburn. A crest of hair on the head is common.

Phalène

ORIGIN France
HEIGHT 8–11 in (20–28 cm)
WEIGHT 4–9 lb (1.8–4.1 kg)
EXERCISE LEVEL
COAT CARE
REGISTERED KC, FCI, AKCs
COLORS White with a range of colors

The drop-eared twin of the Papillon (*see* p. 127), this breed has a lower profile, but a longer history. Portraits and statuettes show that the pets of the doomed Marie-Antoinette were Phalènes.

GOLD AND WHITE   BLACK AND WHITE   TAN AND WHITE

BREED ORIGINS

This breed shares the origins of the Papillon in the Spanish Dwarf Spaniel and northern spitzes. Some registries call both the Continental Toy Spaniel; others relegate this to a variety of the Papillon. The Phalène was almost extinct during the 20th century, but it has recently recovered somewhat in numbers. Ears of both types can be produced in the same litter, and this breed is every bit as lively and intelligent. Both types can suffer from slipped kneecaps.

NOVEL NAMES Phalène means "moth," referring to the way moths' wings are folded down at rest and complementing the name Papillon. The plumed and curled tail once earned both types the name "Squirrel Dog."

Pomeranian

ORIGIN Germany

HEIGHT 8–11 in (20–28 cm)

WEIGHT 4–7 lb (1.8–3.2 kg)

EXERCISE LEVEL

COAT CARE

REGISTERED KC, FCI, AKCs

COLORS White, cream, gray, blue, red, brown, black

It resembles nothing so much as an animated powder puff, but this dog believes it is still as big as its ancestors. The Pomeranian is also called the Zwergspitz or Dwarf Spitz and the Loulou.

 BLACK   CREAM   RED/TAN   GOLD

BREED ORIGINS

The Pomeranian takes its name from a region along the Baltic coast that has been part of many countries over the centuries: once German, it is now in Poland. The German Spitz family was first brought to the United Kingdom by Queen Charlotte at the start of the 19th century, and British breeders succeeded in diminishing its size through the century. This may have been helped by a Volpino

BEST BRUSHED The long, straight coat has a dense undercoat and needs frequent attention with a damp brush to prevent tangles forming.

brought back from Italy by Queen Victoria; her patronage insured the popularity of the fledgling type.

BREED QUALITIES

Smart and energetic, this is a good family companion and suits city life. It is protective of its territory and will bark noisily, so makes an effective watchdog, although unable to do much physical damage to an intruder. It will also challenge larger dogs, seemingly unaware of its size. These are long-lived dogs, although they do suffer from several health problems including slipping kneecaps and eye problems.

COLOR INFLUENCES SIZE The earliest Poms tended to be both white and larger, but as an ever smaller size has been pursued, red and sable tones have become most common.

Poodle (Miniature and Toy)

ORIGIN France
HEIGHT 9–15 in (23–38 cm)
WEIGHT 4–18 lb (1.8–5.5 kg)
EXERCISE LEVEL
COAT CARE
REGISTERED KC, FCI, AKCs
COLORS Any solid color

The full-sized or Standard Poodle (*see* p. 354) can still be seen as a working breed, but these smaller types were created purely for the pleasure of their company.

 BLACK
 CREAM
 BLUE
 GOLD
 DARK BROWN

BREED ORIGINS

Wherever the full-sized Poodle originated, there is no doubt that the smaller versions of the breed were developed in France. These dogs were never intended to be gundogs, although they will point and show all the instinctive drives of their larger ancestors. They have been, and still are, popular as circus dogs, at least in part for their great intelligence. Since the 18th century they have danced, acted out comedies, tragedies, and battles, reportedly walked tightropes, and even played cards and performed magic tricks, responding to the slightest signals from their trainers.

BREED QUALITIES

If they are allowed, these small poodles will make responsive and entertaining companions. Treated as fashion accessories, they can become bored and destructive. Grooming depends on the clip; some health problems—such as ear infections— can be more troublesome.

KEEPING IT SIMPLE Puppies may be shown in a plain, all-over clip. For adults, show rules are stricter, but there is nothing to stop an owner keeping this easy-care look.

TOY POODLE The very smallest of the sizes, this is the ultimate choice for bijou urban homes. The smallest are the longest lived, lasting around 14 years.

MINIATURE POODLE This size was highly popular in the circus ring, and was a must-have pet in the mid-20th century. Overbreeding meant that it slipped from pole position, but this has been a good thing for the quality of the breed.

Pug

ORIGIN China
HEIGHT 10–11 in (25–28 cm)
WEIGHT 14–18 lb (6.4–8.2 kg)
EXERCISE LEVEL
COAT CARE
REGISTERED KC, FCI, AKCs
COLORS Silver, apricot, fawn, black

They look frowning, but these mini mastiffs are full of energy and cheer. The name may come from an old English word for a mischievous devil; some European countries call them "Mops."

BLACK

GRAY

GOLD

BREED ORIGINS

This breed was miniaturized at least 2,000 years ago in China, where it was known as the Lo-Chiang-Sze or Foo, and kept by nobles and monks. In the 16th century it reached Europe on ships of the Dutch East Indies Trading Company, and is said to have saved the life of William of Orange by barking at an assassin. It arrived in the United Kingdom when Dutch royalty took the throne in the 17th century, and remained a royal pet, owned by Queen Victoria.

BREED QUALITIES

The word pugnacious might have been taken from this breed; they are intelligent and can be quite obstinate. Their stare looks defiant and stern, but it masks a playful personality, and a pug can be an enlivening and enchanting companion.

ANCIENT LIKENESS This breed still bears some resemblance to the foo dog or lion dog statues that are seen defensively flanking the doors of palaces and temples in China.

CHANGING FASHIONS The original Pug face, seen in paintings such as Hogarth's self-portrait with his Pug, Trump, was longer. The flat profile of today's dog leads to breathing and eye problems.

CHIC COLORS Pale-colored Pugs were the most fashionable until the 19th century, when traveler and author Lady Brassey is thought to have brought new black dogs back from the East.

Shih Tzu

ORIGIN Tibet/China
HEIGHT 8–11 in (20–28 cm)
WEIGHT 9–16 lb (4.1–7.3 kg)
EXERCISE LEVEL
COAT CARE
REGISTERED KC, FCI, AKCs
COLORS Any color

While the pronunciation of the name is a matter of some dispute and not a little humor, the translation is "lion dog." This breed lives up to it, being courageous and sometimes a little haughty.

 BLACK
 BLUE
 GOLD
 BLACK AND WHITE
 TAN AND WHITE

BREED ORIGINS

It was thought that this breed was a cross between the Pekingese and the Lhasa Apso, which is what it looks like, but recent DNA analysis showed it to be one of the most ancient breeds in its own right. It seems to have come from Tibet to China, where it became a favorite in the court, and spread from there, which is why it is generally regarded as a Chinese, rather than Tibetan breed. They

PERFECT SYMMETRY Bicolored Shih Tzus are commonly seen, and in this coat a white blaze extending from the nose over the face and head and a white tip to the tail are highly desirable.

FLOWER-LIKE FACE The long hair on the brow, which gives the nickname "Chrysanthemum Dog," can be tied up in a topknot; some owners trim it, but this is not allowed for showing.

arrived in Europe in the early 20th century, and have become well loved and established across the world.

BREED QUALITIES

The abundant coat has a long topcoat and a woolly undercoat, so needs regular and thorough grooming. Once brushed, this is a good-natured family dog, relaxed around other dogs and well-behaved children, although occasionally stubborn. It also makes an alert watchdog, and although it is usually quiet indoors, it will bark vociferously at anything it feels is wrong.

BLACK-AND-WHITE ADULT The fine undercoat of the Shih Tzu can become easily matted, so this is definitely not a breed for owners averse to grooming.

Tibetan Terrier

ORIGIN Tibet

HEIGHT 14–16 in (36–41 cm)

WEIGHT 18–30 lb (8.2–13.6 kg)

EXERCISE LEVEL

COAT CARE

REGISTERED KC, FCI, AKCs

COLORS Any color except liver and chocolate

Clubs love to proclaim it 'the Holy Dog of Tibet," an ancient breed originating in a lost valley, kept by monks, and always given as a gift, not sold. There is some truth to all of this romance.

 BLACK   CREAM   BLUE   GOLD   TAN AND WHITE

BREED ORIGINS

Genetic analysis recently confirmed the Tibetan Terrier as one of the oldest breeds in existence. Also called the Tsang Apso, it comes from Tsang province, the religious heart of Tibet, and was both a companion and a guard in monasteries; but it was also used by nomadic Tibetans to herd livestock. As a vital part of everyday life, the early exports were usually gifts, and some of the early arrivals in the United Kingdom were puppies given to a doctor by a grateful patient. The breed is well established as a lively and affectionate companion, fairly biddable and needing conveniently little exercise. It is still something of a wary guard, and surprisingly noisy.

DESCRIPTIVE NAME The Tibetan name of Do Kyi Apso seems to identify this breed simply as a longhaired tied dog or watchdog.

LAID BACK This breed makes an affectionate companion, can act as a small sentry, and shows the intelligence of a herder, but nothing in its relaxed nature comes from a terrier heritage. The name was mistakenly given by Westerners simply because of its size.

Tibetan Spaniel

ORIGIN Tibet
HEIGHT 10 in (25 cm)
WEIGHT 9–15 lb (4.1–6.8 kg)
EXERCISE LEVEL
COAT CARE
REGISTERED KC, FCI, AKCs
COLORS Any color

Affectionately known as Tibbies, these dogs are not really spaniels at all, never having been used in hunting. They are also less purely Tibetan than other breeds that have spread from the region.

 CREAM   GOLD   DARK BROWN   LIVER   BLACK AND WHITE

BREED ORIGINS

Dogs of this type were kept in and around monasteries, and resemble dogs depicted in Chinese bronzes from 2,000 years ago, and known as far afield as Korea from the 8th century. There was some interchange of dogs as gifts between Buddhist centers, and Tibbies certainly show echoes of both the Pekingese and the Japanese Chin. They were kept in part as watchdogs, and even today like to take a high seat, survey the surroundings, and bark at anything out of place. Extrovert and lively, they need more exercise than some other small breeds.

FAMILY LIKENESS The domed head, blunt muzzle, and slightly bowed front legs show links to the Peke and Chin, but are not problematically exaggerated.

Volpino Italiano

ORIGIN Italy
HEIGHT 11–12 in (28–30 cm)
WEIGHT 9–11 lb (4.1–5.0 kg)
EXERCISE LEVEL
COAT CARE
REGISTERED FCI
COLORS White, red; champagne tolerated

This diminutive spitz takes its name from *volpe*, the Italian word for fox. It is similar to the Pomeranian, and is unrecognized in the United States because of similarities to the small American Eskimos.

 CREAM   RED/TAN

BREED ORIGINS

Descended from the same ancient stock as other European spitz breeds, the Volpino has existed in Italy for centuries; Michelangelo probably owned one of its forebears, often reported as a Pomeranian. It was a popular watchdog, particularly with traveling traders, kept to bark and alert bigger mastiffs. It fell out of favor in the 20th century, possibly because its other name, Cane de Quirinale, associated it with the royal palace and the king who supported Mussolini. Today it is bred in Italy and the United States, but is still rare.

PURE COAT The breed was once known in a wider color range, but only solid colors are shown today and almost all are white.

TERRIERS

Tough and tenacious, terriers seize the day and everything in it. These little dogs were miniaturized from hounds to follow prey underground—their name comes from *terre*, French for "earth"—and kill it or drag it out. This work required dogs small in size but big in spirit, and terriers tunnel with enthusiasm and confront opponents from foxes or badgers to dogs many times their size with fearless gusto. While they were described as early as the 16th century as quarrelsome and snappy, terriers are endlessly entertaining, and it is hard not to fall for their sheer lust for life.

BUNDLE OF FUN It is sometimes hard to believe just how much dog can be packed into such a tiny volume. With outsize energy and zest, breeds like this Parson Russell Terrier (*see* p. 156) are loyal and cheerful companions.

Affenpinscher

ORIGIN Germany
HEIGHT 10 in (25 cm)
WEIGHT 7–8 lb (3.2–3.6 kg)
EXERCISE LEVEL
COAT CARE
REGISTERED KC, FCI, AKCs
COLORS Black, gray, silver, red, black and tan, beige, sometimes with white

This little dog's name literally means "monkey biter," but the German word *Pinscher* mostly indicates a dog of terrier type. Comical in looks, it is an energetic and outgoing companion.

BLACK

GRAY

RED/TAN

BLACK AND TAN

BREED ORIGINS

The Affenpinscher's ancestors are unknown, but its looks suggest a cross between German pinschers and a breed with a shortened nose. It has been known since the 17th century, so the Pug may have been a parent. In turn, the Affenpinscher is thought to have contributed to the Belgian Griffon terriers. Originally, there was a larger size, but this disappeared in the early 20th century, and the smaller size is rare. It is more often seen in the United States than its homeland. The breed is friendly to other dogs and suitable for urban and family homes.

FORM AND FUNCTION The shortened face does not hinder this breed in its original role of ratter; it will still efficiently despatch small game and vermin.

Airedale Terrier

ORIGIN United Kingdom
HEIGHT 23 in (58 cm)
WEIGHT 44 lb (20.0 kg)
EXERCISE LEVEL
COAT CARE
REGISTERED KC, FCI, AKCs
COLORS Black and tan

Too large to fit the description of an "earth dog," the Airedale is sometimes called the "King of Terriers." Older names include the Bingley Terrier, pinpointing its earliest roots, and the Waterside Terrier, because of its otter-hunting past.

BREED ORIGINS

The Airedale is a typical terrier in every respect other than size. A cross of the now-vanished Old English Broken-haired Terrier and the Otterhound, it was bred to pursue prey in the water. It has also been a messenger and police dog, but its notorious stubbornness limits its usefulness.

BEST MATE Airedale owners report them to be loyal, brave, and energetic friends.

STREET FIGHTER Although this breed is quiet indoors and makes a good urban companion, it has a tendency to pick fights with other dogs.

American Pit Bull Terrier

ORIGIN United States
HEIGHT 18–22 in (46–56 cm)
WEIGHT 50–80 lb (22.7–36.4 kg)
EXERCISE LEVEL
COAT CARE
REGISTERED AKCs
COLORS Any color

This is the love-it-or-hate it poster child of the fighting breeds and bull terriers class. It is muzzled, microchipped, and barred from housing complexes, parks, cities, and whole countries.

RED/TAN | GOLD AND WHITE | BLACK AND WHITE | TAN AND WHITE | BLACK BRINDLE

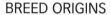

BREED ORIGINS

The history of the Pit Bull is that of the American Staffordshire until the mid-20th century, when the two split. The Pit Bull has come off badly:

IMAGE PROBLEM Pit Bulls are too often bought as a macho accessory by owners who encourage aggression, and suffer from the inevitable results. Cropped ears add to the desired "hard" look.

Limited recognition means no strong common breeding policy, while leash laws preclude them from trials in which they used to excel. They are dog-aggressive, but human-aggressive individuals would have been culled in the breed's past, and in the right hands this loyal dog should be less human-aggressive than a mastiff: No powerful dog should be left alone with children.

American Staffordshire Terrier

ORIGIN United States
HEIGHT 17–19 in (43–48 cm)
WEIGHT 40–50 lb (18.2–22.7 kg)
EXERCISE LEVEL
COAT CARE
REGISTERED FCI, AKCs
COLORS Any color, with or without white

Not identical to the original Staffordshire Terrier in the United Kingdom, this heftier breed is closer to the American Pit Bull. This fighter is gentle around people, but remorseless with other dogs.

BLACK | DARK BROWN | BLACK AND WHITE | TAN AND WHITE | BLACK AND TAN

BREED ORIGINS

Bull terriers, including the Staffordshire, were brought to the United States in the 19th century and kept as fight and farm dogs. In the 20th century, with fighting outlawed, some turned respectable as Staffies—with "American" added later to avoid confusion with the British breed—while others are known as Pit Bulls. It is still possible for dogs to be registered as one breed in one association and the other elsewhere. Fighting dogs were once renowned for their gentleness around humans, but their owners were experienced handlers who spent much time socializing them as pups; with the same care today, this powerful little dog is an affectionate companion.

SMALL BUT STRONG Although the mastiff guard breeds are bigger, the strong jaws and tenacious grip of these dogs can do as much damage.

American Toy Terrier

ORIGIN United States
HEIGHT 10 in (25 cm)
WEIGHT 4–7 lb (1.8–3.2 kg)
EXERCISE LEVEL
COAT CARE
REGISTERED AKCs
COLORS Black and white, tan and white, tricolor

Registered by AKC as the Toy Fox Terrier, but known elsewhere as the American Toy or Amertoy, this miniature dog is less energetic than some other terrier breeds.

BLACK AND WHITE

TAN AND WHITE

BREED ORIGINS

This is a miniaturized Fox Terrier, created in the early 20th century from the smallest of the breed judiciously crossed with Chihuahuas and English Toy Terriers. Originally a ratter, it is now an intelligent, ebullient, and athletic companion that suits city life.

CLOSE SHAVE A very short coat makes this an easy-care dog, but a winter coat is appreciated. There is no working need for docking today.

Australian Terrier

ORIGIN Australia
HEIGHT 10 in (25 cm)
WEIGHT 12–14 lb (5.5–6.4 kg)
EXERCISE LEVEL
COAT CARE
REGISTERED KC, FCI, AKCs
COLORS Sand to red, blue and tan

This breed is the rough-and-ready working ancestor of the Australian Silky Terrier companion breed. A useful household dog in rural Australia, it doubled as ruthless vermin exterminator and alert, noisy watchdog.

BREED ORIGINS

The exact brew that created the Australian Terrier is not recorded, but included the same ancestors as British terriers such as the Yorkshire, Cairn, and Skye, which arrived with settlers in the early 19th century. It was the first native Australian breed to be shown, and had a breed club by 1880. Today, it is a useful watchdog and makes an outgoing companion, although feisty around other animals.

WASH AND WEAR Although long, the coat is wiry, and this is a fairly easy breed to care for. It is not as long lived as some other terriers.

Bedlington Terrier

ORIGIN United Kingdom
HEIGHT 15–17 in (38–43 cm)
WEIGHT 17–23 lb (7.7–10.5 kg)
EXERCISE LEVEL
COAT CARE
REGISTERED KC, FCI, AKCs
COLORS Blue, sandy, liver, may have tan markings

Also once known as the Rothbury Terrier, this breed hails from Northumberland. It has had a varied history as a ratter, hound, retriever, and even a fighting dog.

 GRAY
 GOLD

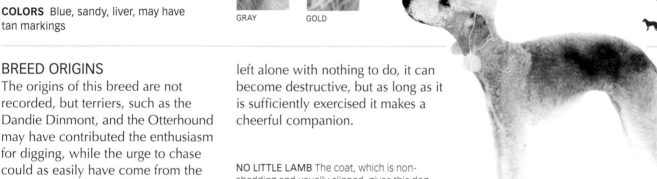

BREED ORIGINS

The origins of this breed are not recorded, but terriers, such as the Dandie Dinmont, and the Otterhound may have contributed the enthusiasm for digging, while the urge to chase could as easily have come from the Whippet input seen in its silhouette. The result is a dynamo of a breed; if left alone with nothing to do, it can become destructive, but as long as it is sufficiently exercised it makes a cheerful companion.

NO LITTLE LAMB The coat, which is non-shedding and usually clipped, gives this dog a mild, sheep-like appearance that is entirely misleading.

Belgian Griffons

ORIGIN Belgium
HEIGHT 7–8 in (18–20 cm)
WEIGHT 7–15 lb (3.2–6.8 kg)
EXERCISE LEVEL
COAT CARE
REGISTERED KCC, FCI, AKCs
COLORS Black, red, black and tan

Depending on the registry, these can be one or three breeds. One or all, they are tolerant and amiable companions, gentler than many terriers. Ravaged by two World Wars, they remain rare.

 BLACK
 RED/TAN
 BLACK AND TAN

BREED ORIGINS

In Europe, the wirehaired dogs are either Griffon Bruxellois or Griffon Belge according to color, and all the smooth-coated dogs are called Petit Brabançon. Elsewhere, the smooth-coated dogs are a variety within a breed called Brussels Griffon or Griffon Bruxellois. All are descended from the Griffon d'Écurie or Stable Griffon, with probable input from the Affenpinscher, the Dutch Smoushond, the Yorkshire Terrier, toy spaniels from the United Kingdom, and Pugs.

COLOR DISTINCTION The rough, reddish coat makes this a Griffon Bruxellois in Europe; the Griffon Belge is black or black and tan.

LITTLE SMOOTHIES Because "griffon" indicates a rough coat, in Europe these dogs are called Petit Brabançon, after a Belgian province.

Border Terrier

ORIGIN United Kingdom
HEIGHT 10 in (25 cm)
WEIGHT 11–15 lb (5.0–6.8 kg)
EXERCISE LEVEL
COAT CARE
REGISTERED KC, FCI, AKCs
COLORS Gray, wheaten, tan or red, blue and tan

Although it has become a popular family companion, this dog still shows itself to be a true hunting type. It has a compact build, persistent but amenable temperament, and hardy constitution.

GRAY

RED/TAN

GOLD

BREED ORIGINS

Like so many working dogs, this breed comes from undocumented origins. Dogs like these were working in the English-Scottish border area in the late 18th century, killing rats, foxes, and possibly otters and badgers. Their descendants include not only the Border Terrier, but also the less widely recognized Fell and Patterdale Terriers, kept as working dogs. The name Border Terrier was in use for this type by the end of the 19th century, and the breed was recognized in the early 20th century.

BREED QUALITIES

This terrier is popular in the United Kingdom, and is in the top ten breeds. This has happened only recently, and it is less popular elsewhere, so it has not been overbred, and remains true to its original type. It has a more tolerant, less snappy personality than many terriers, and is more trainable and a fine family dog—albeit still terrier enough to need active owners.

PERFECT SIZE The Border is an ideal vermin hunter, leggy enough to run good distances, but small enough to fit down a fox's earth.

COAT CARE The hard coat is weatherproof and easy to maintain, shedding dirt with a quick brush. A sleeker look is achieved by hand-stripping the dead hair twice a year.

Boston Terrier

ORIGIN United States
HEIGHT 15–17 in (38–43 cm)
WEIGHT 15–25 lb (6.8–11.4 kg)
EXERCISE LEVEL
COAT CARE
REGISTERED KC, FCI, AKCs
COLORS Brindle, seal, or black with white markings

With a heritage of mastiffs and fighting dogs, one might expect this to be a bullish breed, but it is one of the most relaxed breeds to carry the "terrier" label, even something of a layabout.

BLACK AND WHITE

BLACK BRINDLE

BREED ORIGINS

The Boston dates back to the late 19th century and is a blend of old English and French Bulldogs and the now-extinct White Terrier, with constant selection for smaller size. The breed was an immediate success, the first American breed to gain recognition, and has remained a favorite with the public ever since due to its engaging, compliant personality.

TRIM LOOKS The ears are naturally erect and batlike, but are sometimes cropped to "improve" the line. The tail is naturally short, and not now docked.

Brazilian Terrier

ORIGIN Brazil
HEIGHT 14–16 in (36–41 cm)
WEIGHT 15–20 lb (6.8–9.1 kg)
EXERCISE LEVEL
COAT CARE
REGISTERED None
COLORS Tricolor

Registered as the Terrier Brasileiro and also called the Fox Paulistinha, this breed is popular in its homeland but almost unknown elsewhere.

BREED ORIGINS

Dating from the 19th or early 20th century, the most likely ancestor of this breed is the Jack Russell Terrier, which it resembles in both its looks and its frisky personality. Miniature Pinschers may have been used to increase its size. It was a farm dog, used for hunting in packs which would surround and overwhelm the prey, or alone for ratting. It is now seen in the cities as well, but the

noisy voice that makes it a good watchdog may not be popular with neighbors. The breed's high energy levels also make plenty of exercise essential.

BRAZILIAN LOOKS The slender, curved lines of this breed distinguish it from a Fox Terrier. The tail, usually docked in its homeland, is naturally above the hocks.

BOSTON TERRIER Not all terriers are bundles of unstoppable energy. Some, like the Boston, have been bred away from their original manic nature and turned into polite, relaxed companions that are fit for any home.

Bull Terrier

ORIGIN United Kingdom
HEIGHT 21–22 in (53–56 cm)
WEIGHT 52–62 lb (23.6–28.2 kg)
EXERCISE LEVEL
COAT CARE
REGISTERED KC, FCI, AKCs
COLORS Any color except blue or liver

Instantly recognizable for its convex Roman nose, this dog was first developed as a fighting breed. It is usually a trustworthy and stable breed, but no powerful dog is ideal for a novice owner.

BLACK AND WHITE

TAN AND WHITE

BLACK, WHITE, AND TAN

BLACK BRINDLE

BREED ORIGINS

This breed was developed by John Hinks early in the 19th century. He crossed the White English Terrier, now extinct, with the Bulldog, and the result was instantly successful as a fighter and as a companion. Active and highly intelligent, Bull Terriers should be kept busy. They are tolerant, and do not bite readily, but also do not let go easily, and young dogs may play too roughly for children.

ORIGINAL COLOR Hinks preferred white, still the only color allowed in some registries, but it carries an increased risk of deafness and health problems. Head markings are not penalized.

Cairn Terrier

ORIGIN United Kingdom
HEIGHT 9–10 in (23–25 cm)
WEIGHT 13–14 lb (5.9–6.4 kg)
EXERCISE LEVEL
COAT CARE
REGISTERED KC, FCI, AKCs
COLORS Cream, wheaten, red, sandy, gray, brindled

This typically compact, shaggy little terrier from Scotland has long been a popular breed. It has a robust constitution and an equally robust temperament.

CREAM

GRAY

BLACK BRINDLE

BREED ORIGINS

The exact origins of the Cairn are uncertain, but are almost certainly linked to those of other breeds such as the Scottish, Skye, and West Highland White Terriers. Its name comes from marker cairns built of stones, and its use in hunting out vermin that took refuge in them. Today, it still loves to chase and dig, and may not be for those who love their lawn. It makes a good watchdog and city companion, with a more obedient character than some other terriers. It is cheerful and entertaining, as long as it is entertained in turn.

COAT CARE The hard, wiry top coat of the Cairn can be trimmed around the eyes, but is best "stripped" by hand, or plucked out to reveal the soft undercoat, in summer.

Cesky Terrier

ORIGIN Czech Republic
HEIGHT 10–14 in (25–36 cm)
WEIGHT 12–18 lb (5.5–8.2 kg)
EXERCISE LEVEL
COAT CARE
REGISTERED FCI
COLORS Blue-gray or red-brown

A relative newcomer on the terrier scene, and a European in a group dominated by British breeds, the Cesky has won great popularity in a short time. It is also called the Bohemian Terrier.

BLUE

RED/TAN

BREED ORIGINS

The Cesky was developed in the mid-20th century, and first recognized in 1963. Its creator was Dr. Frantisek Horak, a Czech geneticist, who wanted a dog that was shorter in the leg, narrower, and more useful in burrowing than the typical German terrier breeds. He crossed the Sealyham with the Scottish Terrier and possibly the Dandie Dinmont, resulting in a compact breed with long hair and a heavily bearded face. Further crosses to Sealyhams, the breed that the Cesky most closely resembles, were made to improve the type in the 1980s; this was also the decade when the breed arrived in the United States.

BREED QUALITIES

The typical terrier temper is obvious: this breed is feisty and can be snappy and stubborn. But Ceskies are also fearless, faithful, protective, and playful, and early training and socialization will help to get the best out of them. They are long lived and fairly healthy dogs, although they can suffer Scotty cramp, a non-life-threatening condition that causes cramp after exercise and is controlled by medication.

CESKY CLIP Unlike most other terriers, the Cesky is clipped on the body, leaving curtains of long, soft hair on the belly and legs.

CESKY HEAD The folded ears, inherited from the Sealyham, are less prone to collecting earth and debris when a dog is underground. The head is partly clipped, leaving a dramatic beard.

Dandie Dinmont Terrier

ORIGIN United Kingdom
HEIGHT 8–11 in (20–28 cm)
WEIGHT 18–24 lb (8.2–10.9 kg)
EXERCISE LEVEL
COAT CARE
REGISTERED KC, FCI, AKCs
COLORS Red, silvered black and tan

This breed is named for a fictional farmer in Sir Walter Scott's novel *Guy Mannering*. The colors are named after the character's dogs, red being "mustard" and the silvered coat "pepper."

RED/TAN

BLACK AND TAN

LOW SLUNG The short legs of the Dandie Dinmont mean it is prone to spinal problems, but it is otherwise healthy.

BREED ORIGINS

Although taking its name from a novel published in 1815, the breed was used to pursue otters and badgers in the Scottish borders before this date. Like many working dogs, it has obscure origins, possibly among gypsy dogs. Association with such a fashionable novelist helped the breed's cause, but it is now very rare. More laid back than many terriers, it is calm around other dogs and children.

Dutch Smoushound

ORIGIN Netherlands
HEIGHT 14–17 in (36–43 cm)
WEIGHT 20–22 lb (9.1–10.0 kg)
EXERCISE LEVEL
COAT CARE
REGISTERED FCI
COLORS Shades of yellow, dark straw color preferred

Also known as the Hollandse Smoushond, this breed originally followed coaches and caught rats in stables, jobs that earned it the names of Gentleman's Stabledog or Coachman's Dog. It is taller than terriers that went to earth, with a sturdy but athletic build.

BREED ORIGINS

The ancestry of the original Smoushond is unknown, although its type suggests descent from German Schnauzers. It was a popular dog in the 19th century, but became less so in the 20th, and World War II took a heavy toll. In the 1970s, a Mrs. H.M. Barkman set out to recreate the breed, guided by old breed standards, photographs, and judges with long memories. Today it is secure in its homeland, but rarely seen elsewhere, and its breeders seem content to keep it as a national figure. A typical terrier, it is a noisy guard and vivacious family dog.

EASY CARE The shaggy coat of the Smoushond should have a tousled, unkempt look. Dead hair is stripped or plucked out twice a year.

English Toy Terrier

ORIGIN United Kingdom
HEIGHT 10–12 in (25–30 cm)
WEIGHT 6–8 lb (2.7–3.6 kg)
EXERCISE LEVEL
COAT CARE
REGISTERED KC
COLORS Black and tan

This tiny breed is similar to, but not quite the same as, the Toy Manchester Terrier recognized in the United States. It is so rare that the American breed is used to widen the gene pool.

BREED ORIGINS
This breed was developed from "runt" Manchester Terriers in the late 19th century for hunting rabbits and rats to ground. It is now kept almost entirely as a lively city companion and watchdog; it can be stubborn, and challenging around other dogs.

DISTINCTIVELY DIFFERENT Unusually for a terrier, this is a dainty miniature with an arched back, tucked up waist, and "candle flame" ears.

German Hunting Terrier

ORIGIN Germany
HEIGHT 16 in (41 cm)
WEIGHT 20–22 lb (9.1–10.0 kg)
EXERCISE LEVEL
COAT CARE
REGISTERED FCI
COLORS Red, brown and tan, black and tan

The Deutscher Jagdterrier, created to work above and below ground, still holds true to its name and original purpose. It lives to hunt, and is kept more as a hunter's dog than a companion.

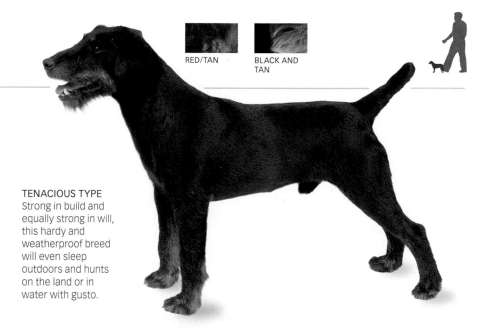

RED/TAN   BLACK AND TAN

BREED ORIGINS
Although it was created in Bavaria, this breed is drawn from an ancestry of old English black-and-tan terriers, Fox Terriers, and Welsh Terriers. It is full of energy and curiosity, ideally suited to rural pursuits, but can become frustrated and even destructive in less active home settings. It makes a fine watchdog and outdoor companion, but is not suitable for city life.

TENACIOUS TYPE Strong in build and equally strong in will, this hardy and weatherproof breed will even sleep outdoors and hunts on the land or in water with gusto.

Glen of Imaal Terrier

ORIGIN Ireland
HEIGHT 14 in (36 cm)
WEIGHT 35 lb (15.9 kg)
EXERCISE LEVEL
COAT CARE
REGISTERED KC, FCI, AKCs
COLORS Blue, wheaten, brindles

Standards for this breed say it "should always convey the impression of maximum substance for size of dog"; in plain terms, this is a small, hairy, good-natured battering ram.

BLUE   GOLD   BLACK BRINDLE

BREED ORIGINS

The breed's roots are unknown, but it may have been employed running in wheels and turning spits before finding favor in vermin hunting and badger baiting. It is a good guard: its sturdy, broad-chested build makes it a breed that many instinctively back away from, and it will not back down easily. It can be as heavy as much larger dogs, so should be treated and trained as such.

ANNUAL MAINTENANCE The rough topcoat should be plucked out by hand in summer.

Irish Terrier

ORIGIN Ireland
HEIGHT 18 in (46 cm)
WEIGHT 25–27 lb (11.4–12.3 kg)
EXERCISE LEVEL
COAT CARE
REGISTERED KC, FCI, AKCs
COLORS Yellow, wheaten, red

These are also called Irish Red Terriers or, by their fans, Daredevils. Even the breed standards mention the breed's "heedless, reckless pluck." They are animated hunters and loyal defenders of the home.

RED/TAN   GOLD

BREED ORIGINS

These dogs emerged from the general stock of guards and vermin hunters through selective breeding in the 19th century, and by the end of the century they had become the first Irish breed recognized by the Kennel Club and been exported to the United States. Still used for hunting in Ireland, they are more often seen as household and family companions. Provided that they are

given enough exercise to use up some of their boundless energy, they can be very civilized indoors: They are tractable with people, but unreliable around dogs or other small pets.

IRISH LOOKS Deeper red coats predominate because they tend to be harder in texture than pale coats. The tail was customarily docked; left natural, it should be held high but not curled over.

Jack Russell Terrier

ORIGIN United Kingdom
HEIGHT 10–12 in (25–30 cm)
WEIGHT 9–15 lb (4–7 kg)
EXERCISE LEVEL
COAT CARE
REGISTERED FCI
COLORS Bicolored or tricolored

These terriers are full of character, and have an adventurous side to their natures that can occasionally lead them into trouble, since they have little fear.

BLACK AND WHITE

BLACK AND TAN

BLACK, WHITE, AND TAN

WELL TRAVELED The first man to walk to both Poles, Ranulph Fiennes, was accompanied by his Jack Russell, Bothie—an extraordinary feat for a rural British hunting breed.

BREED ORIGINS

The Jack Russell Terrier is named after its creator, who obtained a distinctive terrier bitch in May 1819, while studying at Oxford University. He developed a terrier that was bold enough to venture underground to drive out a fox from its lair, and yet could also run well. They were later crossed with a range of other dogs, which helps explain their variable appearance.

BREED QUALITIES

Jack Russell Terriers remain popular, both as companions and working dogs, often being seen on farms. They also prove to be alert watchdogs, with a surprisingly loud bark for their diminutive stature.

PERFECT SIZE To chase foxes into earths, working dogs must never be more than 14 in (35 cm) around the chest.

Kerry Blue Terrier

ORIGIN Ireland
HEIGHT 17–19 in (43–48 cm)
WEIGHT 33–40 lb (15.0–18.2 kg)
EXERCISE LEVEL
COAT CARE
REGISTERED KC, FCI, AKCs
COLORS Blue

Also known as the Irish Blue Terrier, this breed was first noted in Kerry in the southwest, but never restricted to that corner of Ireland. It is traditionally the national dog of Ireland, but surprisingly rare for a breed with such status.

BREED ORIGINS

The origins of this breed are uncertain, and ancestors may include the Soft-coated Wheaten Terrier crossed with the Bedlington Terrier, the Irish Terrier, and even the Irish Wolfhound. The blue, curly coat has attracted the legend that such a dog swam ashore and was considered so fine that he was mated to all the local wheaten-colored terriers; it is not impossible that there is some genetic influence from a Portuguese Water Dog on a

visiting boat. The breed was a farm favorite, used for hunting vermin and otters, but only officially recognized in the late 19th century.

BREED QUALITIES

Today the breed is most likely to be found as a household dog, although it is still sometimes used for hunting. They can be time-consuming to groom, especially if the beard is left full, but make energetic, spirited companions.

YOUTHFUL COLOR Kerry Blues are born black and their coats gradually lighten as they mature. They can stay dark in color until they are fully grown, turning blue as late as two years old.

COAT CARE The wavy coat is soft and silky. Once it would have been allowed to form weatherproof cords, but it is now usually brushed every day or two and trimmed every six to ten weeks.

Lakeland Terrier

ORIGIN United Kingdom
HEIGHT 15–18 in (33–46 cm)
WEIGHT 15–17 lb (6.8–7.7 kg)
EXERCISE LEVEL
COAT CARE
REGISTERED KC, FCI, AKCs
COLORS Black, blue, wheaten, red, liver, red grizzle, blue or black and tan

This hardworking little breed was created to work in the steep, rocky terrain of the Lake District, U.K., dispatching foxes to protect sheep. A keen hunter, it has never achieved widespread popularity.

 BLACK
 BLUE
 RED/TAN
 GOLD
 BLACK AND TAN

BREED ORIGINS

This farm dog is probably descended from extinct black-and-tan terriers, possibly with influence from early Bedlington, Border, and Dandie Dinmont Terriers. It was bred to go to earth after its quarry and despite its ability to learn it can forget its training when in hot pursuit. It is tenacious and fearless of opponents larger than itself, but also confident with strangers, with an ebullient personality. Despite its small size, this is not an ideal choice for the inexperienced owner, but with good training it will make an effective watchdog. "Working Lakeland," Patterdale, or Fell Terriers are working dogs now separate from this breed.

LAKELAND LOOKS The weatherproof coat has a hard, wiry outer coat and a soft undercoat. The tail, once docked, is carried upright.

Lucas Terrier

ORIGIN United Kingdom
HEIGHT 9–12 in (23–30 cm)
WEIGHT 11–20 lb (5.0–9.1 kg)
EXERCISE LEVEL
COAT CARE
REGISTERED None
COLORS Sable; black or gray and tan; white; silver; white and tan, black, or gray; tricolor

These extremely rare terriers have only been around for half a century and never been recognized, but have nonetheless managed to produce a second offshoot breed.

 BLACK AND WHITE
 TAN AND WHITE
 BLACK AND TAN
 BLACK, WHITE, AND TAN

BEST OF BOTH WORLDS The Lucas is enthusiastic on the move, but calm indoors, so makes itself at home in the city or country. It is accounted a healthy and intelligent breed.

BREED ORIGINS

This cross of the Sealyham Terrier and a Norfolk Terrier was created in the 1940s by Sir Jocelyn Lucas to drive game toward guns. He never sought official recognition, a policy pursued by Lucas breeders to this day. Some breeders also crossed to Plummer and Fell Terriers, producing a dog inclined to work underground, and these are now the quite separate Working Lucas Terrier.

Manchester Terrier

ORIGIN United Kingdom
HEIGHT 15–16 in (38–41 cm)
WEIGHT 12–22 lb (5.5–10.0 kg)
EXERCISE LEVEL
COAT CARE
REGISTERED KC, FCI, AKCs
COLORS Black and tan

This breed name means something different on each side of the Atlantic. In the United Kingdom, it has one size, but in the United States there is a Toy version, similar to the English Toy Terrier (*see* p 149).

BREED ORIGINS

Many of the British terrier breeds are descended from old black-and-tan types traceable back to the Middle Ages. The Manchester Terrier was created from this stock in the 19th century, and was the work of John Hulme. He crossed the terriers with Whippets for speed, and the resulting breed, excellent for ratting and rabbiting, was known for a time as "The Gentleman's Terrier." It is still a good outdoor companion, but is inclined to challenge other dogs and is too independent-minded to be a popular household dog.

EAR TYPES British dogs are shown with natural ears, but American dogs may still have them cropped. The end of cropping dented the breed's popularity in the United Kingdom.

Miniature Pinscher

ORIGIN Germany
HEIGHT 15–16 in (38–41 cm)
WEIGHT 12–22 lb (5.5–10.0 kg)
EXERCISE LEVEL
COAT CARE
REGISTERED KC, FCI, AKCs
COLORS Tan, black and tan; some allow blue or chocolate and tan

Also called the Zwergpinscher, this might look like a recent miniaturization of a working breed to make a toy companion, but in fact it has long been a compact working ratter.

RED/TAN   BLACK AND TAN

BREED ORIGINS

This breed was developed from larger German Pinschers at least 500 years ago, but early dogs were tough ratters, since refined into a dog similar to the English Toy Terrier. It will pursue with relish, dig enthusiastically, and challenge dogs far larger than itself. It makes an effective watchdog and lively companion.

CHANGING FASHIONS American standards may still call for a docked tail and cropped ears, but European dogs are now shown undocked with either erect or dropped ears.

Norfolk Terrier

ORIGIN United Kingdom

HEIGHT 10 in (25 cm)

WEIGHT 11–12 lb (5.0–5.5 kg)

EXERCISE LEVEL

COAT CARE

REGISTERED KC, FCI, AKCs

COLORS Gray, wheaten, red, black and tan

This breed is one of the smallest terriers and is mostly identical to the Norwich Terrier. The distinguishing feature of the two breeds is their ears: the Norfolk's are dropped, the Norwich's erect.

 GRAY

 RED/TAN

 GOLD

BLACK AND TAN

BREED ORIGINS

Packs of small red terriers of this type were used by the gypsy ratcatchers of Norfolk for some time before the the Norwich and Norfolk were created from them in the late 19th century. The Norwich was recognized in 1936, and the Norfolk separated nearly 30 years later, in 1964; recognition took another 15 years in the United States. These dogs are too small to be used over any great

distance in a hunt; they were kept on farms to clear rats from barns, and worked in a pack, so are more tolerant of other dogs than many terrier breeds. They are a generally healthy and long-lived breed.

NATURAL FOLD Before the types were separated, the drop-eared dogs could be shown, but their ears were often cropped before that practice was made illegal.

Norwich Terrier

ORIGIN United Kingdom

HEIGHT 10 in (25 cm)

WEIGHT 11–12 lb (5.0–5.5 kg)

EXERCISE LEVEL

COAT CARE

REGISTERED KC, FCI, AKCs

COLORS Gray, wheaten, red, black and tan

This name originally covered both the prick-eared dog we know today and the soft-eared type that is now called the Norfolk. Both ear types had appeared from the breed's earliest days.

GRAY

RED/TAN

GOLD

BLACK AND TAN

BREED ORIGINS

It is thought that local ratters, Cairn Terriers, and short-legged Irish terrier breeds were used to create the Norwich, and either the name Trumpington Terrier was used for this breed, or it was a type used to create it but now extinct. In the late 19th century, the breed was called the Cantab Terrier and was a fashionable pet for students at Cambridge University; it was

exported to the United States as the Jones Terrier. A relatively biddable and calm terrier, it gets along with older children.

SHORT STUFF Although these are active and energetic dogs, their small size means that exercising them is not too time consuming, and they settle well into city life.

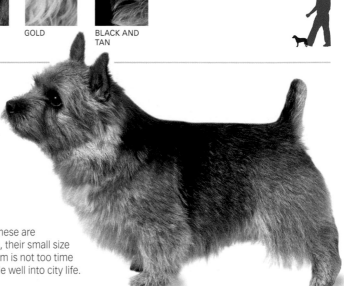

Parson Russell Terrier

ORIGIN United Kingdom
HEIGHT 11–15 in (28–38 cm)
WEIGHT 11–18 lb (5–8 kg)
EXERCISE LEVEL
COAT CARE
REGISTERED KC, FCI, AKCs
COLORS White and black or brown, tricolor

This breed is less popular in rural pursuits but has won wider recognition in show registries than the Jack Russell Terrier. The longer legs allowed dogs to keep up with mounted hunters.

BLACK AND WHITE

TAN AND WHITE

BLACK, WHITE AND TAN

BREED ORIGINS

This and its short-legged near-namesake were developed from white terriers used to pursue foxes underground. These went on to be recognized as Fox Terriers, but moved away from the working type, becoming too large to fit down earths. Reverend John "Jack" Russell developed his own fast and furious dogs from the same stock, and they remain closer to their roots. For a long time both types were classed together, but after much dispute, this breed is now recognized separately.

CHOICE OF COATS This breed has two versions, the wirehaired or broken coat seen here and preferred by Russell himself, and a sleeker smooth-haired type. Both are easy to care for and equally popular.

Patterdale Terrier

ORIGIN United Kingdom
HEIGHT 12 in (30 cm)
WEIGHT 12–13 lb (5.5–5.9 kg)
EXERCISE LEVEL
COAT CARE
REGISTERED None
COLORS Black, bronze, grizzled gray, red with black, liver, or blue; may have tan points

The dogs covered by this breed name can be a varied lot. Patterdale Terriers are working dogs, and as such do not conform tightly to a breed standard for appearance.

BLACK

RED/TAN

DARK BROWN

BLACK AND TAN

BREED ORIGINS

Once, every village or valley in the U.K. would have had its own terrier. Some moved from fields into show halls, some vanished, but some persist. Named after a village in Cumbria, this breed is used to hunt foxes, rabbits, and rats in the Lake District and Yorkshire, and is also known in the United States. Recent legal restrictions on terrier work place the future of such working breeds in doubt.

BROAD STANDARD Patterdales are generally smooth coated and black. Rough-coated dogs are more often called Fell Terriers. As working dogs, size and shape are variable.

Plummer Terrier

ORIGIN United Kingdom
HEIGHT 11–13 in (29–33 cm)
WEIGHT 12–15 lb (5.5–7.0 kg)
EXERCISE LEVEL
COAT CARE
REGISTERED None
COLORS Red and white

This breed is only a few decades old, but it has won itself a band of highly dedicated and partisan followers. It was born out of one slightly eccentric man's passion for ratting, and is named after its creator.

BREED ORIGINS

Brian Plummer embarked on the creation of this breed in the 1960s, using a blend of Jack Russell, Bull Terrier, Beagle, and Fell Terrier to produce a hardy and healthy breed. Today it is larger than the very earliest crosses, but for hunting vermin above ground it is a staunch worker. Most Plummer owners and breeders seem happy for the breed to stay outside major registry recognition, and it is popular with those who use working dogs, but wider acceptance might help to assure its future.

TOUGH CUSTOMER With a breed standard that says "honourable scars permissible," this is a working dog from nose to tail, not a household breed.

Russian Toy Terrier

ORIGIN Russia
HEIGHT 8–11 in (20–28 cm)
WEIGHT 4–7 lb (1.8–3.2 kg)
EXERCISE LEVEL
COAT CARE
REGISTERED None
COLORS Black and tan, red, sable, rarely brown or blue and tan

Also known as the Moscow Toy Terrier, Moscovian Miniature Terrier, and Russian or Moscow Longhaired Toy Terrier, this can be a hard breed to track down. It is not yet recognized outside Russia.

RED/TAN

BLACK AND TAN

BREED ORIGINS

At the turn of the 20th century, the English Toy Terrier was one of the most popular toy breeds in Russia. After a few decades under the Communist regime, the breed had all but vanished, and virtually no recorded pedigree dogs were left.

The remaining dogs of the type were taken in a new direction and became the Russian Toy. They are still active little dogs with a need for a lively life, but gentler and more amenable than most terriers.

LIGHTLY BUILT Slender legs support a lithe body, and the relatively small, fine-muzzled head is carried on a long neck.

FAMILY LIKENESS The shorthair looks like its English ancestor; there is also a longhair with dramatic Papillon-like ears.

Scottish Terrier

ORIGIN United Kingdom
HEIGHT 10–11 in (25–28 cm)
WEIGHT 19–23 lb (8.6–10.5 kg)
EXERCISE LEVEL
COAT CARE
REGISTERED KC, FCI, AKCs
COLORS Black, wheaten, black brindle, red brindle

Once called the Aberdeen Terrier, and also generically called a Skye Terrier, the Scottie was nicknamed "Diehard" by the 19th-century Earl of Dumbarton, who had a famous pack of terriers.

BLACK

GOLD

BLACK BRINDLE

BREED ORIGINS
This breed is descended from terriers of the Scottish Western Isles, known as a type since the 16th century. It was developed in the 19th century, with all Scotties traceable back to one bitch, Splinter. They became hugely fashionable in the United States in the 1930s, possibly helped by President Roosevelt's pet, Fala;

George W. Bush's two Scotties have not worked similar magic. More companions than true terriers, they are loyal, stubborn, and spirited.

SCOTTIE LOOKS Instantly recognizable for its extravagant beard, the Scottie has an insulating double coat and may appreciate clipping or stripping in warmer climates. The ears are naturally pricked and quite narrow.

Sealyham Terrier

ORIGIN United Kingdom
HEIGHT 10–11 in (25–28 cm)
WEIGHT 20–25 lb (10.0–11.4 kg)
EXERCISE LEVEL
COAT CARE
REGISTERED KC, FCI, AKCs
COLORS White, white with lemon, brown, blue, or black on head

Once popular, now rare even in its Welsh homeland, this industrious breed excelled at its original job of hunting otters and other small game, but has not easily made the transition to companion.

GOLD AND WHITE

BLACK AND WHITE

TAN AND WHITE

COAT CARE The show Sealyham coat takes a great deal of time-consuming preparation. Even pet dogs will require proper trimming or stripping three or four times a year.

BREED ORIGINS
The Sealyham Terrier was developed largely by a Captain John Edward in the mid-19th century in southwest Wales. He used Basset Hounds, Bull Terriers, Fox Terriers, the West Highland White Terrier, and the Dandie Dinmont Terrier to create a small but powerful breed to pursue quarry on land, underground, and in water. The dogged determination and enthusiasm for the kill mean that these terriers can be difficult as pets, but they make good watchdogs.

Skye Terrier

ORIGIN United Kingdom
HEIGHT 10 in (25 cm)
WEIGHT 19–25 lb (8.6–11.4 kg)
EXERCISE LEVEL
COAT CARE
REGISTERED KC, FCI, AKCs
COLORS Black, gray, fawn, cream

This breed is immortalized in Grayfriars Bobby, who is said to have spent 14 years sitting on the grave of his master in Grayfriars cemetery in Edinburgh until his own death.

BLACK   CREAM   GRAY   GOLD

BREED ORIGINS

Terriers on the Isle of Skye with hair covering their faces were described in the 16th century, but those could have resembled either this terrier or the Scottish Terrier, which was drawn from island stock. Their dwarf stature may have come from the same roots as the Swedish Vallhund or Welsh Corgis; there are also tales of a Spanish shipwreck and Maltese dogs coming ashore. The terriers were used as vermin hunters and companions, "esteemed, taken up, and made of, in room of the spaniell gentle, or comforter."

BREED QUALITIES

The distinctive long coat of the breed, covering a graceful build, made it popular for showing and as a pet, but numbers have fallen off recently, and the breed is close to extinction in its homeland. It does have the usual terrier feistiness, which can be unappealing next to more biddable and exotic breeds now popular, but it makes a good watchdog and a bright city or rural companion.

COAT CARE The long coat that is part of this breed's appeal is not very prone to matting, but it was kept clipped on working dogs.

UP OR DOWN? The ears of a Skye can be either pricked or dropped. Pricked ears are most common in the majority of countries, but in Australia the restricted number of the breed led to a few drop-eared dogs making the trait more common.

SCOTTISH TERRIER (*see* p. 158) There have been fashions for coat color in this breed over the years. These dogs resemble early examples, which were almost always lighter shades, with black dogs being overlooked at first.

Smooth Fox Terrier

ORIGIN United Kingdom
HEIGHT 10–11 in (25–28 cm)
WEIGHT 15–22 lb (6.8–10.0 kg)
EXERCISE LEVEL
COAT CARE
REGISTERED KC, FCI, AKCs
COLORS White, white and tan, white and black, tricolor

Once classed together with the Wire Fox Terrier, and drawn from the same stock as the Jack and Parson Russell, this breed is now kept almost entirely as a companion, though not suited to city life.

BLACK AND WHITE

TAN AND WHITE

BLACK, WHITE AND TAN

BREED ORIGINS
A fox terrier was any dog that would drive foxes from their earths. This type was shown in the 1860s, and ancestors may include Beagles and even Bull Terriers. Although no longer a working dog, it is energetic and stubborn; it can be snappish, especially with younger children.

COLORING Unlike its black-and-tan ancestors, a white dog could not be mistaken for a fox.

Soft-coated Wheaten Terrier

ORIGIN Ireland
HEIGHT 18–19 in (46–48 cm)
WEIGHT 35–40 lb (15.9–18.2 kg)
EXERCISE LEVEL
COAT CARE
REGISTERED KC, FCI, AKCs
COLORS Wheaten gold

A terrier in name and looks, the Wheaten was originally an all-purpose farm dog, used for herding and guarding livestock as much as hunting, and is one of the more relaxed terriers.

BREED ORIGINS
This versatile breed is thought to be related to both the the Irish and the Kerry Blue Terriers, and was found on farms in southern and southwestern Ireland for centuries. It lacks the over-the-top attitude of its compatriots, however, and perhaps for that very reason has become a more popular companion breed. It is one of the few terriers that is tolerant of children.

WHEATEN VARIATIONS Coats in the United States are generally kept longer, while those of dogs in the United Kingdom tend to be thicker. The coat is copper-red at birth and lightens with maturity.

Staffordshire Bull Terrier

ORIGIN United Kingdom

HEIGHT 14–16 in (36–41 cm)

WEIGHT 24–38 lb (10.9–17.3 kg)

EXERCISE LEVEL

COAT CARE

REGISTERED KC, FCI, AKCs

COLORS Any color except liver; solid or with white

The Staffie, although similar to some banned breeds, has so far not been subject to legislation in its homeland and most of Europe. It may look and walk like a thug, but it can be a pushover.

 BLACK   RED/TAN   GOLD AND WHITE   BLACK AND WHITE   BLACK BRINDLE

BREED ORIGINS
This breed has its roots in dog-fighting, but the Staffie became a respectable recognized breed in the early 20th century. It is sweet-natured with humans but a ruthless fighter of any other dog. They are not recommended as solitary guards, because they should be well socialized; exercising them anywhere near other dogs is tricky.

FIGHTING FACE For dog fights, relatively long muzzles were needed, so short-faced bull baiters were crossed with terriers to produce the breed.

Welsh Terrier

ORIGIN United Kingdom

HEIGHT 15 in (38 cm)

WEIGHT 20 lb (9.1 kg)

EXERCISE LEVEL

COAT CARE

REGISTERED KC, FCI, AKCs

COLORS Black and tan

This breed is a modern representative of an old British type in looks, but less extreme than many terrier breeds in character. Originally a ratter and hunting terrier, it is now an amiable companion.

BREED ORIGINS
This is thought to be descended from the historical type called the broken (meaning rough-coated) black-and-tan terrier, a dog that was once known over much of the United Kingdom. The type was still called the Old English Terrier in the 19th century, but in the 1880s, it was recognized as the Welsh Terrier

and under that name reached the United States, where it is most popular today. Use in hunting packs means this breed is less aggressive toward other dogs than some terrier breeds, and also easier to train.

GROOMING A WELSHIE The coat is easy care except for the beard, which needs regular cleaning to keep it looking good.

West Highland White Terrier

ORIGIN United Kingdom
HEIGHT 10–11 in (25–28 cm)
WEIGHT 15–22 lb (6.8–10.0 kg)
EXERCISE LEVEL
COAT CARE
REGISTERED KC, FCI, AKCs
COLORS White

A perennially popular breed, the Westie has been used as the face of dog food and, along with a black Scottish Terrier, Scotch whiskey. This dog is a bundle of fun that was created for a very sober reason.

BREED ORIGINS

The Westie is derived from white pups in wheaten Cairn Terrier litters. In the 19th century, these dogs flushed out game for guns, and were occasionally mistaken for prey and shot. So a white terrier that was easily distinguished from the quarry at any distance was developed; some credit the breed to Colonel E.D. Malcolm, others to the 8th Duke of Argyll. They are entertaining companions.

ITCHY COAT Although the white coat saved the lives of working dogs, it had a price. White dogs are more susceptible than others to skin problems, and the Westie is particularly prone to allergies due to environmental factors or foods.

Wire Fox Terrier

ORIGIN United Kingdom
HEIGHT 10–11 in (25–28 cm)
WEIGHT 15–22 lb (6.8–10.0 kg)
EXERCISE LEVEL
COAT CARE
REGISTERED KC, FCI, AKCs
COLORS White, white and black, white and tan, tricolor

This bundle of energy was until recently regarded as the Smooth Fox Terrier in another coat in some registries. They share a heritage, and have been crossed, but were always distinct to hunters.

BLACK AND WHITE

TAN AND WHITE

BREED ORIGINS

Starting in the 1860s, fox hunting enthusiasts sought to create their ideal rough-coated terrier, possibly in part from the same rough-coated, black-and-tan terrier stock that produced the Welsh Terrier. The Wire appeared in the show ring some 20 years after the smooth, but surpassed it in popularity in the

1930s when it appeared in the *Thin Man* films and *Tintin* comic strip. It has lost ground recently, possibly because its stubborn personality, an inclination to challenge other dogs, and addiction to digging are harder to accommodate in modern homes.

SIZE MATTERS The ideal terrier could keep up with horseriders and flush out a fox, but the size needed for the first was too great for the second.

Yorkshire Terrier

ORIGIN United Kingdom
HEIGHT 9 in (23 cm)
WEIGHT 7 lb (3.2 kg)
EXERCISE LEVEL
COAT CARE
REGISTERED KC, FCI, AKCs
COLORS Steel-blue and tan

Although most registries now place the diminutive Yorkie in the toy or companion category, it was created as a ratter by miners and mill workers who never envisaged a bow in its hair. It remains a terrier at heart, and will challenge anything.

BREED ORIGINS

In the mid-19th century, Yorkshire was at the heart of the United Kingdom's industrial revolution. Many workers migrated to the area from Scotland, bringing their dogs with them. Clydesdale, Paisley, Skye, and Waterside and English Black-and-tan Terriers may have been involved in its ancestry. From this mix came a dog with an excess of spirit, valued for killing vermin. Today the breed is right at the top of the popularity stakes in the United States, but its size and spirit may be suffering from overexposure. Selective breeding for small size has led to slipped kneecaps and breathing problems in some lines.

EVERYDAY COAT The long, luxuriant, silvered coat takes time to develop. Pet owners usually find it easier to trim dogs back to a shorter length.

MINI DOGS Even the smallest Yorkies still produce the occasional pup larger than themselves. This is no bad thing: Breeding for ever-smaller dogs can lead to health problems.

HOUNDS

Hounds hunt either by sight or by scent. Sighthounds are long-limbed, lean, elegant, and silent hunters. The oldest types have been genetically identified as among the oldest of all dog breeds, originating some 5,000 years ago in southwestern Asia, where they were used to sight, chase, and bring down fleet-footed prey. Scenthounds are relative latecomers, reaching the height of their popularity in the Middle Ages. Their lower build and sensitive noses combine to give unrivalled scenting ability. Alone or in packs, they find and pursue prey, often calling in distinctive voices, but frequently leave the final dispatch to the hunter.

BEAGLE PUP (*see* p. 178) Hounds range from small Beagles, like this pup, to the regal Afghan. Whatever their size and appearance, these are active, interested breeds that provide their owners with plenty of exercise.

Afghan Hound

ORIGIN Afghanistan
HEIGHT 25–29 in (64–74 cm)
WEIGHT 50–60 lb (22.5–27.5 kg)
EXERCISE LEVEL
COAT CARE
REGISTERED KC, FCI, AKCs
COLORS Any color, solid or shaded

The Afghan is perhaps the best known of the sighthounds. Originally at home in the harsh terrain and climate of the Afghan mountain ranges, it became a fashionable companion breed.

BLACK

CREAM

GRAY

GOLD

DARK BROWN

BREED ORIGINS

The Afghan is among the most ancient of all breeds. What is not clear is how thousands of years ago it came to the mountains of Afghanistan, far from the Arabian peninsula where dogs of this type originated. In its homeland, where it is still used for hunting, it is known as the Tazi, and a shorter-haired version exists; it is also called the Baluchi Hound.

In the west, the longhaired version is an established companion breed, prized for its aristocratic appearance and luxurious coat. These dogs lose their poised reserve when exercising and show their ancestors' speed and independence; sound obedience training is recommended if you want them to return to you. They are long lived for large dogs, reaching 12 to 14 years.

ANY COLOR YOU LIKE Although the golden coat is popular and seen as the 'classic' Afghan look, any solid shade or combination is possible and allowed.

REGAL LOOKS The Afghan head is long and elegant, although it must not be too narrow. The ears are carried very low, giving a smooth outline to the head.

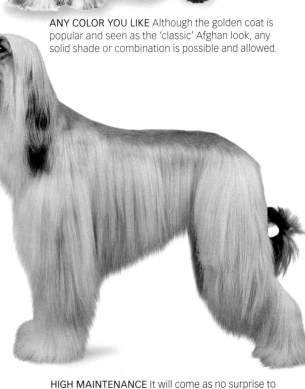

HIGH MAINTENANCE It will come as no surprise to learn that keeping this coat at its best demands a great commitment. Show dogs may be bathed weekly rather than brushed, for maximum shine.

American Foxhound

ORIGIN United States
HEIGHT 21–25 in (53–64 cm)
WEIGHT 65–75 lb (29.4–34.0 kg)
EXERCISE LEVEL
COAT CARE
REGISTERED FCI, AKCs
COLORS Any color

Leaner and lighter than its European counterpart, the American Foxhound will act as an individual hunter or as a pack member, making it adaptable to a wider range of hunting styles.

 GOLD AND WHITE
 BLACK AND WHITE
 TAN AND WHITE
 BLACK AND TAN
 BLACK, WHITE AND TAN

BREED ORIGINS

These dogs are descended from English hunting dogs brought to the United States in the 1860s. Irish and French hounds were added to the mix, taking the breed in a slightly different direction. Today, show lines also find a place as good-natured companions. They are loyal to their family and good with children, but like all hunting dogs are not trustworthy around other non-canine pets. They are a fairly healthy breed, usually living over a decade.

WORKING DOGS When seeking a family companion, choose show bloodlines. Dogs bred for working do not make good pets.

Anglo-Français de Petite Vénerie

ORIGIN France
HEIGHT 18–22 in (46–56 cm)
WEIGHT 35–44 lb (15.8–20.0 kg)
EXERCISE LEVEL
COAT CARE
REGISTERED FCI
COLORS Orange and white, black and white, or tricolor

This smaller version of the Anglo-Français scenthounds is not widely known beyond its French homeland. It has a relatively tractable nature for a hound, and classic good looks.

BLACK AND WHITE
GOLD AND WHITE
BLACK, WHITE, AND TAN

BREED ORIGINS

Once called the Petit Anglo-Français, this breed is a new kid on the block, bred in the 20th century as a smaller counterpart to the Grand Anglo-Français and first given a breed standard as late as the 1970s. It was created by crossing French hunting dogs such as the Poitevin with smaller breeds including Beagles (see p. 178). A lively hound with a cheerful character and a melodious voice, this is nonetheless a calm, and even reserved, household companion.

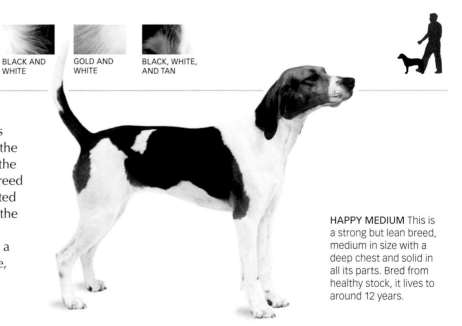

HAPPY MEDIUM This is a strong but lean breed, medium in size with a deep chest and solid in all its parts. Bred from healthy stock, it lives to around 12 years.

Ariégeois

ORIGIN France
HEIGHT 21–24 in (53–61 cm)
WEIGHT 55–66 lb (25–30 kg)
EXERCISE LEVEL
COAT CARE
REGISTERED FCI
COLORS Black and white, some tan on face

Named after the region of southwestern France where it originated, this is a friendly scenthound that is equally at home in a household setting or the thick of a hunting pack.

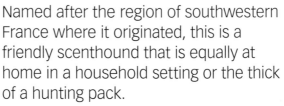

BREED ORIGINS

The Ariégeois was developed in the early 20th century from crossing the Chien d'Artois (*see* p. 185) with other French hunting dogs to create a slightly lighter, smaller type, with the same excellent scenting abilities.

This is a good-tempered breed, which adapts well to family life. It is good with children, and with other dogs, but not so trustworthy around small noncanine pets. It is not

stubborn, but is easily distracted by scents when out exercising, and may be difficult to recall without good training.

A WALKER'S DOG This highly sociable breed is happiest in the company of people or other dogs and engaged in some athletic activity.

Azawakh

ORIGIN Mali
HEIGHT 23–30 in (58–75 cm)
WEIGHT 37–55 lb (17–25 kg)
EXERCISE LEVEL
COAT CARE
REGISTERED KC, FCI
COLORS Brown and white

Also known as the Tuareg Sloughi, this African sighthound is a long-legged, elegant breed. It is alert and independent, a superb guardian dog, and a hunter capable of incredible turns of speed.

GOLD AND WHITE

TAN AND WHITE

BREED ORIGINS

This dog is a breed from antiquity, created in the southern Sahara by the Tuareg, and resembling the similarly ancient Sloughi (*see* p. 220). In its homeland the breed is still used as a hunter, in pursuit of small game and gazelles. It also serves as a guard, and these dogs will sleep on the low roofs of buildings, from which they can rapidly descend and form packs to see off intruders.

This is a highly active breed, which can reach speeds of up to 37 mph (60 kph), and is unsuited to a sedentary indoor life or the company of young children. It needs plenty of outdoor exercise, and a life with a reliable routine.

FAIR WEATHER FRIEND This is a typical warm-climate breed, lightly built and with a very short, fine coat that provides more protection than insulation.

Balkan Hound

ORIGIN Former Yugoslavia
HEIGHT 17–21 in (43–53 cm)
WEIGHT 43–45 lb (19.5–20.5 kg)
EXERCISE LEVEL
COAT CARE
REGISTERED FCI
COLORS Black and tan

This breed has some identity problems. As well as Balkan Hound or Balkanski Gonic, it also goes by the name of Serbian Hound, or Srpski Gonic, but it has long been known over a wider area.

BREED ORIGINS

There are several hound breeds in the countries that once made up Yugoslavia: This may be the oldest of them, and for a long time it was the most popular. Typically, these hounds worked in packs hunting both large game, such as wild boar, and smaller prey. Overlooked by registries and without a written standard, it was maintained faithfully as a breed for over two centuries by the hunters who found it useful, and is still used in hunting today.

The result of their work is a tough, muscular breed, with robust good health. The Balkan Hound adapts to family life, making a dignified companion, but it needs plenty of open space and exercise: this is not a city dog.

VOCAL BREED One of this breed's distinctive characteristics is a high-pitched voice that carries well when hunting.

WORKING CLOTHES Everything about the Balkan Hound, from the dense protective coat to the wide, deep chest, indicates a robust dog with considerable endurance.

Basenji

ORIGIN Zaire

HEIGHT 16–17 in (41–43 cm)

WEIGHT 21–24 lb (9.5–11.0 kg)

EXERCISE LEVEL

COAT CARE

REGISTERED KC, FCI, AKCs

COLORS Black and white, tan and white, black, or brindle

This dog resembles those depicted in tomb paintings from ancient Egypt, and has primitive characteristics, such as a tendency to howl rather than bark, that seem to show it is an ancient breed.

BLACK

BLACK AND WHITE

TAN AND WHITE

BREED ORIGINS

The story of the Basenji breed today begins in the 1930s with dogs brought from Africa to Europe and originally called Congo Dogs. They are not easily trained, but are reliable with children. Although long lived, they are prone to an inheritable disorder of the kidneys.

PRIMITIVE LOOKS These small dogs are muscular and powerful. The tail is typically carried in a curl over the rump.

NO WORRIES A wrinkled face gives this affectionate, intelligent, and energetic breed a misleadingly anxious look.

Basset Artésien-Normand

ORIGIN France

HEIGHT 10–14 in (25–36 cm)

WEIGHT 32–34 lb (14.5–15.5 kg)

EXERCISE LEVEL

COAT CARE

REGISTERED FCI

COLORS Tan and white or tricolor

The forerunner of the more widely known Basset Hound (*see* p. 174), this breed has the same low-slung dwarf build, long ears, drooping lips, and typical coloration, but is a less exaggerated type.

TAN AND WHITE

BLACK, WHITE, AND TAN

BREED ORIGINS

This solemn-looking hound can be traced back to the 1600s. It has the full-length body of larger hounds, but short legs. Originally bred for hunting, by the start of the 20th century the breed had developed into two distinct types, one for working, the other for showing. Work by French breeder Léon Verrier brought the two together again, although two World Wars almost extinguished the breed. Today, this adaptable breed is equally at home as a family or even a city dog.

BASSET BUILD As a hunting dog, this breed has short but straight legs, so is easy to keep up with on foot, while it can still move through undergrowth and over rough terrain without problems.

Basset Bleu de Gascogne

ORIGIN France
HEIGHT 12–14 in (30–36 cm)
WEIGHT 35–40 lb (15.9–18.1 kg)
EXERCISE LEVEL
COAT CARE
REGISTERED FCI
COLORS Blue and white mottle with variable black patches and tan traces

This affectionate breed is more cheerful and energetic than its Basset appearance hints. A fine scenthound, bred for working in packs, its breed standard says it has a "beautiful howling voice."

BREED ORIGINS

The original Basset Bleu de Gascogne, dating back to the Middle Ages, was lost, but was recreated toward the end of the 19th century at the instigation of hunstmen, spearheaded by the breeding work of Alain Bourbon. It is fairly easily trained, and makes a good family or city dog: it can even be trained in guarding, but is sensitive to the cold so appreciates home comforts.

DECEPTIVE LOOKS This is a lively breed, needing plenty of exercise, but easy to keep up with. It is healthy and long lived, but may be susceptible to gastric torsion.

Basset Fauve de Bretagne

ORIGIN France
HEIGHT 13–15 in (33–38 cm)
WEIGHT 36–40 lb (16.3–18.1 kg)
EXERCISE LEVEL
COAT CARE
REGISTERED KC, FCI
COLORS Fawn or red

Also known as the Tawny Brittany Basset, this wiry coated breed is one of the more free-spirited and lively Basset breeds. It thrives on plenty of activity and can be stubbornly determined.

RED/TAN   GOLD

BREED ORIGINS

This breed was created in the 19th century by crossing the longer-legged Griffon Fauve de Bretagne with various short-legged breeds from the Vendée region. It is not widely known outside its native country, but has become an established breed in the United Kingdom. Bred for hunting in packs, it gets along easily with other dogs, and with children, but it is not easy to train.

EASY TO ACCOMMODATE The hard, coarse coat needs little maintenance, and this breed will settle into city life well as long as there are parks nearby for plenty of active exercise.

Basset Hound

ORIGIN United Kingdom

HEIGHT 13–14 in (33–36 cm)

WEIGHT 40–60 lb (18.1–27.2 kg)

EXERCISE LEVEL

COAT CARE

REGISTERED KC, FCI, AKCs

COLORS Any hound color

The best known of all the bassets, this breed has lost any geographical qualification of its name. The exact location of its origin is hazy, but it is regarded as a classically British breed.

GOLD AND WHITE

TAN AND WHITE

BLACK, WHITE, AND TAN

BREED ORIGINS

The Basset is descended from dwarfed bloodhounds, and dates back to at least the 1500s. The first breed description may be Theseus's account of his hounds in Shakespeare's *A Midsummer Night's Dream*: "With ears that sweep away the morning dew/Crook-kneed, and dewlapped like Thessalian bulls/Slow in pursuit, but matched in mouth like bells."

Today the Basset is more often a household dog than a hunting companion. This is an affectionate, amenable breed, good with children. It can be easily distracted, so needs consistent, patient training.

BULKY BUILD The short, crooked legs make the Basset slow, but it should never be clumsy. Lighter types are still used in hunting work, more in the United States than in Europe.

HANGDOG EXPRESSION The Basset is famed for its lugubrious looks. The exaggerated droop of the eyes, ears, and mouth shows a resemblance to bloodhounds in its ancestry.

CLASSIC COAT Although there are no restrictive rules about the Basset coat, with any hound color allowed, by far the most common is the tricolor, followed by tan- or lemon-and-white combinations.

Bavarian Mountain Hound

ORIGIN Germany
HEIGHT 18–20 in (46–51 cm)
WEIGHT 55–77 lb (24.9–34.9 kg)
EXERCISE LEVEL
COAT CARE
REGISTERED FCI
COLORS Brown, red, tan, fawn to biscuit, reddish gray, or brindled

This breed is known in its homeland and recognized under the name of Bayerischer Gebirgsschweisshund. It is an unsurpassed scenthound used by hunters in Germany and central Europe.

RED/TAN

BLACK BRINDLE

BREED ORIGINS

Like all Schweisshunde or "leashhounds," this breed is originally descended from the German scenthounds known as Bracken, and was developed for the purpose of following wounded game. Earlier leashhounds were heavier types, such as the Hanoverian, which proved too cumbersome for work in mountain regions. From the 1870s work by Baron Karg-Bebenburg to produce a lighter, faster type resulted in the Bavarian Mountain Hound. As

firearms improved, the call for this type of dog insured its growing popularity, and it had its own breed club by 1912.

Today this remains almost exclusively a working dog. It is a very mobile and muscular breed, thriving on activity and unsuited to a sedentary or city lifestyle. It is generally calm, devoted to its owner, and responds well to training, but does not make a good guard dog. Bavarian Mountain Hounds are reliable around children, and get on well with other dogs because they have traditionally been worked in small packs, but tend to be reserved with strangers.

LOOSE LIPS Like many scenthounds, the Bavarian has pendulous lips, although not very pronounced. The theory is that these help to trap and intensify scents.

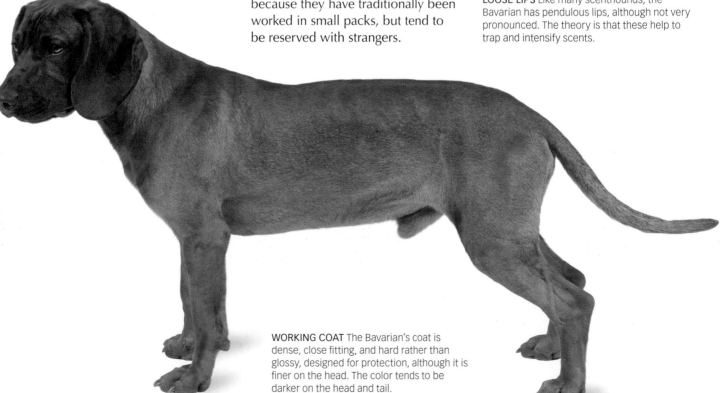

WORKING COAT The Bavarian's coat is dense, close fitting, and hard rather than glossy, designed for protection, although it is finer on the head. The color tends to be darker on the head and tail.

BASSET HOUND (*see* p. 174) This breed's distinctive looks have sold Hush Puppy shoes for five decades. The expressiveness was also the appeal of the British cartoon dog Fred Basset, syndicated around the world under local names.

Beagle

ORIGIN United Kingdom

HEIGHT 13–15 in (33–39 cm)

WEIGHT 18–30 lb (8.2–13.6 kg)

EXERCISE LEVEL

COAT CARE

REGISTERED KC, FCI, AKCs

COLORS Any hound color

The Beagle is most often described in breed standards as a "merry" hound. It has a bell-like baying voice and a lively, curious personality, and can make an excellent family dog.

GOLD AND WHITE

BLACK, WHITE, AND TAN

BREED ORIGINS

The Beagle probably derives from the larger Harrier breed, and has been used for hunting in Britain since the Middle Ages. These small dogs could even be carried by mounted hunters in saddlebags, and were bred to pursue rabbits and birds, either in packs or solo. Today, the breed varies in size from place to place, but has a distinct personality.

ENDEARING LOOKS
The affectionate nature of the Beagle is advertised in its typically appealing expression, but with the exception of Snoopy they are not to be trusted around small animals such as birds.

BEAGLE BODY The Beagle resembles a small Foxhound. It has a sturdy build, with a tail carried high or "gaily," and a short, sleek coat that is easy to care for.

BREED QUALITIES

Beagles are highly sociable, and crave company, either human or canine. If they are to be left alone at all, keep at least two. They may pine alone, and a howling Beagle will make no friends among neighbors.

In the right home, Beagles can be a delight: cheerful, affectionate dogs that are not aggressive and are good with children and friendly with other dogs. They are not the easiest to train, however, and tend to follow their own noses when out and about.

Beagle Harrier

ORIGIN France
HEIGHT 17–19 in (43–48 cm)
WEIGHT 40–44 lb (18.1–20.0 kg)
EXERCISE LEVEL
COAT CARE
REGISTERED FCI
COLORS Tricolor

This French breed is, perhaps oddly, descended from two ancient and very British breeds. It combines many of the best qualities of its forebears, but it remains rare.

BREED ORIGINS

The Beagle Harrier is, as its name suggests, a cross of the Beagle and the larger Harrier. It was created in the 19th century by Baron Gérard, a French sportsman, in an attempt to produce a hound ideal for hunting hares. It is still kept and worked in small packs, but did not fare well in the changing circumstances of the 20th century, and is scarcely seen outside its homeland.

GOOD QUALITIES The Beagle Harrier has the peaceable nature and sociable traits of the Beagle but scaled up into a larger dog. It is also slightly more trainable, and has the same short, dense, easy-care coat.

Berner Laufhund

ORIGIN Switzerland
HEIGHT 18–23 in (46–58 cm)
WEIGHT 34–44 lb (15.4–20.0 kg)
EXERCISE LEVEL
COAT CARE
REGISTERED FCI
COLORS White with black patches or saddle and tan markings on the face

This is the best known of the four surviving types of Swiss Hound, also called Schweizer Laufhund or Chien Courant Suisse. The other varieties, the Jura, Lucerne, and Schwyz, differ mainly in color.

BREED ORIGINS

These attractive scenthounds have accompanied hunters in the mountains of Switzerland since the Middle Ages, tracking roe deer and other smaller prey. Until the end of the 19th century there were five recognized types: two have been lost as hunting declined. A fine working dog, with good health, it makes a good-natured and nonaggressive companion, but can be stubborn and hard to train.

OLD-FASHIONED LOOKS The lean build and a dense, insulating coat of this breed have ancient origins.

Black-and-Tan Coonhound

ORIGIN United States
HEIGHT 23–27 in (58–69 cm)
WEIGHT 55–75 lb (24.9–34.0 kg)
EXERCISE LEVEL
COAT CARE
REGISTERED FCI, AKCs
COLORS Black and tan

Coonhounds are a specialized group of hunting dogs, bred to track and "tree" the raccoon or oppossum and then await the hunter's arrival. They hunt by scent, and have a distinctive baying call.

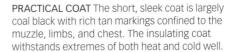

POWER HOUND This large hound has a strong, well-proportioned build, with a deep chest and a strong tail. Long legs and a rhythmic stride give it speed.

BREED ORIGINS

The Black-and-Tan Coonhound was developed in the 18th century in the United States, although it was not officially recognized until 1945. It was created by crossing Bloodhounds and Foxhounds, and the Kerry Beagle may also have contributed to its development. The Coonhound howls as it works, and the following hunter can tell from the sound when the quarry has been treed.

Although intended for hunting raccoons, the breed is a versatile and capable hunter and has also been used very successfully to hunt larger game such as deer and even mountain lion and bears. This is the best known of all the coonhound breeds, and popular for its trainable temperament. It can make a good watchdog, and is an asset to homes that can provide plenty of exercise and interest.

COONHOUND HEAD The head is finely modeled, with no folds in the skin. The ears are set low and well back, hanging in graceful folds; they should reach past the end of the nose.

PRACTICAL COAT The short, sleek coat is largely coal black with rich tan markings confined to the muzzle, limbs, and chest. The insulating coat withstands extremes of both heat and cold well.

Bloodhound

ORIGIN Belgium

HEIGHT 23–27 in (58–69 cm)

WEIGHT 66–110 lb (30.0–50.0 kg)

EXERCISE LEVEL

COAT CARE

REGISTERED KC, FCI, AKCs

COLORS Black and tan, liver/red and tan, red

Developed in Belgium as the Chien de St. Hubert and in England as the Bloodhound, this massive scenthound is synonymous with tracking, and has been used to trace criminals and runaway slaves.

RED/TAN

BLACK AND TAN

BREED ORIGINS

This droopy breed is said to be directly descended from the packs of hounds belonging to St. Hubert, patron saint of hunters, in the 7th century. These dogs were maintained for centuries by Benedictine monks at the Abbaye de Saint-Hubert in the Ardennes, and by tradition six dogs were sent every year to the king of France for the royal packs. Taken to Britain by the Normans, the same lines became known as the Bloodhound, referring not to an ability to scent blood, but to a dog of "pure" blood, belonging to the nobility.

BREED QUALITIES

A gentle, affectionate breed, the Bloodhound needs to be watched around children only because it may bowl them over. It is too easily distracted by interesting scents to be highly trainable, and knows how to use those mournful eyes. Sadly, it can be short lived and is one of the breeds most prone to bloat; joint problems and cancers are also issues, as in most large breeds.

CLASSIC LOOKS Although Bloodhounds now come in a limited range of shades, there was once a wider selection. It included a white strain, known as the Talbot Hound, which had died out by the 17th century.

Borzoi

ORIGIN Russia
HEIGHT 27–31 in (69–79 cm)
WEIGHT 75–105 lb (34.0–47.6 kg)
EXERCISE LEVEL
COAT CARE
REGISTERED KC, FCI, AKCs
COLORS White, golden, tan, or gray with black markings, either solid or mixed

This elegant and reserved dog comes from a heritage of hunting wolves in Russia, and has also been called the Russian Wolfhound. In the last century, it has moved successfully from hunt to home.

CREAM

GOLD

GOLD AND WHITE

BLACK AND WHITE

TAN AND WHITE

BREED ORIGINS

Sighthounds had arrived in Russia from their original home in southwestern Asia by the Middle Ages. Here, they developed into the Borzoi, a Russian term for all sighthounds, including some rarities virtually unknown in the West, such as the Taigan and Chortaj. The Borzoi had spread westward into Europe by the 19th century, where it became favored as a high-status pet and an aristocratic household dog, and was bred for companionship rather than hunting.

Today it is widely known as a household pet, but it has retained all its ancestors' athleticism and free spirit. It remains a hunter at heart, and cannot be trusted to resist the urge to hunt any small animal, so will not live peacefully with noncanine pets. Although this breed needs plenty of exercise, it quickly wearies of very young children's rough and tumble play, and prefers an ordered life.

NOBLE NOSE The head is distinctively long and narrow, with a slightly arched muzzle and ears that lie back on the neck when relaxed.

COAT CARE The silky coat presents a challenge when shed for the summer, but is otherwise not that hard to care for. Brush regularly and clip hair between the toes.

FAST MOVER Like all sighthounds, the Borzoi is capable of amazing feats of speed, and is easily distracted while out and about. Constant vigilance is needed when exercising these dogs.

Bracco Italiano

ORIGIN Italy
HEIGHT 22–27 in (56–69 cm)
WEIGHT 55–88 lb (24.9–39.9 kg)
EXERCISE LEVEL
COAT CARE
REGISTERED FCI
COLORS Chestnut roan, orange and white

The Bracco Italiano, also called the Italian Pointer, is a hunting breed of an ancient type. Long esteemed in their Italian homeland, these dogs have recently become more popular across Europe.

 CREAM

 GOLD AND WHITE

TAN AND WHITE

BREED ORIGINS

Some say that the Bracco is distinguishable in 14th-century frescoes, others that it is descended from the Segugio breed and dates from much later. It was originally bred to drive birds into the nets of hunters. As hunting methods changed, it become a pointing gundog. It makes an even-tempered and loyal companion, good with other dogs and children, but it can be stubborn. Plenty of exercise and mental stimulation are advisable.

ITALIAN STYLE This is a powerful, muscular dog with strong, lean limbs. Together with the low-set ears and pendulous lips, its head is distinguished by "chiselling' of the bones under the eyes.

Briquet Griffon Vendéen

ORIGIN France
HEIGHT 19–22 in (48–56 cm)
WEIGHT 50–53 lb (23.0–24.0 kg)
EXERCISE LEVEL
COAT CARE
REGISTERED FCI
COLORS White and black, white and orange, black and tan, tricolor, fawn with black

The curious name of this breed identifies it as a smallish (briquet) dog, of a type originally bred by a royal clerk, called *greffier* in Old French, and coming from the Vendée region of France.

 CREAM

BLACK, WHITE, AND TAN

BREED ORIGINS

This dog was developed in the late 19th century by the Comte d'Elva. It was almost wiped out by World War II, but today, in its homeland, packs are used to hunt wild boar and deer and do well in trials. It is a hardy breed, tolerant of cold, with a fairly waterproof coat that may show white spotting. It can be stubborn, and some can be snappy, but it makes a loyal if slightly drooling companion.

HAPPY MEDIUM This hardy breed is halfway between the Grand and the Basset Griffon Vendéen.

Chart Polski

ORIGIN Poland
HEIGHT 27–32 in (68–80 cm)
WEIGHT 88 lb (39.9 kg)
EXERCISE LEVEL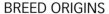
COAT CARE
REGISTERED FCI
COLORS Any color

Across Europe, different types of greyhound developed in different countries. The Chart Polski is also called the Polish Greyhound, and has been preserved by a keen band of breeders.

BLACK CREAM RED/TAN BLACK AND TAN BLUE MOTTLED WITH TAN

BREED ORIGINS

Descended from early sighthounds like the the Asiatic Greyhound, the Chart Polski appears to have existed as a hunting dog since at least the 15th century and possibly earlier; ancient manuscripts show dogs of this type. Not unnaturally, given the troubled politics of the 20th century, there is some animosity over Russian assertions that it is instead descended from the Borzoi, a Russian breed.

In the 20th century, two World Wars dramatically reduced its numbers. After World War II, breeders in Poland worked to revive the breed, but with the Iron Curtain in place it remained unknown in western Europe or beyond until recently.

NO LIGHTWEIGHT Although lean and elegant, the Chart Polski is stronger and less delicate than other shorthaired sighthounds. It withstands heat and cold well.

HUNTER'S HEAD The powerful but refined head is carried high on a long, strong neck. The soulful expression of the expressive eyes, with a lively and appealing gaze, belies the fact that this is a ruthless hunter.

BREED QUALITIES

Even today this slow-to-mature breed remains rare. Like many sighthounds, it is a quiet character, loyal to its family and good with children, but often reserved with strangers. It is quick on its feet and seemingly tireless in pursuit of prey, which will include any small noncanine animals.

Chien d'Artois

ORIGIN France
HEIGHT 20–22 in (51–56 cm)
WEIGHT 40–53 lb (18.1–24.0 kg)
EXERCISE LEVEL
COAT CARE
REGISTERED FCI
COLORS Tricolor

Once called Picard and also Briquet, or 'small dog', this breed works across country or in woodland, aided by its compact build. It is used in small packs to hunt game from hares up to deer or boar.

BREED ORIGINS

Dogs of this type were renowned for their scenting ability from the Middle Ages, and prized as Artois hounds by the 17th century. In the 19th century they were almost lost, but concerted efforts at the turn of the 20th century and again after World War II reestablished the breed. Sociable and musical-voiced, these dogs need to have firm and consistent training.

FRENCH FASHION The distinctive type was almost lost through a trend for cross-breeding to English dogs in the 19th century.

Cirneco dell'Etna

ORIGIN Italy
HEIGHT 20–22 in (51–56 cm)
WEIGHT 18–26 lb (8.1–12.0 kg)
EXERCISE LEVEL
COAT CARE
REGISTERED FCI
COLORS Fawn or fawn with white; also white, white with orange, or brindled fawn

Also called the Sicilian Hound, this breed is similar to the running dogs of ancient Egypt. It remains rare beyond Sicilian shores.

CREAM   GOLD   GOLD AND WHITE

ELEGANT LOOKS The Cirneco dell'Etna has a slender and light build, but is robust and strong.

BREED ORIGINS

This breed's ancestors came to Sicily with Phoenician traders some 3,000 years ago; its name commemorates the island's notable landmark, Mount Etna. It is similar to the Pharaoh and Ibizan Hounds, but smaller, and hunts by sight and scent, specializing in rabbit and hare. This is a lively breed, and is not suited to an indoor life or to the unpredictable ways of children.

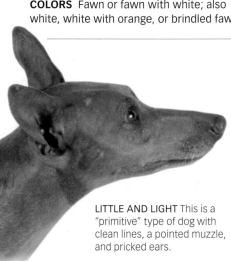

LITTLE AND LIGHT This is a "primitive" type of dog with clean lines, a pointed muzzle, and pricked ears.

Dachshunds

ORIGIN Germany
HEIGHT 7–9 in (18–23 cm)
WEIGHT 15–25 lb (6.8–11.3 kg)
EXERCISE LEVEL
COAT CARE
REGISTERED KC, FCI, AKCs
COLORS One color, bicolor, or dappled or striped; no white

This breed group has a complex set of categories according to both size and coat type that differ from country to country. Dogs bred for working differ from those that are bred for showing.

CREAM　　BLUE　　RED/TAN　　GOLD　　BLACK AND TAN

BREED ORIGINS

Dwarfed or short-legged dogs have been known for thousands of years, and the Dachshund, also called the Dackel or Teckel in Europe, has been known as a type since the Middle Ages. Bred from the hunting dogs known as Bracken, they were selected because their short stature made them suitable for working underground, hence their name, which means 'badger dog'.

Today, these dogs are kept both as hunting companions and household pets. Those bred for working have shorter spines and longer legs than those bred for showing; the latter are more prone to spine problems, always a risk with this build.

FULL OF POTENTIAL The different sizes of Dachshunds are not distinct breeds, so what a puppy may be is always open to chance, although lines tend to produce certain sizes consistently.

WIREHAIRED DACHSHUND This type of Dachshund is reputed to be the best balanced of the three coats, less feisty than the smooth-coated original but bolder than the longhairs.

BREED DIFFERENCES

As well as the various sizes of Dachshunds (*see* box), there are three different coats: the Smooth-haired, the Wirehaired, and the Longhaired. The Smooth-haired is the oldest, the original hunting dog. The Wirehaired was created by crossing with rough-haired Pinschers, and using the Dandie Dinmont Terrier to improve the head type. The Longhaired is thought to come from crosses with short-legged spaniels, with further work to miniaturize the resulting dogs. The differences are more than cosmetic: all of these crosses also affected the temperament.

BREED QUALITIES

Although it is a small dog that can adapt to urban life, needing little space for exercise, some caution is needed when choosing this popular breed. They are variable in temper, and some seem to have the will of a much larger dog in concentrated form. Be prepared to give firm and

SMOOTH-HAIRED DACHSHUND The original coat, this shorthaired type is the most excitable. They can be fearful and snappish.

consistent training when they are young or face a lifetime of challenge—and these robust small dogs often live on into their mid- to late teens.

LONGHAIRED DACHSHUND Spaniel heritage has given this breed not only a silky coat but a tendency to be much less tenacious than their Smooth-haired cousins, and even rather shy.

Sizes of Dachshund

British and American clubs tend to recognize two sizes of Dachshund, the Standard and the Miniature, with the dividing line between the two set at 11 lb (5 kg). Continental European clubs classify by chest circumference—a vital statistic for an earth dog. Dachshunds have a chest of 14 in (35 cm), Miniatures 12–14 in (30–35 cm), and Rabbit Dachshunds or Kaninchen Teckel below 12 in (30 cm).

Deerhound

ORIGIN United Kingdom
HEIGHT 28–30 in (71–76 cm)
WEIGHT 80–100 lb (36.3–45.4 kg)
EXERCISE LEVEL
COAT CARE
REGISTERED KC, FCI, AKCs
COLORS Gray, brindle, yellow, sandy-red, or red fawn with black points; some white allowed

Historically Scottish, this is also called the Scottish Deerhound. Its original purpose was hunting deer, but it is now most often a gentle, friendly, and undeniably impressive companion.

GRAY · RED/TAN · GOLD · BLACK BRINDLE

BREED ORIGINS

Rough-coated hounds have been recorded for over 500 years, probably descended from ancient imported short-coated sighthounds crossed with longer-coated dogs suited to the Scottish Highlands' climate. Packs hunted deer, but with the demise of the clan system and the shift to hunting with guns, the breed declined by the 18th century. It was revived in the 19th century, but remains rare.

This is an intelligent and trainable hound, sociable with both children and other dogs. It does not need a large home, since adults are layabouts indoors, but a good-sized outdoor space and thorough daily exercise are vital.

DEERHOUND LOOKS Everything from the head to the tail has a long, strong, tapering line. The coat is shaggy, never wooly, and much softer on the head, chest, and stomach than elsewhere.

Drever

ORIGIN Sweden
HEIGHT 12–16 in (30–41 cm)
WEIGHT 30–33 lb (13.6–15.0 kg)
EXERCISE LEVEL
COAT CARE
REGISTERED FCI
COLORS Fawn and white, black and white, tricolor

Also called the Swedish Dachsbracke, this accomplished scenthound is among the most popular hunting dogs in its homeland. It is used to track and drive quarry toward the hunters.

GOLD AND WHITE · BLACK AND WHITE · BLACK, WHITE, AND TAN

SLOW BUT STEADY Short legs mean this is not the fastest of hounds, but it has incredible stamina and a tenacious desire to hunt.

BREED ORIGINS

This is a recreation of a historic type, bred from the Westphalian Dachsbracke crossed with local hounds. Its compact size makes it suited to slowly driving flighty deer toward guns, and this hardy, robust breed is a tenacious hunter. When hunting is not available, these dogs make laid-back, amenable companions, although they are self-contained and not the ideal family dog.

TIDY FACE The Drever head is large, but well proportioned. Unlike some other hounds, it has close-fitting eyelids and lips, rather than droopy folds.

Dunker

ORIGIN Norway
HEIGHT 19–22 in (48–56 cm)
WEIGHT 35–49 lb (15.9–22.0 kg)
EXERCISE LEVEL
COAT CARE
REGISTERED FCI
COLORS Black or blue marbled with fawn, with white markings

Not widely found elsewhere, this hound is among the most popular hunting breeds in its native Norway, where it is used to track and retrieve hares by scent. It is friendly and relaxed, but free spirited.

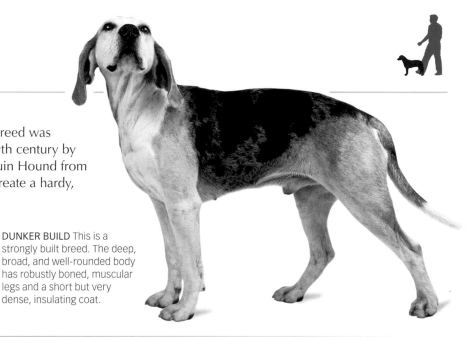

BREED ORIGINS

Also called the Norwegian Hound, this breed was specifically created in the early to mid-19th century by Wilhelm Dunker. He crossed the Harlequin Hound from Russia with Norwegian scenthounds to create a hardy, reliable dog with enormous stamina; the only health problem is a tendency to hip displasia. Dunkers have an easygoing temperament, adapting well to urban and family life as long as they have plenty of exercise to mop up their boundless energy.

DUNKER BUILD This is a strongly built breed. The deep, broad, and well-rounded body has robustly boned, muscular legs and a short but very dense, insulating coat.

English Coonhound

ORIGIN United States
HEIGHT 21–27 in (53–69 cm)
WEIGHT 40–65 lb (18.1–29.5 kg)
EXERCISE LEVEL
COAT CARE
REGISTERED AKCs
COLORS Any hound color; most often red tick

Despite its misleading name, this robust scenthound is an entirely American breed. It was first bred for hunting raccoons and similar quarry, a role that it still fulfills today, mostly in the southern states.

BLUE   RED/TAN   BLACK AND WHITE   TAN AND WHITE   BLACK, WHITE AND TAN

BUILD AND COAT This is a relatively small coonhound, but powerful and strong boned. It slopes from the shoulders to the rump, but the long ears and drooping lips are typical of the type.

BREED ORIGINS

This breed is also sometimes called the Redtick Coonhound, a name perhaps more suitable, since its ancestors included not only English but French dogs, bred in the early 19th century.

This is first and foremost a hunting dog, robust and active with high energy levels. It does make a good-tempered household and family companion, as long as there are no small, noncanine pets to consider.

Finnish Hound

ORIGIN Finland

HEIGHT 22–25 in (56–63 cm)

WEIGHT 44–55 lb (20.0–25.0 kg)

EXERCISE LEVEL

COAT CARE

REGISTERED FCI, AKCs

COLORS Tricolor

The Suomenjokoira or Finsk Stovåre is a versatile tracker used for tracking hare and fox by scent. A medium-sized breed with a resonant voice, it is the most popular of Finland's working dogs.

BREED ORIGINS

Some accounts say this Harrier-like breed dates from the 18th century and was created by a goldsmith named Tammelin using Swedish, German, and French hounds. The official standard, however, dates its origins not further back than the 1890s, after the creation of the Finnish Kennel Club, and merely mentions Finnish dogs that resembled European breeds. However it began, it is an enthusiastic hunter that brings prey to bay for the hunter; it will also find shot birds, but does not retrieve.

BREED QUALITIES

Eager to hunt in any conditions, this lively breed needs plenty of outdoor activity. It is a friendly dog that thrives on human company, so is a good companion for children, but a poor guard. It gets on with other dogs, but males may be more temperamental.

KEEN NOSE This indefatigable hound will relish hunting in all conditions. It works independently, tracking the quarry and bringing it to bay with persistent, short barks to guide the hunter.

SUMMER COAT This breed is strongly built but not heavy. The coat is not particularly dense, and while these dogs will sleep outside in summer, they need more protection in the winter.

Français

ORIGIN France
HEIGHT 24–28 in (60–72 cm)
WEIGHT 75–77 lb (34.0–35.0 kg)
EXERCISE LEVEL
COAT CARE
REGISTERED FCI, AKCs
COLORS White and black or orange, tricolor

Technically there are three different breeds: Blanc et Noir, Blanc et Orange, and Tricolore. All are scenthounds used for small game, lighter in build than the Grand Anglo-Français breeds.

GOLD AND WHITE

BLACK AND WHITE

TAN AND WHITE

BREED ORIGINS

The Français Blanc et Noir owes its existence to Michel Beauchamp, who crossed the Harrier with dogs from Poitou, Normandy, and Saintonge. It won many prizes at trials between the World Wars, and was recognized in 1957. In that year breeder Henri de Falandre first showed tricolored dogs, resembling extinct old French hunting dogs, created from the Anglo-Français, Poitevin, Billy and Bleu de Gascogne. The Blanc et Orange, created using the Billy, came last. All three scenthounds are calm, gentle breeds, good with other dogs and children, but are rarely seen and even more rarely kept as household dogs rather than hunting companions.

POPULAR COLORS The Tricolore is the most commonly seen of the three types. The Blanc et Orange has always been dogged by very low numbers, and may now be completely extinct.

German Hound

ORIGIN Germany
HEIGHT 16–21 in (41–53 cm)
WEIGHT 44 lb (20.0 kg)
EXERCISE LEVEL
COAT CARE
REGISTERED FCI
COLORS Tricolor

Known in its homeland as the Deutsche Bracke, this enthusiastic, robust scenthound is the last remaining example of a hunting dog once common across Germany, with a host of regional varieties.

BREED ORIGINS

This sole surviving variety of Bracke is descended from the Westfälische Bracke. It has the tricolored coat of the variety known as the Sauerländer Holzbracke, which was mixed with local Steinbracken to create a type known simply as the Deutsche Bracke since 1900. A loyal, friendly breed, it is peaceful and calm in the home but a passionate, tenacious hunter once it finds a scent outdoors.

BREED FEATURES The pink nose is a defining trait of the breed. The relatively long-legged Bracken are taller than the Dachsbracken, which in turn stand well above the Dachshund types.

Grand Anglo-Français

ORIGIN France
HEIGHT 24–27 in (61–69 cm)
WEIGHT 66–71 lb (29.9–32.2 kg)
EXERCISE LEVEL
COAT CARE ✏
REGISTERED FCI
COLORS White and black, white and orange, tricolor

The three colors of this large French scenthound are recognized in separate classes, but they are basically the same dog. The tricolor is the most popular, and the white and orange the rarest.

GOLD AND WHITE

BLACK AND WHITE

BLACK, WHITE, AND TAN

BREED ORIGINS
These hounds were bred from crosses of French hounds and English Foxhounds in the 19th century. French wolf-hunting Poitevins contributed the colors of the tricolore coat, while the Bleu de Gascogne or Gascogne Saintongeois may lie behind the blanc et noir. This ancestry has produced a dog with a strong but compact type that was traditionally used in packs for hunting large game.

These dogs have a relaxed, nonaggressive temperament, settling into city and family life, although they are dogs of enormous stamina and retain a hunter's need for exercise and stimulation. They are generally healthy and can be expected to live around ten years.

POPULAR CHOICE The handsome coat of the tricolor type has insured that it is the most often seen away from the hunting environment.

Grand Basset Griffon Vendéen

ORIGIN France
HEIGHT 15–16 in (38–41 cm)
WEIGHT 40–44 lb (18.1–20.0 kg)
EXERCISE LEVEL
COAT CARE ✏
REGISTERED FCI
COLORS White and black, black and tan, white and orange, tricolor, fawn shades

The Grand Basset, or large Basset, is smaller than its antecedents but taller than many basset breeds. It was created for the hunting of hares, and bred to a precise size to excel in this role.

GOLD AND WHITE

BLACK AND TAN

BLACK, WHITE, AND TAN

BREED ORIGINS
This breed was created at the end of the 19th century, through the work of the Comte d'Elva, also involved in the Briquet Griffon Vendéen, and Paul Dezamy. Like all French Bassets, it is derived from larger hounds, in this case the Grand Griffon. Adaptable and good tempered, it makes a pleasing urban companion or family dog, although it demands copious exercise and regular grooming of its wiry coat.

SMALL BUT POWERFUL This Basset breed was deliberately bred to be small enough for effective pursuit of hares, although it can also be used to track much larger game.

Grand Bleu de Gascogne

ORIGIN France

HEIGHT 25–28 in (64–71 cm)

WEIGHT 71–77 lb (32.2–34.9 kg)

EXERCISE LEVEL

COAT CARE

REGISTERED FCI

COLORS Mottled black and white, with tan markings on face, legs, and beneath tail

A successful French export, this breed is now more widespread in the United States than it is in France, where it is less common since the wolf that was its quarry was driven to extinction.

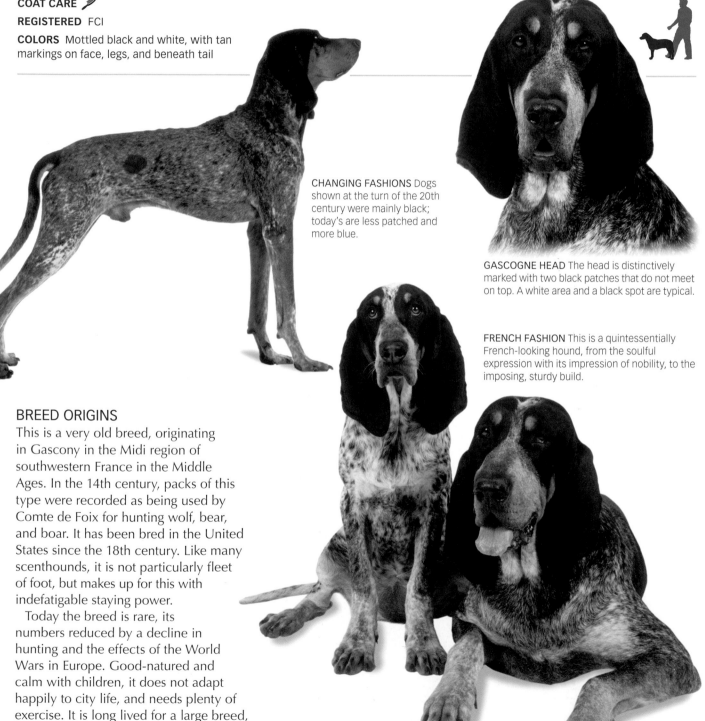

CHANGING FASHIONS Dogs shown at the turn of the 20th century were mainly black; today's are less patched and more blue.

GASCOGNE HEAD The head is distinctively marked with two black patches that do not meet on top. A white area and a black spot are typical.

FRENCH FASHION This is a quintessentially French-looking hound, from the soulful expression with its impression of nobility, to the imposing, sturdy build.

BREED ORIGINS

This is a very old breed, originating in Gascony in the Midi region of southwestern France in the Middle Ages. In the 14th century, packs of this type were recorded as being used by Comte de Foix for hunting wolf, bear, and boar. It has been bred in the United States since the 18th century. Like many scenthounds, it is not particularly fleet of foot, but makes up for this with indefatigable staying power.

Today the breed is rare, its numbers reduced by a decline in hunting and the effects of the World Wars in Europe. Good-natured and calm with children, it does not adapt happily to city life, and needs plenty of exercise. It is long lived for a large breed, often reaching its teens.

Grand Griffon Vendéen

ORIGIN France

HEIGHT 24–26 in (61–66 cm)

WEIGHT 66–77 lb (29.9–34.9 kg)

EXERCISE LEVEL

COAT CARE

REGISTERED FCI

COLORS White and black, black and tan, white and orange, tricolor, shades of fawn

The oldest and largest of the Griffon Vendéen group, this was originally bred for hunting wild boar and roe deer. Its fall in popularity may be due to the scarcity of this game today.

GOLD AND WHITE   BLACK AND WHITE   BLACK, WHITE AND TAN

BREED ORIGINS

The original hound of the Vendée region was the Grand Vendéen, an ancient shorthaired breed. The wirehaired Grand Griffon Vendéen, dating back to the Middle Ages, is descended from this, with input from other breeds such as the Griffon Fauve de Bretagne. The smaller Griffon breeds, their names qualified by the diminutives Briquet and Grand and Petit Basset, followed this larger breed.

Today this is the rarest of the group, perhaps due to its larger size. Although it is obedient, calm, and reliable around children and other dogs, it needs space to roam and plenty of stimulating exercise.

WETSUIT A wiry topcoat and downy undercoat is an excellent combination for hunting in wet environments, but this breed needs good grooming to prevent a "doggy" smell developing.

Greek Harehound

ORIGIN Greece

HEIGHT 19–22 in (48–56 cm)

WEIGHT 38–44 lb (17.2–20.0 kg)

EXERCISE LEVEL

COAT CARE

REGISTERED FCI

COLORS Black and tan, some white allowed on the chest

Also known as the Greek Hound, Hellenic Hound, or Hellenikos Ichnilatis, and breeding true due to its natural isolation, this was the first Greek breed to be internationally recognized, in 1996.

BREED ORIGINS

This is a very old breed, refined in antiquity from sight and scenthounds. Its ancestors were known as *laconikoi* or *lagonikoi*, meaning hare dogs, and spread with traders; similar hounds are found across the Balkans.

Today it makes a fine companion for hunting hare and boar, but can become destructive if bored, so is only a suitable companion for an involved, enthusiastic owner.

ANCIENT LOOKS A robust, healthy breed, moderate in all its parts, the Greek Harehound has a close fitting skin and a sleek, easy-care coat.

Greyhound

ORIGIN United Kingdom
HEIGHT 27–30 in (69–76 cm)
WEIGHT 60–70 lb (27.2–31.7 kg)
EXERCISE LEVEL
COAT CARE
REGISTERED KC, FCI, AKCs
COLORS Black, white, red, blue, fawn, fallow, or brindle, with or without white

There are Italian, Hungarian, Russian, and other Greyhounds, and this member of the group is also known as the English Greyhound. Closely resembling dogs in ancient art, it is renowned for its speed.

 BLACK

 BLUE

 RED/TAN

 GOLD

 BLACK AND WHITE

BREED ORIGINS

Ancient Egyptian art shows dogs similar to the modern Greyhound, and is seized upon as evidence of the breed's antiquity. However, DNA analysis in 2004 put it surprisingly close to herding dogs, implying that while this deep-chested, narrow-waisted, finely tapered type of dog has been around for millennia, the modern breed sprang from a wider genetic base more recently.

The "grey" does not refer to color, but comes from Old English, and is thought to mean "fine." Greyhounds were used in hunting large and small game, and today are principally used in racing.

BREED QUALITIES

Despite their speed in pursuit, the Greyhound at home can be a relaxed and relaxing companion, although not ideal for city life and families with young children. It tends to forget its training when it sights potential prey, but is otherwise tractable.

BUILT FOR SPEED Greyhounds can reach speeds of 43 mph (69 kph); retired racing dogs can find it hard to break the habits of a lifetime when they see small animals.

LIVE FAST, RETIRE YOUNG Racing dogs have a short working life, and rescue organizations often have adult dogs to home. Away from the track, the Greyhound is typically quiet and gentle.

Griffon Fauve de Bretagne

ORIGIN France
HEIGHT 19–22 in (48–56 cm)
WEIGHT 40–49 lb (18–22 kg)
EXERCISE LEVEL
COAT CARE
REGISTERED FCI
COLORS Fawn shades, from wheaten to red

This intelligent and adaptable scenthound was originally used for hunting wolves. They are sociable and affectionate dogs, but have not achieved great popularity beyond their hunting role.

RED/TAN   GOLD

BREED ORIGINS

This breed from Brittany is one of the oldest French scenthounds, known from the 14th century when a pack belonging to Huet des Ventes was recorded. Its numbers declined in the 19th century when wolves became extinct, and was very rare when efforts began to revive it after World War II. The breed club's motto of "hunting first" guides the development and the use of this hound, which is almost always kept as a hunting companion and rare outside its homeland.

BRETAGNE QUALITIES This hardy breed has a bony, muscular build clothed in a rough, weatherproof coat. They are tenacious when on a scent, using their "chopping" voice of repeated short barks.

Griffon Nivernais

ORIGIN France
HEIGHT 21–25 in (53–64 cm)
WEIGHT 50–55 lb (22.7–24.9 kg)
EXERCISE LEVEL
COAT CARE
REGISTERED FCI
COLORS Sand to fawn overlaid with black or blue

A recreation of an ancient type from central France, this slightly sad-looking scenthound is an energetic and good-natured breed that needs early training to overcome its will to follow a scent.

BREED ORIGINS

This was a popular medieval hunting breed, but was dropped from the royal packs in the 16th century in favor of white hounds. It lived on in Nivernais, but died out during the French Revolution at the close of the 18th century. At the end of the 19th century, it was recreated from the dogs of the region, together with the Griffon Vendéen, Foxhound, and Otterhound.

SHAGGY DOG This is a hardy and muscular breed, built for stamina rather than speed, and used in packs for wild boar. The tousled coat is called *barbouillaud* in French.

Hamiltonstövare

ORIGIN Sweden

HEIGHT 18–24 in (46–61 cm)

WEIGHT 50–60 lb (22.7–27.2 kg)

EXERCISE LEVEL

COAT CARE

REGISTERED KC, FCI

COLORS Tricolor

This scenthound, also called the Hamilton Hound, was created by Swedish Kennel Club founder Count Adolf Patrik Hamilton. First used for hunting hare and fox, it has more recently won an audience beyond its homeland and original purpose.

BREED ORIGINS

Hunting in Sweden was only for royalty and the gentry until the end of the 18th century, when restrictions were lifted. Old hound breeds became more widespread, and new ones were created in the following decades. When the first dog show was held in Sweden in 1886 almost 200 hounds were exhibited. Among them were a pair called Pang and Stella, owned by Count Hamilton, who are considered to be the founders of the breed. Created from crosses of Foxhounds, Harriers, and the best of breeds from southern Germany and Switzerland, the breed was at first called the Swedish Hound. In 1921 it was renamed in honor of its creator.

BREED QUALITIES

In hunting, it is used singly for tracking and flushing small game. It is calm around children and other dogs, and has begun to be seen as a companion breed, but it needs plenty of exercise.

NEAT PACKAGE A well-proportioned breed, the Hamiltonstövare is athletic and muscular, built for stamina rather than speed or strength. The coat is hard and sleek, lying close to the body.

Hanoverian Hound

ORIGIN Germany

HEIGHT 20–24 in (51–61 cm)

WEIGHT 85–99 lb (38.6–44.9 kg)

EXERCISE LEVEL

COAT CARE

REGISTERED FCI

COLORS Light to dark, brindled red, with or without mask; white patches on chest allowed

Recognized as the Hannoverscher Schweisshund or "leash hound" and also called the Hanover Hound, this sturdy scenthound is the closest German equivalent to the Bloodhound or St. Hubert Hound.

 RED/TAN

 BLACK AND TAN

BREED ORIGINS

Leash hounds, also referred to as Leithunder or liam hounds, were used to track quarry over 1,000 years ago. They belonged to the general type of hunting dogs known as Bracken. Later, when hunting with guns became more common, these dogs were used to track wounded game so that it could be properly despatched. Although today's breed is claimed to be an almost unchanged descendant of ancient leash hounds, intensive breeding work was undertaken in the Hanoverian hunting estates, giving us a hound of unsurpassed scenting ability that is almost exclusively a working dog.

HEAVYWEIGHT HUNTER This sturdy breed has determination and stamina; the Bavarian Mountain Hound was developed from it.

DEDICATED DESIGN The nose and drooping lips of the breed are designed to catch scent, and even the pendent ears may waft scents to the nose.

Harrier

ORIGIN United Kingdom
HEIGHT 19–22 in (48–56 cm)
WEIGHT 48–60 lb (21.8–27.2 kg)
EXERCISE LEVEL
COAT CARE
REGISTERED FCI, AKCs
COLORS Any hound color; usually white with yellow, red, or black

This classic English scenthound dates back through the Middle Ages, yet it was in danger of extinction in the 20th century, and is without official breed recognition in the main British registry.

GOLD AND WHITE   BLACK AND WHITE   TAN AND WHITE   BLACK, WHITE, AND TAN

HARRIER TYPE The description "Beagle on steroids" aptly sums up this essentially larger scale but similar breed.

BREED ORIGINS

The name Harrier comes from the French *harier* or hunting dog, and the earliest written record is a reference to the Penistone pack in the west of England in 1260. This breed is close to the Beagle and the English Foxhound, and when its numbers declined it was revived using crosses to the Foxhound. Its future is now secure, and it is found in hunting packs and homes, where it makes a sociable companion, relaxed with children and other dogs.

GENIAL DOG This active breed is happiest when out sniffing and exploring in company; it is a good-natured and compliant companion.

Hungarian Greyhound

ORIGIN Hungary
HEIGHT 25–28 in (64–71 cm)
WEIGHT 50–68 lb (22.9–30.8 kg)
EXERCISE LEVEL
COAT CARE
REGISTERED FCI
COLORS Any hound color

Smaller than the classic Greyhound, this elegant, powerful breed is rare outside its homeland, where it is called the Magyar Agar. Some claim it is faster than the Greyhound over some distances.

CREAM   BLACK AND WHITE   TAN AND WHITE   BLACK, WHITE, AND TAN

BREED ORIGINS

Believed to derive from Asian Greyhounds brought to Hungary by the Magyars in the 9th century, the breed was used to hunt small game. It was crossed with the Greyhound to improve its speed in the 19th century, and is a tough and seemingly tireless hound. In the home it is gentle, affectionate, and biddable.

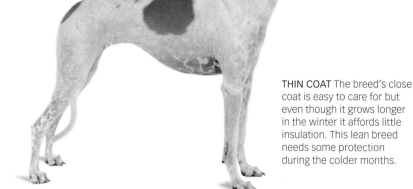

THIN COAT The breed's close coat is easy to care for but even though it grows longer in the winter it affords little insulation. This lean breed needs some protection during the colder months.

Hygenhund

ORIGIN Norway
HEIGHT 19–23 in (48–58 cm)
WEIGHT 44–53 lb (20.0–24.0 kg)
EXERCISE LEVEL
COAT CARE
REGISTERED FCI
COLORS Red shades, black and tan, both with white allowed, white and red, tricolor

This compact scenthound is named after its creator, and is also called the Hygen Hound. It is not widely known outside Norway, and remains a working dog rather than a home companion.

RED/TAN   BLACK AND WHITE   TAN AND WHITE   BLACK AND TAN   BLACK, WHITE AND TAN

BREED ORIGINS

The Hygenhund was created in the early 19th century by crossing north German hounds with Scandinavian breeds, including the now extinct Ringerike Hound. The aim was to create a small breed ideal for hunting hares, and the result was a lively dog with tremendous stamina over long distances. It does not adapt well to city life; although it gets on with other dogs, its tendency to snap makes it an unreliable family dog.

OUTDOOR TYPE Despite its short, tight coat, this is a hardy breed and is content to live outside in the company of other dogs in all but severe cold.

Ibizan Hound

ORIGIN Ibiza
HEIGHT 23–28 in (58–71 cm)
WEIGHT 42–55 lb (19.0–24.9 kg)
EXERCISE LEVEL
COAT CARE
REGISTERED KC, FCI, AKCs
COLORS White and red, white, red

This primitive-looking sighthound has a variety of names, including Podenco Ibicenco, Ibizan Warren Hound, Ibizan Podenco, Balearic Dog, and Charnique. On Ibiza it is called Ca Eivissec.

CREAM   RED/TAN   TAN AND WHITE

PRIMITIVE HEAD The long, tapering face of the Ibizan is similar to that of the Pharaoh Hound and the Cirneco dell'Etna.

BREED ORIGINS

This breed was thought to descend directly from ancient hounds brought from North Africa by traders, breeding true in isolation on the Balearic islands. A genetic study in 2004 revealed that it diverged from common canine stock much more recently.

Like most sighthounds that are traditionally run in packs, these are relaxed around other dogs and good with children, but are not the most biddable and tend to take off after anything that moves.

ART NOT NATURE Even if the DNA evidence shows the ancient origins of the Ibizan Hound to be a fiction, it is a perfect reproduction of an antique type.

Irish Wolfhound

ORIGIN Ireland

HEIGHT 32–34 in (81–86 cm)

WEIGHT 105–120 lb (47.6–54.4 kg)

EXERCISE LEVEL

COAT CARE

REGISTERED KC, FCI, AKCs

COLORS Gray, steel gray, brindle, red, black, pure white, fawn, wheaten

This massive breed makes it easy to imagine the fearsome Celtic hounds known as Cú Faoil used for hunting wolves, elk, and boar, and partly responsible for the local extinction of all three.

GRAY

RED/TAN

SHAGGY DOG The coarse, wiry top coat is best stripped out by plucking in summer, leaving a sleek, soft undercoat for the warmer months.

THE EYES HAVE IT For all its size and power, this is the original gentle giant, most likely to lick you to death.

BREED ORIGINS

The ancestors of this hound probably came to Ireland via the Roman Empire, and large, shaggy hounds are prominent in ancient Irish writing. By the 19th century numbers were seriously depleted; this is not a dog suited to hunting with a gun.

The breed was saved by a Captain Graham, who used Deerhound, Great Dane, and Borzoi lines to inject new blood.

Today, the breed is a mellow household companion, good with children and other dogs and perhaps less inclined to chase than some other sighthounds. Sadly, it is not long lived, and is prone to bone cancer and gastric torsion, like other giant and deep-chested breeds.

IRISH WOLFHOUND The breed motto is "gentle when stroked, fierce when provoked" but in truth this mellow-natured breed is hard to provoke—which is just as well, because it weighs more than many adults.

Istrian Coarse-haired Hound

ORIGIN Croatia

HEIGHT 18–23 in (46–58 cm)

WEIGHT 35–53 lb (15.8–24.0 kg)

EXERCISE LEVEL

COAT CARE

REGISTERED FCI

COLORS White with ears and limited body markings of lemon-orange

This quiet but lively hunter is called the Istarski Ostrodlaki Gonic in its homeland and breed standard, and also termed the Istrian Rough-coated, Rough-haired, and Wirehaired Hound or Scenthound.

BREED ORIGINS

The Istrian Coarse-haired Hound was created from the much older Istrian Smooth-haired hound by crossing with the French hunting breed the Griffon Vendéen in the 19th century, when they were known as "barbini."

Although the breed almost vanished due to World War I, it recovered and has been recognized since 1948.

Like its shorthaired antecedent, it was created for hunting fox and hare, and it is still almost exclusively kept as a hunting dog today, either running freely or tracking on a leash. The original aim of the crossbreeding that brought in the long hair was to improve the hound's voice, and this breed does have a deep, sonorous call. It can make a good guard dog, and mixes well with other dogs and children, but is not suited to city life.

SERIOUS FACE The breed standard's description of a "stern, gloomy and sometimes even sombre" expression belies this dog's gentle, calm character when it is not working.

ROBUST TYPE This breed is suited to hunting in the harsh mountain terrain of the region. The long, bristly top coat and thick, short undercoat give weather-resistant protection.

Istrian Smooth-haired Hound

ORIGIN Croatia

HEIGHT 18–21 in (46–53 cm)

WEIGHT 35–50 lb (15.8–22.7 kg)

EXERCISE LEVEL

COAT CARE

REGISTERED FCI

COLORS White with ears and limited body markings of lemon-orange

This breed is called the Istarski Kratkodlaki Gonic in its homeland. The Istrian peninsula in the Balkans is partly Croatian, partly Slovenian, and both lay some claim to this scenthound, whose origins long predate modern politics.

SMOOTH LOOKS This hound should give a noble impression, with clean lines and a supple gait. Only very limited markings are allowed, and the quality of the rich, bright orange is much prized.

BREED ORIGINS

The Istrian Smooth-haired, also sometimes called the Istrian Setter, is thought to be the oldest of the Balkan hounds, arising from crosses between Asian sighthounds and European scenthounds. It has existed at least since the Middle Ages, with local frescoes from the 15th century, painting, and writings all recording

dogs of this type. It was from the start used for hunting relatively small quarry, such as fox and rabbit, and is still an enthusiastic and competent hunter today, and kept as such across the region.

BREED QUALITIES

Although energetic in pursuit, this is a gentle, calm breed when off duty, and becomes very attached to its owner. It is comfortable around other dogs and children, obedient and easy to care for, but not happy with an urban lifestyle. It has a penetrating and rather sharp voice.

MASKED HOUND A divided 'mask' over the eyes and ears is characteristic; ears flecked with orange are particularly prized. A small 'star' marking on the top of the forehead is also typical.

Italian Spinone

ORIGIN Italy

HEIGHT 24–26 in (61–66 cm)

WEIGHT 71–82 lb (32.2–37.2 kg)

EXERCISE LEVEL

COAT CARE

REGISTERED KC, FCI, AKCs

COLORS White, white with solid and/or speckled markings of orange or brown

This breed is a versatile hunting dog, with a thick, wiry coat that protects it when moving though thorny undergrowth to track or flush game.

CREAM

GOLD AND WHITE

TAN AND WHITE

NATURAL SCRUFFS The drawbacks of this breed are a shaggy coat that can become pungent if not regularly and rigorously groomed, and the production of copious resilient drool.

BREED ORIGINS

The Spinone can be traced back to the 13th century, when it emerged in the region of Piedmont, in northwestern Italy. It may be descended from the older Segugio, a dedicated scenthound. It was Italy's most popular hunting dog until the 20th century, when other pointers and setters overtook it, and the breed all but disappeared during World War II. Today it is popular again, particularly for hunting in dense scrub or near water.

BREED QUALITIES

Spinones are used to find and retrieve, but not to hunt to a kill, and are classified as gundogs in the United Kingdom. This heritage has given it a tractable nature, and it is less likely to take off on its own at high speed than most hounds—its favored pace seems to be a comfortable amble, ideal for walking. These qualities and its patient nature help to make it an attractive household companion.

FRIENDLY FACE This is a good-natured breed, with very low levels of aggression. This means that despite its size and deep bark, it is born to be a loyal companion, not a guard dog.

Jura Laufhund

ORIGIN Switzerland
HEIGHT 18–23 in (46–58 cm)
WEIGHT 34–44 lb (15.4–20.0 kg)
EXERCISE LEVEL
COAT CARE
REGISTERED FCI
COLORS Black and tan, sometimes with a small white patch on the chest

Like the Berner, Luzerner, and Schwyzer Laufhund breeds, this is one of the scenthounds recognized under the group name of Swiss Hound, Schweizer Laufhund, or Chien Courant Suisse.

BREED ORIGINS
Developed in the Jura Mountains on the border with France in the Middle Ages, and also called the Bruno Jura Hound or Laufhund, this breed is used for hunting small game, but is not the most popular of the Swiss types. It is easy-going with children and dogs, but also stubborn and needs firmness.

FRENCH INFLUENCE
Distinguished from the other Schweizers by its broader head and more wrinkled appearance, the Jura bears a resemblance to the related St. Hubert Hound.

Kerry Beagle

ORIGIN Ireland
HEIGHT 22–24 in (56-61 cm)
WEIGHT 44–55 lb (20.0–24.9 kg)
EXERCISE LEVEL
COAT CARE
REGISTERED None
COLORS Black and tan, blue and tan, white and tan, tricolor

Although it is not recognized by any major registry this is one of Ireland's oldest breeds. It was used for centuries, hunting in packs or alone, in the county of Kerry and through the southwest.

TAN AND WHITE

BLACK AND TAN

BLACK, WHITE AND TAN

BLUE MOTTLED WITH TAN

BREED ORIGINS
The Kerry Beagle has existed since the Middle Ages. It is thought that it was bred down in size from larger hounds, used to hunt stags, to create a type suitable for smaller game, specifically hares. Although a well-recorded breed, with detailed pedigrees surviving from the 18th century, it almost died out by the 20th century; today it is enjoying something of a comeback in drag-hunting trials and as a lively, friendly family or household companion.

NOT JUST A PRETTY FACE The looks and the scenting ability of the Kerry Beagle found their way into American hound breeds through dogs taken to the United States by emigrants.

NO MIDGET The name Beagle suggests a small hound, but these dogs are closer in size to English or American Foxhounds.

Lurcher

ORIGIN United Kingdom
HEIGHT 26–30 in (65–75 cm)
WEIGHT 49–70 lb (22.0–32.0 kg)
EXERCISE LEVEL
COAT CARE
REGISTERED None
COLORS Any color

The Lurcher is a breed unlike any other—indeed, it is debatable whether it is a breed at all. Long before the current trend for designer crossbreeds, the Lurcher was the original melting pot.

BLACK   GRAY   BLUE   BLACK AND WHITE   BLACK BRINDLE

BREED ORIGINS

For centuries, Gypsies kept crosses of greyhounds and collies or terriers. The name "lurcher" is from the Roma word for thief, *lur*: A fitting title for a fleet-footed, silent hound that became the classic poacher's dog.

For those who can keep up with these speedy animals, they are the ultimate country dog, and prove to be surprisingly peaceable once they are at rest.

VARIABLE TYPE Today, lurcher-to-lurcher breedings are more usual, but those dogs are still very diverse in size, color, and coat type.

Luzerner Laufhund

ORIGIN Switzerland
HEIGHT 18–23 in (46–58 cm)
WEIGHT 34–44 lb (15.4–20.0 kg)
EXERCISE LEVEL
COAT CARE
REGISTERED FCI
COLORS Black and white speckle, looking blue, with black patches and tan markings

Originating in central Switzerland, this breed is one of four grouped as the Schweizer Laufhund, Swiss Hound, or Running Hound. The Berner and Jura are from the west, the Schwyzer from the east.

BREED ORIGINS

Bred in the Swiss mountains, the exact origins of the Luzerner, or Lucernese Hound, are not known; it has existed since the Middle Ages. Like the other Schweizers, it is fairly small, suitable for mountain terrain, used to track game of all sizes.

The Luzerner Laufhund makes a placid family companion, and although cold resistant is a home lover, not a guard dog.

TRUE COLORS The striking coat color and pattern of the Luzerner suggest that it has a heritage in common with the French scenthound the Petit Bleu de Gascogne.

Neiderlaufhunde

ORIGIN Switzerland
HEIGHT 13–16 in (33–41 cm)
WEIGHT 30–40 lb (13.6–18.1 kg)
EXERCISE LEVEL
COAT CARE
REGISTERED FCI
COLORS White with black and tan, black and tan, black and white, white with orange

The four Schweizer Laufhund types—Berner, Jura, Luzerner, and Schwyzer—each have rare short-legged counterparts, collectively known as the Schweizer Niederlaufhunde or Small Swiss Hounds.

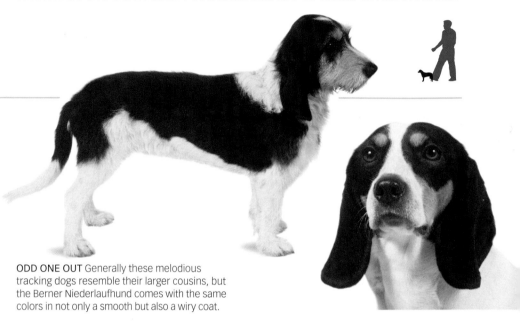

BREED ORIGINS

At the end of the 19th century, smaller hunting territories were introduced in much of Switzerland. The existing Laufhund types seemed too fast to keep game within these confines, so smaller types were bred through selection and crosses to dwarf breeds to track the quarry more slowly. Easy-going at home, they need a surprising amount of activity, and are tireless and passionate on a trail.

ODD ONE OUT Generally these melodious tracking dogs resemble their larger cousins, but the Berner Niederlaufhund comes with the same colors in not only a smooth but also a wiry coat.

Otterhound

ORIGIN United Kingdom
HEIGHT 23–27 in (58–69 cm)
WEIGHT 65–120 lb (29.5–54.4 kg)
EXERCISE LEVEL
COAT CARE
REGISTERED KC, FCI, AKCs
COLORS Any color

Today, otters are rare and protected, but once they were common enough to be regarded as pests. The Otterhound was the specialist solution to the problem.

GRAY

RED/TAN

GOLD

TAN AND WHITE

BREED ORIGINS

The exact origins of the Otterhound breed are uncertain, but it has existed for at least 1,000 years. Bloodhounds, early foxhounds, and rough-coated terrier breeds or the Nivernais Griffon may have contributed. Reliable and calm, if hard to call back from any body of water, it makes a good rural companion.

WATER RESISTANT The rough, insulating coat allows this hound to follow otters into rivers and their dens. A hardy breed with stamina and a love of water was vital for all-day hunts.

Petit Basset Griffon Vendéen

ORIGIN France
HEIGHT 13–15 in (33–38 cm)
WEIGHT 25–35 lb (11.3–15.9 kg)
EXERCISE LEVEL
COAT CARE
REGISTERED FCI
COLORS White, white and orange, tricolor

Diminutive in comparison with the Grand, Briquet, and even the Grand Basset Griffon Vendéen, this dwarfed scenthound is today the most popular breed of the whole group.

CREAM

GOLD AND WHITE

BLACK, WHITE AND TAN

BREED ORIGINS

This breed came into existence before the Grand Basset, emerging in the 18th century as a dog for coursing hares. It has a more truly "basset," meaning low or dwarfed, build than the Grand Basset, with a body of the same size but carried on markedly shorter legs. Popular as a hunting dog in France for over a century, it has more recently found favor as a companion breed and won friends abroad. This intelligent breed has an independent streak and can clamor for attention. It needs scrupulous grooming and plenty of activity, but is a cheerful, busy companion.

COUNTRY COUSIN The shaggy coat gives this breed a slightly unkempt, rustic look, but it will settle into city life as long as there are plenty of parks for daily activity.

LOW-SLUNG LOOK The dwarfed legs should be straight and strong, but the combination of a long body and short legs inevitably gives this breed a tendency to spinal problems.

Petit Bleu de Gascogne

ORIGIN France

HEIGHT 20–23 in (51–58 cm)

WEIGHT 40–44 lb (18.1–20.0 kg)

EXERCISE LEVEL

COAT CARE

REGISTERED FCI

COLORS Mottled black and white, with or without black patches, with tan markings

Not exactly small, but midway in size between the Grand Bleu and the Basset Bleu, this scenthound was bred for hunting hares. It is not common, and is mostly known in its native land.

BREED ORIGINS

Like its larger counterpart, this hound dates back to the Middle Ages. It is still mostly found in its original homeland of southwestern France. Bred to track the difficult scent of the hare, it has an excellent nose and obsessive concentration once it is on a trail. Coupled with seemingly boundless stamina, this can make it a time-consuming dog to exercise, but for those with the inclination to take long walks with varied routes, this makes a fine country companion. Once at home, this breed settles down happily with other dogs or children.

STAYING POWER With a deep-chested, powerful, and muscular build, this is a healthy and long-lived dog. It needs wide open spaces, and does not settle well into city life.

Petit Griffon de Gascogne

ORIGIN France

HEIGHT 17–21 in (43–53 cm)

WEIGHT 40–42 lb (18–19 kg)

EXERCISE LEVEL

COAT CARE

REGISTERED AKCs

COLORS Mottled and patched black and white, with tan markings

This rustic-looking scenthound breed is officially recognized as the Petit Griffon Bleu de Gascogne, coming in only one coat pattern, and is the shaggy-coated version of the Petit Bleu de Gascogne.

BREED ORIGINS

The provenance of this rough-coated hound is uncertain: The breed standard claims ancient origins in a cross of the Petit Bleu and a Griffon type, but some sources consider it an 18th-century creation. Although employed as a hardworking hunter for centuries, it had almost disappeared by the late 20th century, but in recent years has enjoyed a revival. It is a friendly and easy-going household or family dog.

PROTECTIVE BUT PUNGENT Thick skinned and coarse coated, this is an excellent dog for overgrown countryside, but neglected shaggy coats will mean a 'doggy' smell.

Pharaoh Hound

ORIGIN Malta
HEIGHT 21–25 in (53–64 cm)
WEIGHT 45–55 lb (20.4–24.9 kg)
EXERCISE LEVEL
COAT CARE
REGISTERED KC, FCI, AKCs
COLORS Tan with small white markings

RED/TAN

TAN AND WHITE

This breed's original name in Malta is Kelb Tal-Fenek, meaning "rabbit dog." The English name refers to the breed's assumed ancient origins, and was once also used for the Ibizan Hound.

BREED ORIGINS

The English name of this breed was chosen because of its strong resemblance to dogs appearing in ancient Egyptian art: The dog is variously classed as a hound or a primitive pariah type, according to registry. It was generally assumed to be directly descended from these ancient dogs, having been spread across the Mediterranean by Phoenician or Carthaginian traders and then continued to breed true in isolation on the island of Malta. However, genetic research in 2005 seems to show that this breed is in fact of much more recent origin, a coincidental or artful recreation of the ancient type. It is also kept as a companion, but managing a highly active, intelligent breed with a mind of its own and an overwhelming urge to chase is not for the inexperienced.

FAIR-WEATHER FRIEND The strong, clean lines of this breed reflect its good health and sound structure, but a thin coat provides little insulation, and the thin ears can suffer frostbite.

Polish Hound

ORIGIN Poland

HEIGHT 22–26 in (56–66 cm)

WEIGHT 55–71 lb (24.9–32.2 kg)

EXERCISE LEVEL

COAT CARE

REGISTERED FCI

COLORS Black and tan with touches of white

Known in its homeland as the Ogar Polski, this handsome and substantial scenthound was virtually unknown in the West for much of the Communist era, and even today remains relatively obscure.

BREED ORIGINS

This breed can be traced back at least to the 18th century, when it was developed for tracking large game, but its exact origins remain unknown. Its appearance hints strongly at the involvement of the French bloodhound breed the St. Hubert Hound, and it may also be related to German hounds of similar coloring. It suffered in World War II, when it narrowly escaped extinction; another smaller hound, the Polski Pies Gonczy, was not so lucky. Today its future seems assured in and to some extent beyond its homeland. It is still used for tracking and also kept as a family dog: it is reliable with children and can adapt to city life, but needs plenty of activity.

WELL BUILT Everything about this breed is broad, strong, and heavy, from the deep chest and well-muscled legs to the thick, low-set tail. Even its gait is heavy.

POLISH COLORS The black or near-black color of the body was called *podzary*, meaning "burnt," in old Polish hunting terminology. The tan comes in various shades, with a warm cinnamon being favored.

Porcelaine

ORIGIN France
HEIGHT 22–23 in (56–58 cm)
WEIGHT 55–62 lb (24.9–28.1 kg)
EXERCISE LEVEL
COAT CARE
REGISTERED FCI
COLORS Very white, with restricted orange spots and black pigmented spots of skin

This elegant scenthound is named for the translucent, glossy finish of its coat; it is also sometimes called Chien de Franche-Comté. It remains a quintessentially French breed.

BREED ORIGINS

This may be the most ancient of all French hound breeds, descended from the extinct Montaimboeuf. It was a popular pack hound before the French Revolution virtually wiped it out. In the 19th century, breeders revived it from a few dogs. An energetic hunter with a musical voice, it makes a sociable family dog, although not suited to urban apartment life.

UNIQUE PATTERN Orange-flecked ears and a ghostly pattern of dark spots are typical of the breed.

Portuguese Podengo

ORIGIN Portugal
HEIGHT 8–28 in (20–71 cm)
WEIGHT 10–60 lb (4.5–27.2 kg)
EXERCISE LEVEL
COAT CARE
REGISTERED FCI
COLORS Yellow, fawn, or black with white

Recognized under the name Podengo Portugueso, this breed comes in Grande (large), Medio (medium), and Pequeno (small). Each of these has a short- and a long- or wirehaired variety.

GOLD AND WHITE

TAN AND WHITE

BREED ORIGINS

The origins of these primitive sighthounds are obscure. They may be descended from the same lines as the Pharaoh Hound, or from small Iberian wolves. They are sometimes still used for small game, giving the other names of Portuguese Warren Hound or Rabbit Dog. The Medio is by far the most common. Off-duty, they make loyal family companions, although they may fight other dogs.

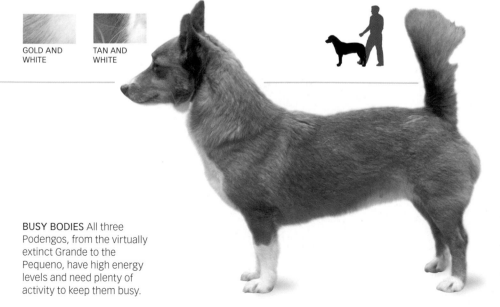

BUSY BODIES All three Podengos, from the virtually extinct Grande to the Pequeno, have high energy levels and need plenty of activity to keep them busy.

Posavac Hound

ORIGIN Croatia

HEIGHT 17–23 in (43–58 cm)

WEIGHT 35–45 lb (15.9–20.4 kg)

EXERCISE LEVEL

COAT CARE

REGISTERED FCI

COLORS All shades of reddish-wheaten with white

This breed is recognized as the Posavski Gonic; the anglicized version of its name is also spelled Posovaz or Posovatz. It is a tough scenthound, ideally adapted to forests and undergrowth.

GOLD AND WHITE

TAN AND WHITE

BREED ORIGINS

The origins of this ancient hound breed are lost in the mists of time. It is indigenous to Croatia, and lays claim to being shown in the same 15th-century frescoes as the similar Istrian Smooth-haired Hound. Local to Posavina, the Sava river valley southeast of Zagreb, these dogs were known as "boskini," becoming known by their current name after

FAMILY LIKENESS The breed is close to the Istrian hounds, but has a different coat, with white limited to markings on the head, neck, chest, lower limbs and tail tip.

recognition in the 20th century. A robust, sure-footed, and tireless hunter, it has a high, ringing voice. It is still used free or on a leash to track hare and fox, but also makes a gentle companion.

TAILORED FIT The skin of this breed fits tightly, without the wrinkles and drooping lips and eyelids that are often seen in breeds from Western Europe.

LOCAL TRAIT The Posavac head is fairly long and narrow. The divided mask, although seen in breeds from elsewhere, is particularly characteristic of hounds from the Balkan region.

Rampur Greyhound

ORIGIN India
HEIGHT 22–30 in (55–75 cm)
WEIGHT 58–66 lb (26.5–30.0 kg)
EXERCISE LEVEL
COAT CARE
REGISTERED None
COLORS Black, gray, grizzle, brindle, particolor

Although rare beyond India, this breed is the best known of the subcontinent's indigenous breeds. Its name comes from its original home, the district of Rampur in Uttar Pradesh, northeastern India.

BLACK GRAY BLACK BRINDLE

BREED ORIGINS
Hunting dogs have been kept in India for millennia. When the Afghans came to India in the 18th century they brought the Tazi, a ferocious, independent-minded sighthound. Crossed with more obedient English Greyhounds, this produced the Rampur: loyal, but still feisty enough to take on boars and leopards. Hardy and adaptable, they are instinctive hunters but peaceable companions.

INDIAN TYPE The narrow pointed head and slender body are shared by the Rajapalyam, once used to attack British cavalry, and the Mudhol or Caravan Hound.

Saluki

ORIGIN Iran
HEIGHT 20–28 in (51–71 cm)
WEIGHT 44–66 lb (20.0–29.9 kg)
EXERCISE LEVEL
COAT CARE
REGISTERED KC, FCI, AKCs
COLORS Any color or colors except brindle

Also called the Arabian Greyhound, Persian Greyhound, or Gazelle Hound, this swift and elegant sighthound has been known in the Middle East and used in the hunt for millennia.

BLACK GOLD GOLD AND WHITE

BREED ORIGINS
The Saluki closely resembles ancient images of hunting dogs, and recent DNA analysis confirmed that it is not a modern recreation but a truly ancient breed. It predates Islam, and while dogs are generally regarded as unclean in the religion, the Saluki was always an exception; the white spot often found on its chest is known as "the kiss of Allah" by the Bedouin. It was first brought to the

United Kingdom in the 1840s, but only became popular at the start of the 20th century. Today it is established across the world as a graceful companion, at ease in family and city homes.

NATURAL VARIATION Because the breed was historically scattered across a wide area, a range of geographically isolated local types emerged. The coat varies in color between places, and both smooth and feathered types exist.

Schillerstövare

ORIGIN Sweden

HEIGHT 20–24 in (51–61 cm)

WEIGHT 40–53 lb (18.1–24.0 kg)

EXERCISE LEVEL

COAT CARE

REGISTERED FCI

COLORS Black and tan

The Schiller Hound might be seen as the rural workers' counterpart to the Hamiltonstövare; it is also a scenthound from Sweden, bred in the 19th century, and carrying the name of its creator.

CONSISTENT COLOR The original dogs shown by Per Schiller were rather small, and black and tan with limited white markings. Today's breed is larger and reliably black and tan.

BREED ORIGINS

When ancient restrictions in Sweden were lifted to allow commoners to hunt at the end of the 18th century, both the numbers and the breeds of hounds increased. At the first national dog show in 1886, a young farmer, Per Schiller exhibited Tamburini and Ralla I, siblings descended from Swedish scenthounds from the Kaflås estate. These in turn were descended from black-and-tan German hounds that came to Sweden with returning soldiers from the 16th century. These two dogs were the founders of this breed, which was further developed using primarily British Harriers but also Swiss hounds.

BREED QUALITIES

This dog is used alone to hunt small game in Swedish fashion. It tracks the quarry and brings it to bay for the hunter, barking all the time. It remains almost entirely a hunting companion, although its friendly nature would suit a wider role. It is a friendly breed, calm around children, and obedient, but it does take a lot of exercise and is not suitable for city life.

RARE BREED Although recognized at the start of the 20th century, the Schillerstövare is still uncommon outside its homeland, and very rare beyond Scandinavia.

SALUKI (*see* p. 216) One of the oldest of all breeds, this graceful sighthound was created to hunt the fleet-footed gazelle. It has a flying gallop and a zest for hunting that belies its delicate appearance.

Sloughi

ORIGIN Morocco
HEIGHT 24–28 in (60–70 cm)
WEIGHT 44–59 lb (20.0–27.0 kg)
EXERCISE LEVEL
COAT CARE
REGISTERED KC, FCI, AKCs
COLORS Sand to fawn, may have black shading or white markings

Although it is sometimes called the Arabian Greyhound and classed with the Saluki, recent DNA analysis has shown the Sloughi to be a distinctively African breed.

GOLD

GOLD AND WHITE

BREED ORIGINS

When looking at the relationships between animals, a mixture of archeology, written records, and the looks of the breed have in the past been the only tools available. Beyond a certain distance, these can give no great certainty. The advent of genetic studies has shone a new light on the history of dog breeds, and revealed some surprises. Although it looks close to the other breeds

sometimes called greyhounds, the Sloughi appears to have spent all of its genetic history in Africa, almost entirely untouched by any new input. It has needed none: A slender, sand-colored dog, it is in many ways the perfect hound for its home. A slightly high-strung breed and suspicious of strangers, it is content as the companion of a consistent, quiet owner but not a choice for a rowdy household with children.

HAPPY MEDIUM The Berbers kept two lines of Sloughis: the small, fine desert Sloughi, and a larger mountain Sloughi. Elsewhere, the breed has developed as a blend of the two.

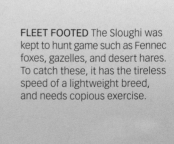

FLEET FOOTED The Sloughi was kept to hunt game such as Fennec foxes, gazelles, and desert hares. To catch these, it has the tireless speed of a lightweight breed, and needs copious exercise.

Slovakian Hound

ORIGIN Slovakia
HEIGHT 16–20 in (40–50 cm)
WEIGHT 33–44 lb (15.0–20.0 kg)
EXERCISE LEVEL
COAT CARE
REGISTERED KC, FCI, AKCs
COLORS Black and tan

Known in its homeland as the Slovensky Kopov, this breed is also sometimes called the Black Forest Hound, a name that has more German than Slovakian connotations for many people; confusion over the breed's identity may have contributed to its low profile abroad.

HOMING DOG Spirited and with stamina to spare, this breed will enthusiastically follow a trail for hours, and may be hard to call back when it finds a scent. It has an excellent sense of direction, so will find its way back eventually.

BREED ORIGINS
This hound has much in common with other central European scenthounds and resembles some of the German leash hounds. It existed as a type rather than a breed for almost all of its history, maintained as a working dog by the hunters who valued its skills. An accomplished tracker with a fine voice, it was used to find big game such as wild boar, through remote and harsh mountain regions.

Only after World War II did breeders select the individuals seen as the best and formally produce a new hound.

BREED QUALITIES
The Slovakian is happiest doing what it knows best. It is not suited to city life, and unlikely to appreciate the attentions of children. Young dogs can be unruly, but given firm and consistent training this loyal breed is a fine companion for rural pursuits.

Spanish Greyhound

ORIGIN Spain
HEIGHT 26–28 in (66–71 cm)
WEIGHT 60–66 lb (27.2–29.9 kg)
EXERCISE LEVEL
COAT CARE
REGISTERED FCI
COLORS Any color

Recognized as the Galgo Español and also called the Spanish Galgo, this greyhound is smaller than its English counterpart. It is bred as a companion or show dog rather than a professional racer.

BLACK

RED/TAN

BLACK AND WHITE

TAN AND WHITE

BLACK BRINDLE

BREED ORIGINS

This is an old greyhound breed, thought to be descended from the African sighthound the Sloughi and greyhounds from the Near East, and possibly dating back to antiquity as a distinct type. Although it has been used to hunt a range of game from wild boar to rabbits, and vermin such as foxes, it was principally intended for hunting hare. Today, these hunting dogs may be crossed with English Greyhounds to give greater speed.

This is a healthy dog, but not one of the most tractable. It makes a quiet, somewhat shy companion, unsuited to small homes or families with young children.

ROUGH COAT Compact but never small, with the typical greyhound build, this breed has a hard coat that comes in both short and semilong options.

Spanish Hound

ORIGIN Spain
HEIGHT 18–22 in (46–56 cm)
WEIGHT 45–55 lb (20.4–24.9 kg)
EXERCISE LEVEL
COAT CARE
REGISTERED FCI
COLORS White and orange, black and white

Known in its homeland and registered under the name Sabueso Español, this scenthound is a tireless hunting dog. It is primarily used for small game but sometimes also for larger quarry.

BLACK AND WHITE

GOLD AND WHITE

BREED ORIGINS

The Sabueso dates back to the Middle Ages, and is described in a treatise on hunting by the 14th-century King Alfonso XI of Castile. It is particularly good at tracking hare, and is usually used alone rather than in packs. A medium-sized dog, generally long in its proportions, its favoured gait is an economical trot with long strides, which it can sustain all day. This makes it particularly useful for tracking wounded game. At a walk, it tends to keep its head low, and it can look rather lugubrious. This breed can be temperamental, and is not recommended for homes with other dogs or children.

GENDER GAP There is a marked difference between the sexes in this breed, with all but a few of the very smallest males being larger than the largest females.

Swedish Elkhound

ORIGIN Sweden

HEIGHT 23–25 in (58–64 cm)

WEIGHT 66 lb (29.9 kg)

EXERCISE LEVEL

COAT CARE

REGISTERED FCI

COLORS Shades of gray with cream to white markings

The official national breed of Sweden, this dog is also known by the name of Jämthund. Once there were many more regional elkhounds, and this one originated in Jämtland in northern Sweden.

WORKING ANIMAL The wolf-like appearance identifies this as one of those spitz breeds that are happiest when they have a job to do, and are frustrated just hanging around.

WARMLY DRESSED The rugged good looks of this breed show excellent adaptation to its chilly northern environment, with small, well-covered ears and a dense, insulating coat.

BREED ORIGINS
This dog dates back many centuries, and was traditionally used for hunting not only elk but bears, wolves, and even the agile Scandinavian lynx, driving the quarry until it was trapped and then awaiting the hunters' arrival. It was only recognized in the latter part of the 20th century; until then it was judged as part of the Norwegian Elkhound breed, a politically unpopular union. In truth, many physically isolated communities developed their own slightly different strains of hunting dog over the centuries; this one simply survived and got itself noticed.

BREED QUALITIES
This heritage has created a strong, hardy dog of enormous stamina. It is also intelligent, and has found alternative employment in herding, guarding, sled-pulling, military roles, and simply as a household pet. Elkhounds are friendly with children, but they may have dominance disputes with other dogs.

Schwyzer Laufhund

ORIGIN Switzerland
HEIGHT 18–23 in (46–58 cm)
WEIGHT 34–44 lb (15.4–20.0 kg)
EXERCISE LEVEL
COAT CARE
REGISTERED FCI
COLORS White with orange

This breed, with the Berner, Jura, and Luzerner, completes the quartet of Swiss scenthounds recognized as types of the Schweizer Laufhund, also called the Swiss Hound or Chien Courant Suisse.

BREED ORIGINS

Although it takes its name from the canton of Schwyz in the eastern part of Switzerland, this hound shares a resemblance to French hounds with the other Schweizer Laufhund varieties. Those seeking to establish their antiquity point to a Roman mosaic found in the western Swiss town of Avenches, apparently showing pack hounds corresponding to the four modern strains. This breed is also kept as a household pet in rural homes and is friendly with children and other dogs, but it can be stubborn and demanding.

OLD SMOOTHIE The Schwyzer was the only one of the Laufhunds to have a wirehaired variant, but this has vanished, along with other Laufhund strains, in the 20th century.

Transylvanian Hound

ORIGIN Hungary/Romania
HEIGHT 22–26 in (55–65 cm)
WEIGHT 66–77 lb (30.0–35.0 kg)
EXERCISE LEVEL
COAT CARE
REGISTERED FCI, AKCs
COLORS Black and tan, tricolor

Also called the Hungarian Hound, and registered as the Erdélyi Kopó, this scenthound came in a long-legged and a short-legged version. The taller type is still rare; the short-legged is now extinct.

BLACK AND TAN

BLACK, WHITE, AND TAN

BREED ORIGINS

This breed is thought to date back to 9th-century crosses of local hounds with Magyar dogs. Sadly, these dogs were killed in large numbers in Romania after World War II as scapegoats for territorial conflicts. A reserved personality, it is happy with other dogs and children.

LOCAL SPECIALITY This is a typical hound of the region in form and color. It has a biddable nature and a high-pitched, ringing voice.

Treeing Walker Coonhound

ORIGIN United States
HEIGHT 20–27 in (51–69 cm)
WEIGHT 45–70 lb (20.4–31.8 kg)
EXERCISE LEVEL
COAT CARE
REGISTERED AKCs
COLORS White and tan, black and white, tricolor

Named for its breeder, rather than its pace, the Treeing Walker was bred to scent, pursue, and trap small prey such as raccoons in trees, to be despatched by the following hunter with a gun.

BLACK AND WHITE

TAN AND WHITE

BLACK, WHITE, AND TAN

BREED ORIGINS

This breed is descended from a hunting dog of unknown origin crossed with the English Foxhound of the Walker family in Virginia in the 19th century. The result was an enthusiastic hunter of impressive speed that will almost climb trees to reach the quarry.

These dogs are happiest when working. They are sociable with children and other dogs, but if kept as household dogs need copious activity, and have a tendency to run off in pursuit of any scent. They are loyal, and eager to please, if slightly excitable, and are reputed to have no road sense.

UNSTOPPABLE Although it resembles its Foxhound ancestors, this is a breed apart. This is an obsessive hunter for whom the hunt is not its work, but its life.

Whippet

ORIGIN United Kingdom
HEIGHT 17–20 in (43–51 cm)
WEIGHT 28 lb (12.7 kg)
EXERCISE LEVEL
COAT CARE
REGISTERED KC, FCI, AKCs
COLORS Any color

This Greyhound in miniature is one of the fastest sighthounds in existence. Both its official name and the nickname 'snap dog' are said to refer to it moving as fast as a snapped or cracked whip.

BLACK

CREAM

BLUE

RED/TAN

BREED ORIGINS

The Whippet was created in the north of England in the 19th century. Hare coursing was a popular sport, and crossing Fox Terriers with the Greyhound—which was too large for the sport—created the Whippet. Despite its graceful, slight appearance, this is a hardy hunter, with all the tenacity of its terrier antecedents when on a scent. At home, this is a gentle, affectionate breed, relaxed around children and other dogs and even something of a couch potato, especially in winter.

TAKE COVER Thin skin and a fine, close coat provide little protection or insulation. A jacket in cold weather is practical, not a fashion statement.

GUNDOGS

The earliest uses that humans found for dogs—hunting, guarding, and companionship—were extensions of their natural behavior. As hunting developed, so did a need for dogs that could carry out actions quite against their nature: pointers and setters that could find quarry but then hold back from pursuit and freeze or crouch to leave an open shot; spaniels to flush game out from cover; and retrievers to find the fallen bodies and gently carry them back. All these tasks needed highly trainable, obedient, and patient dogs, and so many gundog breeds are also excellent family companions and assistance dogs.

ADAPTABLE NATURE An excellent nose and a soft mouth are essential in the working Labrador (*see* pp. 254–55); its biddable nature and strong desire to please are more important to nonhunting owners. This is the most popular of all dog breeds, for good reason.

American Cocker Spaniel

ORIGIN United States
HEIGHT 14–15 in (36–38 cm)
WEIGHT 24–28 lb (10.9–12.7 kg)
EXERCISE LEVEL
COAT CARE
REGISTERED KC, FCI, AKCs
COLORS Black, cream, red, brown; solid or with white; tan points

In the United States this breed is simply the Cocker Spaniel, and the original type is known as the English Cocker Spaniel (*see* p. 236), but international registries give each their national identity.

BLACK   RED/TAN   GOLD   GOLD AND WHITE   BLACK AND WHITE

BREED ORIGINS

This breed has the same early history as the English Cocker, but American breeders pursued a prettier dog, with longer, silkier hair, rather than working qualities. In 1936 a group broke away and formed an "English Cocker Spaniel" club. Some solid colors may suffer "avalanche of rage" syndrome, but otherwise these are affectionate, gentle companions, rarely seen as working dogs.

BEAUTY REGIME The dense coat is prone to dry or oily seborrhea, and hair on the ears must be trimmed to let air reach the ear canals, minimizing infections. The hairy feet are magnets for debris.

American Water Spaniel

ORIGIN United States
HEIGHT 15–18 in (38–46 cm)
WEIGHT 25–45 lb (11.3–20.4 kg)
EXERCISE LEVEL
COAT CARE
REGISTERED FCI, AKCs
COLORS Liver, brown, or dark chocolate

Although recognized internationally, this breed is rare outside the United States, and still primarily found as a working dog. It is hard to know how popular it is, because many working dogs are not registered.

BREED ORIGINS

The exact origins of this breed are not recorded, but early colonists took hunting dogs with them, and the American Water Spaniel is likely to be descended from Curly-coated Retrievers and Irish Water Spaniels among others. It has been known as a general-purpose farm and hunting dog since the 19th century in the midwest, notably in Wisconsin, where it is the state dog, and in Minnesota.

BREED QUALITIES

This breed excels as a "bird dog," flushing and retrieving feathered game, and is an enthusiastic swimmer, suited to working in swamps, lakes, and rivers. It is a generally obedient and tolerant breed, making a fine family companion.

FORM AND FUNCTION Early spaniels were classed by where they worked best—land, field, or water. The curly, water-repellent coat marks out this breed as designed for work in water.

Ariège Pointer

ORIGIN France
HEIGHT 24–26 in (61–66 cm)
WEIGHT 55–66 lb (24.9–29.9 kg)
EXERCISE LEVEL
COAT CARE
REGISTERED FCI
COLORS Pale fawn or brown with white

Known in France as the Braque de l'Ariège, this breed is used for hare and bird pointing and retrieving, and shows an independent-minded tracking heritage beneath the gundog mentality.

BREED ORIGINS

This breed comes from older braques or pointers, such as the Saint-Germain Pointer, which were crossed with southern breeds in the 19th century. It had almost disappeared early in the 20th century, but was preserved by a few huntsmen and taken up by dedicated breeders in the 1990s, although it is rare outside southwestern France. It is lively and enthusiastic, but needs firm training.

TRUE TO TYPE With great presence, today's robust but elegant breed is believed to closely resemble the original; either color or white may predominate in the coat.

Barbet

ORIGIN France
HEIGHT 18–22 in (46–56 cm)
WEIGHT 33–55 lb (15.0–24.9 kg)
EXERCISE LEVEL
COAT CARE
REGISTERED FCI
COLORS Black, gray, fawn, chestnut, white, pied

Also called the French Water Dog, this breed's name comes from its *barbe*, or beard. It was once the most popular water dog in Europe, and an ancestor of several other breeds, but is rare today.

BLACK   GRAY   RED/TAN   GOLD

BREED ORIGINS

This breed was described as early as the 16th century, when it was used for hunting waterfowl and may have retrieved fallen arrows as well as fallen prey. It may be related to the Briard, griffon breeds, the Irish Water Spaniel, and the Poodle. Although tolerant and affectionate, it is not a popular family dog.

CURLY COAT The distinctive coat, which offers such excellent protection against cold water, demands considerable care.

AMERICAN COCKER SPANIEL (*see* p. 228) This breed and specifically the golden color were made famous in Disney's *Lady and the Tramp*, and it is still one of the most popular breeds in the United States today.

Blue Picardy Spaniel

ORIGIN France
HEIGHT 22–24 in (56–61 cm)
WEIGHT 42–44 lb (19.1–20.0 kg)
EXERCISE LEVEL
COAT CARE
REGISTERED FCI
COLORS Black and white

Called the Epagneul Bleu de Picardie in France, this breed is more like a setter than a spaniel in both looks and actions. It is related to English Setters through a complex set of cross-Channel exchanges.

BREED ORIGINS
Picardy Spaniels were almost certainly used to create the English Setter, and this in turn was crossed back to dogs in Picardy to create this breed, first recorded in the 1870s. An active sporting dog, it is particularly used as a water dog for pointing and retrieving snipe in the marshes of northeastern France. Playful but gentle enough to be a good family companion, it is rarely seen beyond this region.

FAMILY LIKENESS This breed is a recent arrival, dating back no further than the late 19th century, but strongly resembles early engravings of older setter breeds from the United Kingdom. Mingled black and white hairs give the blue coat color.

Boykin Spaniel

ORIGIN United States
HEIGHT 15–18 in (38–46 cm)
WEIGHT 30–38 lb (13.6–17.2 kg)
EXERCISE LEVEL
COAT CARE
REGISTERED AKCs
COLORS Liver, dark brown, chocolate

This curly-coated brown spaniel of uncertain parentage is only just on the road to general recognition, but is the state dog of South Carolina where it was developed as a small water dog that literally wouldn't rock the boat.

BREED ORIGINS
This breed began with a spaniel-type stray found in Spartanburg, South Carolina at the start of the 20th century by Alexander Lawrence White. He took the

LIFE JACKET This breed is an excellent swimmer, and its wavy or curly coat is less bulky than that of many spaniels, and waterproof.

dog, named Dumpy, to his hunting partner, "Whit" Boykin. Boykin provided dogs for visiting hunters who went out on the swamps in boats, where a small dog was ideal. Dumpy was bred to a curly-coated spaniel-type female of equally obscure origins, found at a train station, and the breed was underway. A working dog, it needs plenty of stimulation to avoid destructiveness, but it is goodnatured and obedient.

Brittany

ORIGIN France

HEIGHT 19–20 in (48–51 cm)

WEIGHT 35–40 lb (15.9–18.1 kg)

EXERCISE LEVEL

COAT CARE

REGISTERED KC, FCI, AKCs

COLORS Black and white, orange and white, liver and white, tricolor

A favorite gundog in France, this breed is also popular abroad. Although it is known as the Epagneul Breton in its homeland, elsewhere the "spaniel" is usually omitted; it is more of a setter.

BLACK AND WHITE

TAN AND WHITE

BLACK, WHITE, AND TAN

BREED ORIGINS

One of the oldest breeds of this type in France, this was almost extinct at the start of the 20th century, when it was revived by breeder Arthur Enaud through outcrossing and renewed selections. Its popularity is as much due to its relaxed tolerance of children and other dogs as its working abilities, and this is an obedient, affectionate companion for anyone who can provide sufficient activity.

TRUE COLORS In the United States, only brown and red shades, seen as "classic" French colors, are allowed. In Europe, black is also allowed, since it was in the original French breed standard that was drawn up in 1907.

Cesky Fousek

ORIGIN Czech Republic

HEIGHT 24–26 in (61–66 cm)

WEIGHT 62–75 lb (28.1–34.0 kg)

EXERCISE LEVEL

COAT CARE

REGISTERED FCI

COLORS Brown, brown mixed with white

This breed may be found under several names, from Bohemian Wirehaired Pointing Griffon to Czech Coarsehaired Pointer, Slovakian Wirehaired Pointer, or Rough-coated Bohemian Pointer.

BREED ORIGINS

Wirehaired Bohemian dogs, similar to this breed, were used in hunting as long ago as the 14th century, and were described as excellent water dogs in the 18th century. But the breed's illustrious story almost ended with World War I, and in the 1920s it had to be rejuvenated with the use of German pointers, breeds to which it may have contributed in the past. Today it is a very popular hunting

dog in its homeland but still not widely known abroad. Loyal and gentle with people, it is a natural and multi-talented hunter, and may not co-exist peacefully with other small pets.

TRIPLE COAT The waterproof coat consists of a thick, close-fitting, water-repellent undercoat, a longer overcoat, and hard and wiry longer hair particularly on the body.

Chesapeake Bay Retriever

ORIGIN United States
HEIGHT 23–26 in (58–66 cm)
WEIGHT 64–75 lb (29.0–34.0 kg)
EXERCISE LEVEL
COAT CARE
REGISTERED KC, FCI, AKCs
COLORS Gold, red-gold, brown

Webbed toes, a slightly oily, wavy coat, and a tireless, tough personality distinguish this stalwart water dog, known to its fans as the Chessie. It shares many traits with the Curly-coated Retriever.

RED/TAN

GOLD

BREED ORIGINS

Nobody is sure of the exact ancestry of this breed. It can be traced back to Sailor and Canton, male and female pups rescued from a foundering ship in Maryland in 1807, said by the captain to be "a pair of pups of the most approved Newfoundland breed, but of different families." They were noted as excellent water dogs and bred with local retrievers. This is a rural dog, excellent for active families.

CAMOUFLAGE COLORING The coat color should match the dog's working environment as closely as possible, and breed standards describe the desired shades as 'brown, sedge or dead grass."

Clumber Spaniel

ORIGIN United Kingdom
HEIGHT 19–20 in (48–51 cm)
WEIGHT 40–65 lb (18.1–29.5 kg)
EXERCISE LEVEL
COAT CARE
REGISTERED KC, FCI, AKCs
COLORS White with lemon to orange

This is the largest of the spaniels, in terms of bulk, rather than height. Perhaps inevitably, it is slower than some others, but its less boisterous style is coupled with quiet determination, and this is a stoic, steady breed characterized by greater dignity than is typical for spaniels.

BREED ORIGINS

The breed takes its name from Clumber Park, home of the Duke of Newcastle; one tale says that the Duc de Noailles sent his prized spaniels there in the French Revolution, another that it is a British creation from older spaniel breeds.

ADAPTABLE TYPE Used in packs to flush pheasant, this is an excellent country dog but also quiet and calm enough for city life.

Curly-coated Retriever

ORIGIN United Kingdom
HEIGHT 25–27 in (64–69 cm)
WEIGHT 70–80 lb (31.8–36.3 kg)
EXERCISE LEVEL
COAT CARE
REGISTERED KC, FCI, AKCs
COLORS Black, brown

This distinctive English breed, with its all-over tightly curled coat, is both the largest of the retrievers and, together with the Flat-coated Retriever, one of the first to be officially recognized.

BLACK

DARK BROWN

BREED ORIGINS

The precise ancestry of this breed is not recorded, but it is thought to be descended from the now extinct English Water Spaniel or Irish Water Spaniel, crossed with Lesser Newfoundland dogs, the forerunners of the Labrador, which were brought to the United Kingdom by fishermen. Used for hunting waterfowl, it was an established type by the start of the 19th century and was shown in 1860. Once it was a highly popular breed as both working dog and companion, but today it is perhaps the scarcest of all the retrievers.

BREED QUALITIES

As a retriever, this breed is robust and enthusiastic, with great stamina. As a companion it is calm, even serious, but affectionate. It will make an alert guard, but does not like being left alone, and is more a rural than a city breed because plenty of outdoor activity is essential. Eyelid problems, hip dysplasia, and epilepsy do occur.

TAILOR MADE The tiny, tight curls of the coat need brushing a couple of times a week to remove any tangles; wetting the coat after will remove frizziness and return the curly look. The dense, waterproof coat is perfect for a water dog, and this breed is an excellent swimmer.

Dutch Partridge Dog

ORIGIN Netherlands
HEIGHT 22–28 in (56–70 cm)
WEIGHT 45–50 lb (20.4–22.7 kg)
EXERCISE LEVEL
COAT CARE
REGISTERED FCI
COLORS White with brown

Also known as the Drentse or Drentsche Patrijshond, and more familiarly called the Drent, this rare breed represents a historical type part way between the spaniel and the pointer. A typical versatile European hunting dog, it is used to both point and retrieve all kinds of small, furred game.

BREED ORIGINS

This breed is thought to spring from 16th-century Spioenen or Spanjoelen—Spanish dogs arriving via France—and to be related to the Small Munsterlander and the Epagneul Français. In the sparsely populated province of Drenthe, these dogs were popular and kept purebred. When working, the breed can be a relentless hunter, but at home it is more relaxed, and makes a good companion for active families, even adapting to city life.

TAIL SIGNALS Longer hair furnishes the neck, chest, ears, legs, and especially the tail. A characteristic of the breed is that when working, the tail swings in a circle, especially when a scent is found.

English Cocker Spaniel

ORIGIN United Kingdom
HEIGHT 15–17 in (38–43 cm)
WEIGHT 26–34 lb (11.8–15.4 kg)
EXERCISE LEVEL
COAT CARE
REGISTERED KC, FCI, AKCs
COLORS Black, cream, red, brown, solid or with white, tan points

In the United Kingdom, this breed is simply the Cocker Spaniel, but elsewhere its nationality is added to distinguish it from the American Cocker Spaniel. Side by side, nobody could mistake the two today.

 BLACK
 RED/TAN
 GOLD
 GOLD AND WHITE
 BLACK AND WHITE

BREED ORIGINS

Spaniels were used to flush game into nets as early as the 16th century. Cockers, specializing in woodcock, were described in the 19th century. These dogs are now the second most popular breed in their homeland, and show and working lines have diverged. Working dogs are smaller, with shorter coats, and boundless energy, while show dogs need more coat care but less mental and physical stimulation.

COLOR AND TEMPERAMENT A rare condition called "avalanche of rage" syndrome can affect solid-colored, but not bicolored, dogs.

English Pointer

ORIGIN United Kingdom

HEIGHT 21–24 in (53–61 cm)

WEIGHT 44–66 lb (20.0–29.9 kg)

EXERCISE LEVEL

COAT CARE

REGISTERED KC, FCI, AKCs

COLORS White and black, liver, lemon, or orange

Many registries officially list this aristocratic-looking dog simply as the Pointer, but given the number of pointing breeds in the world, it is widely given its national identity for the sake of clarity.

GOLD AND WHITE

BLACK AND WHITE

TAN AND WHITE

BREED ORIGINS

At first, pointers were worked with sighthounds that would pursue the game once found; as guns became more popular they worked in tandem with retrievers. It is thought that Greyhounds, Bloodhounds, setters, foxhounds, and even bulldog breeds contributed to their development. Pointers are recorded in England as far back as 1650, but continental breeds such as the Spanish Pointer were involved in their creation. By the 18th century these were perhaps the most popular hunting dog, and became popular in the United States by the 1900s.

A fast and reliable scenter that can quickly cover a wide area, the Pointer is especially adept at finding feathered game, and is used for hunting and in competitive trials, in which they excel. As companions, they are serious and sensitive but also biddable and gentle.

FINELY HONED Pointers need to have a balance of strength, stamina, and speed to work swiftly over long distances for a long day's hunting, Breeding for these requirements has produced a strong but graceful build of athletic curves.

English Setter

ORIGIN United Kingdom
HEIGHT 24–25 in (61–64 cm)
WEIGHT 40–70 lb (18.1–31.8 kg)
EXERCISE LEVEL
COAT CARE
REGISTERED KC, FCI, AKCs
COLORS White and black, orange, lemon, or liver, tricolor

This elegant breed combines old-fashioned looks with old-fashioned manners. It is a proficient tracker, setter, and retriever of birds, but just as happy as an active family dog, and a peaceful companion.

GOLD AND WHITE

BLACK AND WHITE

TAN AND WHITE

BREED ORIGINS

The first setters were developed in France from Spanish and French spaniels, and were in England by the 16th century, but the modern breed was developed by Sir Edward Laverack in the 19th century. It is now split into the show lines and the often lighter-built working or field lines, which include the strain known as Llewellin Setters.

BREED LOOKS Like all the British setter breeds, the English has a feathery coat that comes in its own distinctive pattern, an all-over fleck that is known as "belton" by breeders.

English Springer Spaniel

ORIGIN United Kingdom
HEIGHT 19–20 in (48–51 cm)
WEIGHT 49–55 lb (22.2–24.9 kg)
EXERCISE LEVEL
COAT CARE
REGISTERED KC, FCI, AKCs
COLORS Liver and white, black and white, tricolor

One of the oldest surviving spaniel breeds, this is still a popular working dog and household companion in the United Kingdom, and also among the top breeds registered in showing circles.

BLACK AND WHITE

BLACK AND TAN

BREED ORIGINS

Dogs of this type can be seen in paintings from the 17th century, but were then simply spaniels, not springers, used on furred game, and cockers, used for birds. In fact, this breed has been shown by American hunters to be a proficient bird dog. It is strongly split into working and show lines, but show lines still need exercise and stimulation, or, for all their gentleness, they may become destructive.

SHOW AND FIELD This is a show type dog, with pendulous ears and lips, and a long coat that is mainly colored. Field types are lighter and more wiry with a fairly short, feathery coat, predominantly white for visibility.

Field Spaniel

ORIGIN United Kingdom
HEIGHT 18 in (46 cm)
WEIGHT 35–50 lb (15.9–22.7 kg)
EXERCISE LEVEL
COAT CARE
REGISTERED KC, FCI, AKCs
COLORS Black, liver, roan; solid or with tan or small white markings

BLACK   DARK BROWN

Several hunting breeds have split into working and show lines, but for this breed the change was more dramatic. Show breeding led to its effective demise as a working dog, and almost made it extinct.

BREED ORIGINS
The Field Spaniel was originally part of the Cocker Spaniel, but was separately recognized at the end of the 19th century. An instant success in the show ring, it was then bred for a long back and short legs, using Sussex Spaniels and even Bassets. The result was a dog that could no longer work effectively and an explosion of health problems, and by the end of World War II the breed had all but disappeared. Carefully rejuvenated with a healthier conformation through crosses to Cocker and Springer Spaniels, it remains rare but is found as an affectionate and active family companion.

SHOW LOOKS The Field Spaniel was developed when dog showing was becoming fashionable. Most working spaniels were a mix of white and a color, and a "classier" solid coat was the goal.

Flat-coated Retriever

ORIGIN United Kingdom
HEIGHT 22–23 in (56–58 cm)
WEIGHT 55–79 lb (25.0–36.0 kg)
EXERCISE LEVEL
COAT CARE
REGISTERED KC, FCI, AKCs
COLORS Black, liver

BLACK   DARK BROWN

Together with the Curly-coated Retriever, these glossy black dogs were the first retrievers with show recognition in their homeland. They are making a comeback as outgoing companions.

BREED ORIGINS
Developed in the mid-19th century for flushing and retrieving, this breed is descended from crosses of the now extinct Lesser Newfoundland or St. John's Water Dog and setters. It was popular as a gamekeeper's dog, and spread abroad, but was almost extinct after World War II. Since 2000, Scandinavian Flat-coats have won the UK Gundog Group twice, encouraging a rise in breed numbers.

HANDSOME COMPANIONS Although it is no longer found in great numbers in field trials, or as a working dog, the breed has modest popularity in a new role as a lively but good-natured family dog.

ENGLISH SPRINGER SPANIEL (*see* p. 238) Although their name comes from their role of "springing" furred game from cover, these dogs live up to it in other ways. Whether bred for work or companionship, gundogs are a joy to exercise.

French Gascony Pointer

ORIGIN France

HEIGHT 23–27 in (58–68 cm)

WEIGHT 44–70 lb (20.0–32.0 kg)

EXERCISE LEVEL

COAT CARE

REGISTERED FCI

COLORS Chestnut; solid or with white or tan

Originating in southwestern France, this breed is still largely unknown beyond its homeland, where it is very methodically named the Braque Français, type Gascogne. It is one of the oldest pointer breeds still surviving today.

BREED ORIGINS

Setters were recorded from the Middle Ages, when the Chien d'Oysel was used on partridge caught with nets, and this pointer is an early descendant. After the French Revolution, British breeds became popular in northern France, but older types survived in the south. Almost extinct at the start of the 20th century, the Gascony was revived by Dr. C. Castets, first president of Le Club du Braque Français de France.

Today, modest numbers are found as working dogs and household companions. It is intelligent, loyal, and easy to train, but its sensitive nature needs encouragement.

EARLY BREED STANDARD In the 17th century, Selincourt described pointers as tall dogs, "strongly built, large-headed with long ears, square muzzle, large nose, hanging lips and a brown and white coat."

French Pyrenean Pointer

ORIGIN France

HEIGHT 19–23 in (47–58 cm)

WEIGHT 40–53 lb (18.0–24.0 kg)

EXERCISE LEVEL

COAT CARE

REGISTERED FCI

COLORS Chestnut; solid or with white or tan

Known in its homeland as the Braque Français, type Pyrénées, this is the most popular of the braques, and the only one to reach North America. It is popular with hunters, but not known in many show registers.

BREED ORIGINS

This breed's history is essentially that of the French Gascony Pointer; a smaller type was known in the Pyrénées, suited to the mountainous terrain. When the southwestern braques were revived, M. B. Sénac-Lagrange, second president of the breed club, favored this type. It has the same gentle temperament as the Gascony, making an affectionate family companion that responds superbly to "soft" training.

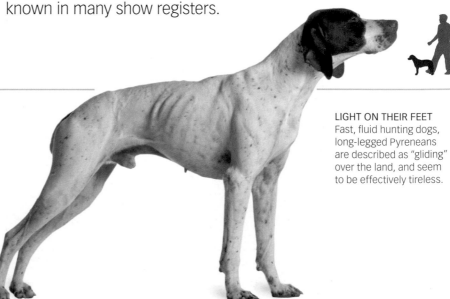

LIGHT ON THEIR FEET Fast, fluid hunting dogs, long-legged Pyreneans are described as "gliding" over the land, and seem to be effectively tireless.

French Spaniel

ORIGIN France

HEIGHT 22–24 in (55–61 cm)

WEIGHT 44–55 lb (20.0–25.0 kg)

EXERCISE LEVEL

COAT CARE

REGISTERED FCI, AKCs

COLORS White and brown, from cinnamon to dark liver

This breed is known as the Epagneul Français in its homeland, where it is also patriotically claimed by its admirers to be the origin of all the diverse varieties of hunting spaniels.

FRENCH COAT The coat is generally flat and silky, softened by longer feathering on the ears, legs, and tail, usually seen with medium brown spotting.

As with other French breeds, it lost out in favor of British breeds in the 19th century and was on the verge of extinction, but it was rescued by a priest, Father Fournier. The breed remained almost unknown outside France until the 1970s, when it was introduced to Canada, where it has become a popular bird dog with hunters.

BREED QUALITIES

Rustic in looks, this is an ideal country dog that will encourage long walks, but it is calm indoors and rarely barks, so can adapt to city life too. It is gentle and obedient, and like most of the French gundogs has a sensitive temperament that craves affection and needs soft words to give its best.

BREED ORIGINS

Despite its name, this old breed, which dates back to the 17th century, is more of a pointer or setter than a spaniel. Early dogs of this type would set or point very low, so a hunter behind them could throw a net over them onto the game ahead. As hunting methods changed, the higher pointing style was developed, and this breed is still a fine pointer and retriever. It is also good for flushing game in water and over wild, rugged terrain, although it is not the fastest of spaniels.

SIMILAR FEATURES This breed is thought to be related to the Small Munsterlander and the Dutch Partridge Dog. While conventional thought has it that this type of dog spread from Spain to France and beyond, some believe that it is fundamentally Danish.

German Shorthaired Pointer

ORIGIN Germany

HEIGHT 23–25 in (59–64 cm)

WEIGHT 55–70 lb (24.9–31.8 kg)

EXERCISE LEVEL

COAT CARE 🪥

REGISTERED KC, FCI, AKCs

COLORS Black, brown; solid or with white in variable mixes of specks and patches

Known as the Deutsch Kurzhaar in its homeland and a GSP to hunters, this is a versatile and tireless hunting dog. It will retrieve as well as point, and works in all kinds of terrain.

BLACK

DARK BROWN

BLACK AND WHITE

TAN AND WHITE

BREED ORIGINS

The ancestry of the German Shorthaired Pointer goes back to pointers that came to Germany from Spain and France. Once sophisticated shotguns were in use, bringing down distant birds in flight, these specialized dogs needed to expand their repertoire to include retrieving. Intensely focused breeding activity in Germany in the late 19th century saw British and French breeds mixed with the national stock to create a versatile hunting

BREED LOOKS The coat may be patched, flecked, or both. Conformation and constitution are more important: A dog must be able to carry out any and all hunting activities.

SOFT MOUTH Because this breed retrieves as well as points, the muzzle must be long, broad, deep, and strong so that the dog can carry game gently without damaging it.

dog. The result of this was the range of German Pointers, of which the Shorthaired is the most successful. They are popular hunting dogs, with the intelligence to work independently.

BREED QUALITIES

Like most gundog breeds, these are loyal and affectionate dogs, gentle to handle and devoted to their family; they have always been household as well as hunting dogs. But they are powerful, with limitless energy, and need as much exercise as they can get. Neglected GSPs can be destructive or hyperactive, and they may become ardent escape artists.

German Spaniel

ORIGIN Germany
HEIGHT 16–20 in (41–51 cm)
WEIGHT 44–66 lb (20.0–29.9 kg)
EXERCISE LEVEL
COAT CARE
REGISTERED FCI
COLORS Brown or red; solid or with white

This is also called the Deutscher Wachtelhund or German Quail Dog. It is a remarkably versatile dog, performing all activities from tracking to retrieving anywhere from high moors to marshes.

BREED ORIGINS
This breed was developed in Bavaria in the 19th century to create a Stöberhund, literally a rummaging dog, capable of finding and tracking air and ground scents, and flushing, driving, and retrieving varied game. A superlative hunting dog, the breed is treated as a house dog by its owner, not kennelled outdoors, and makes an obedient and intelligent companion.

NOT FOR SALE In Germany this dog is still bred "exclusively by hunters for hunters," solely with regard to its tested hunting abilities.

German Wirehaired Pointer

ORIGIN Germany
HEIGHT 24–26 in (61–66 cm)
WEIGHT 60–70 lb (27.2–31.8 kg)
EXERCISE LEVEL
COAT CARE
REGISTERED KC, FCI, AKCs
COLORS Brown, brown or black roan with or without patches, light roan

The start of the German standard for the Deutsch Drahthaar says it "must be usable for all the work in the field, in the woods and in water before and after the shot." This is no showhall breed.

DARK BROWN   BLACK AND WHITE   TAN AND WHITE

BREED ORIGINS
This breed dates back to the 19th century and is derived in part from the German Shorthaired Pointer. The Griffon Korthals from Hessen, and the Pudelpointer were also involved in a systematic effort to create an assertive, efficient, and versatile wirehaired gundog that could withstand all weathers. The resulting breed has risen to the top of the popularity stakes for gundog breeds

in its native land, and is also gaining a following abroad. Away from the working field, they are loyal to their family but can be aloof with strangers. They are highly active, with an inclination to roam alone if not accompanied out.

WEATHERPROOF The wiry coat is quite water repellent making this the most weather resistant of the German pointers. The Longhaired, or Stichelhaar is seen far less than the other two.

Golden Retriever

ORIGIN United Kingdom
HEIGHT 22–24 in (56–61 cm)
WEIGHT 60–75 lb (27.2–34.0 kg)
EXERCISE LEVEL
COAT CARE
REGISTERED KC, FCI, AKCs
COLORS Gold

Having ruled the popularity stakes for years, the gregarious and genial Golden Retriever has begun to decline in numbers. It may be fashion, lifestyles making them harder to accommodate, or simply "too much of a good thing" turning sour.

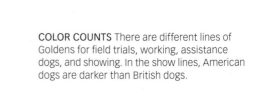

BREED ORIGINS

Developed in Scotland from the 1860s by Sir Dudley Majoribanks, Goldens started with Nous, a yellow puppy from a litter of black retrievers, and Belle, from the now extinct Tweed Water Spaniel breed. The results were first shown in 1906 as "any other color" retrievers, and became a breed within a few years: recognition in North America came in the 1920s and 1930s. As with other highly popular dogs, overbreeding of this friendly, "live-to-please" breed has led to health and temperament problems in some lines.

BIGGER AND BETTER
Improvements in guns in the 19th century meant a powerful retriever was needed to bring back birds downed over long distances, and the Golden fulfilled this role.

COLOR COUNTS There are different lines of Goldens for field trials, working, assistance dogs, and showing. In the show lines, American dogs are darker than British dogs.

Gordon Setter

ORIGIN United Kingdom
HEIGHT 23–27 in (58–69 cm)
WEIGHT 45–80 lb (20.4–36.2 kg)
EXERCISE LEVEL
COAT CARE
REGISTERED KC, FCI, AKCs
COLORS Black and tan

This black-and-tan setter is a tireless runner, bred to cover great tracts of the Scottish Highlands in pursuit of grouse, ptarmigan, and partridge. Less often seen as a working dog than in the past, it makes an ebullient companion.

CHANGING LOOKS
Although black-and-tan setters were known in England and Scotland in the 16th century, this breed was originally a tricolor; white is now limited to small markings.

BREED ORIGINS

Setters find birds that freeze to escape notice, and then similarly freeze: Falcons or a thrown net accomplish the rest. This breed was developed by the Duke of Richmond and Gordon in Scotland in the early 19th century. Better guns and a decline in partridge in the 20th century made retrievers more useful, so this is usually a household companion today. Loyal and obedient, they can be bouncy.

Hungarian Vizsla

ORIGIN Hungary
HEIGHT 22–24 in (56–61 cm)
WEIGHT 49–62 lb (22.2–28.1 kg)
EXERCISE LEVEL
COAT CARE
REGISTERED KC, FCI, AKCs
COLORS Chestnut-gold

This breed is called simply the Visla in the United States, and the Hungarian Short-haired Pointer or Rövidszörü Magyar Vizsla in Europe. It is now popular both at home and abroad.

BREED ORIGINS

Pointers working with falcons were recorded in the 14th-century "Vienna Chronicle" of Hungarian codes and laws. At first called the Yellow Pointer, it became the Hungarian Pointer, and by the 16th century the Vizsla, a name that may come from an old Hungarian word meaning "search." An influx of English and German pointers in the 19th century almost made the breed extinct, as did World War II, but today it is popular at home and abroad, and has given rise to the Hungarian Wirehaired Vizsla.

LOOKS FAMILIAR The Vizsla was used in development of other breeds of similar lines, most notably the German Shorthaired Pointer and the Weimaraner; in turn, these same breeds may have been among the dogs used to re-establish the Vizsla after numbers fell in the 19th century.

Hungarian Wirehaired Vizsla

ORIGIN Hungary
HEIGHT 22–24 in (56–61 cm)
WEIGHT 49–62 lb (22.2–28.1 kg)
EXERCISE LEVEL
COAT CARE
REGISTERED KC, FCI, AKCs
COLORS Gold

Also known in Europe as the Hungarian Wirehaired Pointer or Drotzörü Magyar Vizsla, this breed is less familiar than its shorthaired parent. However, its popularity is spreading in the United Kingdom, North America, and Australia.

BREED ORIGINS

The Hungarian Wirehaired Vizsla was developed in the early 20th century. Wanting a dog with a thicker coat and heavier frame, suitable for working in less favourable weather, breeders crossed the Vizsla with the German Wirehaired Pointer. Although it is not reliably recorded, it may be that griffon breeds, the Pudelpointer, and even the Red Setter were also used in the early stages. In all respects but the coat, the two Vizsla breeds are alike, sharing not only their looks but their deeply affectionate, gentle character and lively enthusiasm for games; they have always been part of the family.

WIREHAIRED AND SHORTHAIRED The Wirehaired is now regarded as a completely separate breed from its more commonly seen smooth-coated cousin.

GAINING GROUND The Wirehaired lacks an undercoat, so it is not a breed that can live outdoors. A medium-paced pointer that also retrieves well, this versatile breed is likely to spread as a hunting dog as much as a companion.

Irish Red-and-White Setter

ORIGIN Ireland

HEIGHT 24–27 in (61–69 cm)

WEIGHT 60–70 lb (27.2–31.8 kg)

EXERCISE LEVEL

COAT CARE

REGISTERED KC, FCI, AKCs

COLORS Tan and white

This breed is the original Irish hunting setter from which the Irish Red Setter was derived. It was eclipsed by its offspring, but over the years this athletic, impulsive breed has been regaining a popularity little by little, both at home and abroad.

BREED ORIGINS

Before the mid-19th century, almost all the hunting setters in Ireland were red and white. With the advent of shows, as opposed to field trials, solid-colored coats were seen as glamorous and desirable. This trend can be seen in other working breeds, from the Field Spaniel to the balance of color in the coat of the English Springer. The red-and-white dogs almost became extinct, but were rescued by a clergyman, Noble Huston, in County Down.

LIVE WIRE The Red-and-White is still a versatile gundog that will retrieve as well as set. Some individuals are impulsive and highly strung, others more reflective, but all are affectionate and intelligent, with exuberance and energy.

Irish Setter

ORIGIN Ireland
HEIGHT 25–27 in (64–69 cm)
WEIGHT 60–70 lb (27.2–31.8 kg)
EXERCISE LEVEL
COAT CARE
REGISTERED KC, FCI, AKCs
COLORS Red-tan

In Irish, it is Modder rhu or Madra rua, the red dog, and although it is the most recent of the nine dog breeds native to the country, it is perhaps the best known.

BREED ORIGINS

This breed is sometimes called the Irish Red Setter, in deference to its Red-and-White antecedent. The solid coat existed by the 18th century, but only became fashionable in the 19th century. In the United States there are large Irish Setters, found in show halls, and smaller Red Setters, bred to be true to the working origins. Harder to train than other gundogs, it makes a good-natured, spirited companion.

GOOD LOOKS A silky, flowing coat has made this redhead a perenially popular companion.

Irish Water Spaniel

ORIGIN Ireland
HEIGHT 21–24 in (53–61 cm)
WEIGHT 45–65 lb (20.4–29.5 kg)
EXERCISE LEVEL
COAT CARE
REGISTERED KC, FCI, AKCs
COLORS Dark brown

Quite unlike any other Spaniel in looks, this is the sole survivor of three water spaniel breeds once known in Ireland. It is a dynamic water dog that dives unhesitatingly into freezing water, and has a reputation as a clown.

BREED ORIGINS

This breed's ancestry is a mystery, but input from the Poodle, Barbet, and Portuguese Water Dog are suggested. It was created by Dublin breeder Justin McCarthy in the 1830s, and he left no records. Variously classed as a retriever or spaniel, this adaptable working dog makes an ideal companion for those who love long walks, but is too energetic for many, despite its gentle, loyal nature.

TRUE WATER DOG Described by those who know and love it best as "a bundle of rags in a cyclone," this breed's superb swimming abilities and use in marshes have earned it the nickname "Bogdog." The founding father of the breed even bore the nautical name Boatswain or Bo'sun.

Italian Pointer

ORIGIN Italy

HEIGHT 22–26 in (56–66 cm)

WEIGHT 55–88 lb (24.9–39.9 kg)

EXERCISE LEVEL

COAT CARE

REGISTERED FCI

COLORS White, white speckled or patched with orange or chestnut

This versatile breed is popular in its homeland but relatively rare abroad. It is recognized in most registries by its native name, Bracco Italiano, linguistically close to the "braque" pointing breeds of France.

GOLD AND WHITE

TAN AND WHITE

BREED ORIGINS

This breed goes back to the Middle Ages and its exact origins are not recorded. Like the Segugio, it is thought to be a blend of coursing hound and Asian mastiff, although some point to the ancient Bloodhound, the St. Hubert Hound. Fashionable during the Italian Renaissance, it was bred by the Medicis, among others, for hunting birds with nets. Its popularity subsequently declined; it was almost extinct by the turn of the 20th century, and was revived by breeder Ferdinando Delor de Ferrabouc. It has spread abroad more recently and very slowly: It

has been recognized in the United Kingdom for 20 years, but there are still very few registered each year, and although it has some loyal fans in North America it is virtually unknown there.

BREED QUALITIES

On the move, the Bracco has a distinctive extended trot, with head held high, and a tendency to disappear on a scent. In character they are affectionate, gentle, and loyal dogs, although they can be stubborn. They are active dogs that need plenty of time, and are perhaps too boisterous for confined spaces or small children.

TWO TYPES This breed has historically had two regional types; and although there is only one breed standard, the variations can still be seen today. The Piedmontese dogs were lighter in both color and build, while the Lombard Pointer was darker-coated and heavier set.

Kooikerhondje

ORIGIN Netherlands
HEIGHT 14–16 in (35–41 cm)
WEIGHT 20–24 lb (9.0–11.0 kg)
EXERCISE LEVEL
COAT CARE
REGISTERED KC, FCI, AKCs
COLORS Tan and white; black shading on ears

You may find this dog described as the Small Dutch Waterfowl Dog, Kooiker Dog, or Dutch Decoy Spaniel, but unless you live in its homeland you will be lucky to find one in the flesh at all.

BREED ORIGINS

This breed has existed since at least the 17th century, when it can be found in the paintings of Rembrandt. It was bred for a role similar to that of the extinct English Red Decoy Dog or the Nova Scotia Duck-tolling Retriever: to play busily but silently and lure ducks toward hunters. In this breed's case, it had to lure them not just within the range of guns, but into a tunnel of nets over a *kooi* or canal, the end of which was then sealed behind the hapless birds. Rescued from extinction by Baroness van Hardenbroek van Ammerstol after World War II, it is growing in popularity, although low numbers mean it is subject to inherited health problems.

WHITE FLAG The breed's appearance is tailored to its role, with a white tail preferred. The high visibility of this "flag" acts as a powerful decoy. Some individuals are still employed to lure birds today, but now for ringing and study.

READY TO ROMP As might be expected from its background, the Kooikerhondje is an active, agile, and playful breed with a love of water. They are good-tempered, especially with their family, but may be aloof or noisy with strangers.

Labrador Retriever

ORIGIN United Kingdom
HEIGHT 22–24 in (51–61 cm)
WEIGHT 55–75 lb (24.9–34.0 kg)
EXERCISE LEVEL
COAT CARE
REGISTERED KC, FCI, AKCs
COLORS Golden, chocolate, black

Anyone in search of a genial companion or family dog is likely to be advised "if in doubt, get a Lab," and it seems most do. This is undoubtedly the most popular breed in the English-speaking world.

BLACK

GOLD

DARK BROWN

BREED ORIGINS

The ancestor of this breed was the St. John's Dog, a precursor of the Newfoundland. Brought to the United Kingdom by fishermen, it was the start of the Curly-coated, Flat-coated, and Labrador Retrievers, its proven ability in pulling nets ashore by their floats now applied to safely retrieving game. Labradors were named by the early 19th century and became common by the end of the century, appearing in the United States early in the 20th century.

BREED QUALITIES

The trainable, obedient nature of this breed has made it the world's favorite assistance dog, and individuals have learned to do everything from negotiating traffic to putting their owner's cash cards into machines for them. They make wonderfully happy, exuberant family dogs, but have boundless energy and a boundless appetite.

COLOR TRENDS Brown and yellow pups occurred from the start and were eventually recognized. The yellows have become ever paler, until almost all are pale cream today, although shades down to "red fox" are allowed.

ORIGINAL COLOR Labs were at first strongly preferred in black, as shown by the first painting of one, *Cora, a Labrador Bitch* by Edwin Landseer.

IT'S NOT WORK As in many other gundog breeds, there are distinct show lines and separate, usually more rangy, working dogs. Labs from working lines have even higher energy levels. Even a show Lab will retrieve anything with gusto.

Large Munsterlander

ORIGIN Germany
HEIGHT 23–26 in (58–65 cm)
WEIGHT 64–68 lb (29.0–31.0 kg)
EXERCISE LEVEL
COAT CARE
REGISTERED KC, FCI, AKCs
COLORS Black and white

At home this is the Grosser Münsterländer, but it loses its accent abroad, and this spaniel-type German pointer has been quite a successful export. Although it is seen in modest numbers in show halls, it is appreciated as a versatile breed by hunters.

BREED ORIGINS

Ultimately these dogs are descended from medieval white or bicolored bird dogs, but the modern breed dates back to the 19th century breeding that produced the German Shorthaired, Wirehaired, and Longhaired Pointers. The last type of these is very rarely seen, but is the parent of this dog. Unwanted black-and-white puppies turned up in Longhaired Pointer litters, and in the 1920s they became a separate breed in Münster, named to distinguish them from the Small Munsterlander.

BREED QUALITIES

Field trials show this breed to be slow-maturing but worth the wait, since it works close to the hunter and is very responsive to training. It has always lived in the home, and is a calm, gentle character, reliable with children and other dogs.

BREED LOOKS The long, dense coat of this breed allows it to move through dense cover without problems, and also provides good insulation. The head should be solid black, but the rest of the coat is flecked and patched.

Nova Scotia Duck-tolling Retriever

ORIGIN Canada
HEIGHT 17–21 in (43–53 cm)
WEIGHT 37–51 lb (16.8–23.1 kg)
EXERCISE LEVEL
COAT CARE
REGISTERED FCI, AKCs
COLORS Red shades; solid or with white markings

This dog's unusual name comes from its unusual hunting role of attracting or "tolling" birds; it is also known as the Yarmouth Toller and Little River Duck Dog, pinning down the location of its origin.

RED/TAN   TAN AND WHITE

BREED ORIGINS

Tollers belong to a category of dogs bred to romp and play silently between a concealed hunter and a body of water. When curious ducks are attracted by the activity, the hunter calls back the dog and takes aim, and then sends the dog out to retrieve. Such "decoy dogs" were taken to Nova Scotia by British settlers, and gave rise to this breed. The breed is quiet and obedient, but highly playful and a superb companion for games in parks or fields.

WORKING FEATURES A moderate and athletic build is required for these dogs, covered with a water-repellant, medium length double coat with a soft dense undercoat, to allow them to retrieve from icy water.

Old Danish Pointer

ORIGIN Denmark
HEIGHT 20–23 in (51–58 cm)
WEIGHT 40–53 lb (18.1–24.0 kg)
EXERCISE LEVEL
COAT CARE
REGISTERED FCI
COLORS White and brown

In Danish this is the Gammel Dansk Hønsehund, which translates to its other names, the Old Danish Chicken Dog or Old Danish Bird Dog. Popular in its homeland, it is almost unknown abroad.

BREED ORIGINS

This breed is descended from crosses of Danish hounds with pointing dogs from southern Europe imported in the 17th century. In northern Denmark in the early 18th century, a man named Morten Bak crossed gypsy dogs, probably descended from the pointers, and local farm dogs derived from scenthounds to produce this breed. The result is a tenacious tracker, pointer, and retriever, which is also a gentle, loyal, and affectionate companion. As with most breeds created for a task, owners should be prepared for plenty of walking and stick-throwing in wide, open spaces.

TOUGH SURVIVOR This breed is hardy, despite its short, close coat, and a versatile worker over all terrains and in water. Almost extinct after World War II, it is now one of Denmark's most popular breeds.

Perdiguero de Burgos

ORIGIN Spain
HEIGHT 26–30 in (66–76 cm)
WEIGHT 55–66 lb (24.9–29.9 kg)
EXERCISE LEVEL
COAT CARE
REGISTERED FCI
COLORS Liver and white

Also called the Burgos Pointing Dog or Spanish Pointer, this breed is a preserved moment in gundog history: the transformation of scenthounds into pointers and setters.

BREED ORIGINS

Spanish Pointers influenced all other European pointers, and this is a last representative of those dogs. The Burgos is thought to be a blend of the larger Perdiguero de Navarro and the Spanish Hound. In northern Spain, it survived for centuries in low numbers but is now increasing in popularity. Mostly used to point and retrieve birds and hares today, for much of its history it was used on large game such as deer. It is gentle, intelligent, and obedient if trained.

LOOKS DECEIVE Spanish Hound heritage gave this breed an excellent nose and loose skin. It is lighter than it looks, nimble on challenging terrain.

Perdigueiro Português

ORIGIN Portugal
HEIGHT 20–22 in (51–56 cm)
WEIGHT 35–60 lb (15.9–27.2 kg)
EXERCISE LEVEL
COAT CARE
REGISTERED FCI
COLORS Yellow or brown; solid or with white

In English, this dog is usually called the Portuguese Pointer, although "Perdigueiro" translates as "quail dog." It is better known in North America than its Spanish counterpart, the Perdiguero de Burgos.

RED/TAN   GOLD   TAN AND WHITE

BREED ORIGINS

The origins of this breed are uncertain due to its antiquity, but it is thought to be derived from the Perdigueiro types of Spain, and to be an ancestor of the English Pointer. Known since the 13th century as a tracker and pointer, it was first used with falcons or nets, later with guns, and also retrieves. It is still popular in Portugal as a tenacious and cunning hunter, and although gentle enough for family life has high energy levels that make it happiest as a working dog or a companion for a highly active owner.

PRACTICAL COAT The coat is dense and fairly hard in texture to provide protection. It is shorter and softer on the face and ears, where it has a velvety texture.

Saint-Germain Pointer

ORIGIN France
HEIGHT 21–24 in (54–62 cm)
WEIGHT 40–57 lb (18.0–26.0 kg)
EXERCISE LEVEL
COAT CARE
REGISTERED KC, FCI, AKCs
COLORS White with tan

This is known as the Braque Saint Germain in France, which is where almost all are to be found. A rare dog even in its homeland, with fewer than 100 born each year, this royal creation is virtually unknown abroad.

HUNTING QUALITIES The Saint-Germain is said to be more predictable than the English Pointer but faster than other French braques, with a good gallop and range. It is used mainly to hunt pheasant and rabbit, and retrieves well.

BREED ORIGINS

Orange-and-white hunting dogs existed in France for centuries; surviving examples are the French Gascony and French Pyrenean Pointer. Further north, they fell from favor during the French Revolution. In the 1820s, local white-and-orange braques were crossed with English Pointers, a gift from King George IV, in the royal kennels. As political unrest flared, they were sent to Compiègne, and then to Saint Germain, where the breed took its name. Two World Wars almost wiped it out; today it is maintained by a small group of enthusiasts.

BREED QUALITIES

In personality, this is a gentle, loyal, and affectionate breed. Hunting, it is swift and keen in fields, woods, and marshes, but not coldhardy. Recent years have seen a rise in numbers, a renewed focus on working, and an acknowledgment that new blood from other pointers is needed.

FRENCH LOOKS
This breed resembles a leggier English Pointer in build, but the orange-and-white coloring is pure French style. Some mottling of the two colors is tolerated.

Small Munsterlander

ORIGIN Germany

HEIGHT 20–22 in (50–56 cm)

WEIGHT 31–35 lb (14.0–16.0 kg)

EXERCISE LEVEL

COAT CARE

REGISTERED KC, FCI, AKCs

COLORS Brown and white

Although both come from the province of Münster, where this is called the Kleiner Münsterländer, this breed is not directly related to the Large Munsterlander. The two spring from different origins and differ in color and size—although in North America this "small!" breed is becoming quite large.

BREED ORIGINS

The exact origins of the Small Munsterlander are unclear. Relaxed hunting laws and many new hunters in the 19th century brought an explosion in German breeding of pointers and retrievers. Adaptable hunting dogs called Wachtelhunds or German

Spaniels were recorded in Münster; the breeders involved in turning these dogs into a breed included heath poet Hermann Löns, the Baron of Bevervörde-Lohburg, and a teacher named Heitmann. Still primarily a hunting companion, these make lively, affectionate pets for active households.

OLD-FASHIONED LOOKS Bred since the 1920s to a standard written by Friedrich Jungklaus, this dog has traits that were once common in all European hunting dogs.

IN DEMAND This breed is rare beyond Germany. Only a handful of dogs have been registered so far in the United Kingdom, while in the United States, hunters snap up available dogs quickly.

Stabyhoun

ORIGIN Netherlands
HEIGHT 19–22 in (48–55 cm)
WEIGHT 42–55 lb (19.0–25.0 kg)
EXERCISE LEVEL
COAT CARE
REGISTERED KC, FCI, AKCs
COLORS Black, brown, or orange, with white

Also called the Frisian Pointing Dog or sometimes Beike, this breed's native name describes its behavior. The first part means "stay by," while the second part, pronounced "hoon," means dog.

GOLD AND WHITE

BREED ORIGINS

Regarded as a piece of national heritage, this dog has been known since at least 1800 and is probably descended from 16th-century Spanish spaniels. The hunting dog of farmers, it is an adaptable, obedient breed that tracks, points, and retrieves; today it is seen hunting or in canine sports, and also makes a good pet for active families. It is very rare outside the Netherlands.

HEALTH FIRST This is a healthy and robust breed with a natural build; the typically feathered tail is not traditionally docked. Despite relatively low numbers, breeders enforce strict rules to avoid inbreeding, and have controlled an inherited epilepsy.

Sussex Spaniel

ORIGIN United Kingdom
HEIGHT 15–16 in (38–41 cm)
WEIGHT 40–50 lb (18.0–22.5 kg)
EXERCISE LEVEL
COAT CARE
REGISTERED KC, FCI, AKCs
COLORS Golden-shaded liver

Although it is a spaniel, this breed has some distinctly hound-like traits, from its slightly sad-looking face to its tendency to give tongue when following a scent. Designed for a narrow role in hunting, today it is very rare.

BREED ORIGINS

This breed was created at the end of the 19th century by a Mr. Fuller in East Sussex, United Kingdom, who wanted a dog to work in dense undergrowth; for this it needed to be small, and to call while working as it would largely be hidden from sight. Calling was not a desirable trait in existing spaniel breeds, so Fuller used a range of dogs to produce his new breed. The breed was never highly popular, and by the end of World War II was virtually extinct in the United Kingdom. Today it is more often to be seen in the United States, and it makes a solid, affectionate companion, less playful than other spaniels.

LOW AND SLOW The short stature of the Sussex gives it a rolling movement, and it is a tenacious rather than brisk breed. American dogs are smaller than those bred to the British standard.

Weimaraner

ORIGIN Germany
HEIGHT 23–28 in (58–71 cm)
WEIGHT 70–85 lb (31.8–38.6 kg)
EXERCISE LEVEL
COAT CARE
REGISTERED KC, FCI, AKCs
COLORS Gray

The word "Vorstehhund," meaning pointer, is now usually dropped from this breed's name, and it is much more of an all-purpose dog, also competent in tracking and retrieving. They are sometimes nicknamed Gray Ghosts.

BREED ORIGINS

Some claim the Weimaraner is an ancient breed, discernable in a 17th-century painting by Van Dyck, but at this time it was still more a leash-hound, used to track and bring down large game. Its history only becomes certain at the start of the 19th century, when it was popular in the Weimar court of Karl August, Grand Duke of Saxe-Weimar-Eisenach, an enthusiastic huntsman. By this time hunting of boar and stags was in decline, and a pointer for use against small game was much more useful. The older hound was crossed with Hühnerhund or bird-dog types to create the oldest of the German pointing breeds.

BREED QUALITIES

The Weimaraner is popular as a companion in many countries; overbreeding has led to temperament problems such as aggression and anxiety separation in some lines. The best Weimaraners are active, intelligent, cheerful companions, but they can be reserved with strangers.

BREED LOOKS Besides the more common shorthair, there is a longhair with a smooth or slightly wavy coat.

SPLIT PERSONALITY The Gray Ghost nickname comes not only from the breed's color but its silent, stealthy action when working. In contrast, the off-duty Weimaraner is full of bounce and enthusiasm.

Welsh Springer Spaniel

ORIGIN United Kingdom
HEIGHT 18–19 in (46–48 cm)
WEIGHT 35–40 lb (15.9–18.1 kg)
EXERCISE LEVEL
COAT CARE
REGISTERED KC, FCI, AKCs
COLORS Tan and white

This energetic spaniel lags far behind the English Springer Spaniel in popularity, but still has devoted followers who keep it both as a hunting dog and simply as an active, enthusiastic companion.

BREED ORIGINS

The Welsh Springer was recognized on both sides of the Atlantic at the turn of the 20th century. Before this it was classed together with the English Springer, but the two breeds are quite distinct. The Welsh is lighter, and both its conformation and its coat have led some to point to the Brittany Spaniel as a close relation. The Welsh also has a greater love of water than the English. Unlike many other hunting breeds, it has not split into working and show lines: The same dogs are used fairly equally as either. Although they can be aloof with strangers, Welsh Springers are affectionate and energetic with their families.

HISTORIC TYPE Historical evidence shows that this type of red-and-white dog was certainly known in Wales in the 18th century.

Wirehaired Pointing Griffon

ORIGIN France
HEIGHT 22–24 in (56–61 cm)
WEIGHT 50–60 lb (22.7–27.2 kg)
EXERCISE LEVEL
COAT CARE
REGISTERED FCI, AKCs
COLORS Steel gray with brown (liver) patches, or solid brown (liver)

This is the breed's American name; in Europe, its French name of Griffon d'Arrêt à Poil Dur Korthals is more usually translated as French Wirehaired Korthals Pointing Griffon.

DARK BROWN

BREED ORIGINS

This breed was created in the late 19th century by Edward K. Korthals, a Dutchman breeding in Germany; his dogs contributed to the German Shorthaired Pointer. He also worked as an agent for the Duke of Penthièvre in France, where this breed was adopted. Imported into the United States in the early 20th century, it was not as popular as faster dogs in the open landscape, but ever more restricted hunting space has made the lively but more biddable and reliable European dogs bred for such conditions more popular.

RUGGED BREED This intelligent and affectionate dog is quiet in the home, but needs plenty of exercise. The wiry coat requires minimal grooming.

WEIMARANER (*see* p. 262) This distinctive dog has made an impact on the hunting field and in the home; their soulful expressions have even brought them success as comedy characters in commercial art and on children's television.

HERDING DOGS

One of the characteristics of herding dogs is their hardy nature. While they may not display the obvious athleticism associated with hounds as a group, these dogs are nevertheless equipped with considerable stamina as well as natural intelligence. Although they will work under the general control of a handler, they need to be able to anticipate the movements of the sheep or other livestock that they are herding, and react accordingly. By far the best-known member of this group is the German Shepherd Dog, which also used to be called the Alsatian. It has since become popular not just as a pet and in the show ring, but also for a wide variety of tasks, ranging from police and military service to aiding the visually impaired. However, a number of herding breeds are still kept primarily for working purposes and are rarely seen in the show ring or, indeed, anywhere outside of their native lands.

BELGIAN SHEPHERD DOG (*see* pp. 272–73) The Tervuren is one of a group of four Belgian Shepherd Dogs that are distinguishable by their coat type, coloration, and length.

Anatolian Shepherd

ORIGIN Turkey
HEIGHT 28–32 in (70–80 cm)
WEIGHT 90–141 lb (41.0–64.0 kg)
EXERCISE LEVEL
COAT CARE
REGISTERED KC, FCI, AKCs
COLORS Any color

This dog was bred to protect rather than herd flocks. It is a hardy breed, at home living outside through the hot summers and cold winters on the arid heights of the Anatolian Plateau in Turkey.

BLACK

CREAM

BLACK, WHITE, AND TAN

BLACK BRINDLE

BREED ORIGINS

Large herd guardians first arrived in Anatolia some 1,000 years ago with Turkic tribes from further east. Descended from those early arrivals, the Anatolian has some similarity to the Pyrenean Mastiff or Mountain Dog, Tatra Mountain Sheepdog, and particularly the Kangal or Turkish Shepherd. It retains the loyalty, intelligence, and possessiveness of a herd guardian.

BREED QUALITIES

This is a muscular breed, capable of great speed and endurance, and needing plenty of activity. It naturally defends its home against any strangers, and while not quick to attack, does not back down easily once roused. Care is needed around guests and children, and early training and socialization are essential; this breed looks for a leader and needs to know where it stands. They take up to four years to become fully mature and live to about ten.

ANATOLIAN COAT The most frequent color is fawn, with a darker mask, and white and brindle are also common. The smooth coat is medium to long, depending on the lineage, and longer on the ruff and tail.

MELLOW MOOD Cropped ears traditionally added to the imposing appearance, but made it harder to read the dog's mood. When the Anatolian is alert, the high-set tail is carried curled over the back; when relaxed, it hangs low.

Australian Shepherd

ORIGIN California

HEIGHT 18–23 in (45–58 cm)

WEIGHT 35–70 lb (16.0–32.0 kg)

EXERCISE LEVEL

COAT CARE

REGISTERED KC, FCI, AKCs

COLORS Blue merle, black, red merle, red; with or without white and tan markings

Despite its name, the Australian Shepherd is not Australian at all, but was created and developed entirely in the United States and, until recently, was relatively unknown outside its native land.

BLACK

BLACK AND WHITE

TAN AND WHITE

RED/TAN

BLUE MOTTLED WITH TAN

BREED ORIGINS

In the 19th century, Californian ranchers needed a tough herding dog that could work in the hot climate. Among the initial breeding stock were dogs from Australia and New Zealand, and dogs originally from the Basque region of Spain that arrived with Merino sheep; hence its misleading name. As well as herding, this breed is used as a search-and-rescue dog and a sniffer dog in the prevention of narcotics smuggling.

BREED QUALITIES

This hardy, intelligent, and capable breed makes a genial family companion, although it is happiest if allowed to use its talents in agility, obedience, or other competitive trials, and suits an active household with plenty of

COAT COLORS In dogs that have white in their coat pattern, the hair around the ears and eyes should be colored. White hair in these areas is associated with sight and hearing problems.

interesting walks. If bored, it may become destructive or decide to start herding members of the family.

The moderately long, coarse coat needs occasional brushing. Living to about 13 years, these dogs have few health concerns, most of which will be avoided by careful breeders. As in other breeds, the merle color gene carries risk of hearing and sight problems, and breeding two bobtailed individuals can result in some offspring with serious spinal defects. Some lines are also prone to hip dysplasia.

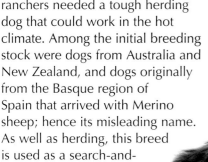

FULL COAT The coat is medium in length and quite full, with feathering on the backs of the legs and a mane and frill at the neck. Most dogs are naturally bobtailed; those that are not have traditionally been docked.

Bearded Collie

ORIGIN United Kingdom
HEIGHT 20–22 in (50–56 cm)
WEIGHT 40–66 lb (18.0–30.0 kg)
EXERCISE LEVEL
COAT CARE
REGISTERED KC, FCI, AKCs
COLORS Gray, black, fawn, brown, either solid or with white

A long coat and gentle expression give the impression that this breed is a big softie, and it does have a gentle, reliable personality. But beneath the coat is a lean body packed with spirit and energy.

BLACK

CREAM

GRAY

DARK BROWN

BLACK AND WHITE

BREED ORIGINS
According to the breed legends, a Polish sea captain traded three of his Polish Sheepdogs to a Scottish shepherd for a valuable ram and ewe in the early 16th century. When these dogs interbred with the local herding stock, the Bearded Collie breed was born. There may have been two sizes of the breed originally: a smaller, lighter one for gathering and herding in the highlands, and a heavier type for droving in the lowlands. They were used for centuries, variously called Highland Sheepdog, Highland Collie, and Hairy Moved Collie. The breed was described in the late 19th-century book *Dogs of Scotland* as "a big, rough, 'tousy' looking tyke, with a coat not unlike a doormat." They may have been involved in the creation of the Old English Sheepdog.

Although shown at the turn of the 20th century, the breed then all but vanished. After World War II a Mrs. Willison started its revival, and by the 1960s it was once again recognized and even exported to the United States, although it is still not common.

ALL CHANGE The coat changes shade over the life of the dog. Black, blue-gray, brown, or fawn at birth, it fades to lighter gray or cream by about a year. With maturity, it darkens to somewhere between the two.

FRIENDLY FACE The head is broad, with a short muzzle and wide-set eyes. The shaggy coat is long even under the chin, giving the breed its beard and name.

What is a collie?

Although the name collie conjures up a small black and white dog to most British people, and a Rough Collie to Americans, it is applied to a range of herding breeds, especially from the upland areas of northern England and Scotland. Most say the word comes from early Scots *col*, meaning black, referring to either the dog's color or black-faced sheep; some claim it is an ancient Celtic word meaning "useful."

BREED QUALITIES

That long, high-maintenance coat is no fashion accessory; the weatherproof outer layer covers an insulating undercoat. The owner of a Beardie must be willing to go out in all weathers, because nothing will dissuade this dog. It is renowned for its "bounce" and apparently boundless energy, and it needs access to an outdoor space.

The breed is also famed for its cheerful, enthusiastic, humorous personality, and a tail said to never stop wagging. It thrives on human company, pines without it, and makes an excellent family dog; despite its loud bark, it is not a good watchdog. Intelligent and sometimes headstrong, it benefits enormously from training, and enjoys tracking, competitive obedience or agility trials, or simply performing tricks. Although prone to hip dysplasia, this is a generally healthy breed that lives to about 12 years.

WELL HIDDEN Although set high, the ears are pendent and lie very close to the head, giving such a smooth line that they cannot be discerned at all on a well-groomed dog.

Belgian Shepherd Dog

ORIGIN Belgium
HEIGHT 22–26 in (56–66 cm)
WEIGHT 44–66 lb (20.0–30.0 kg)
EXERCISE LEVEL
COAT CARE
REGISTERED KC, FCI, AKCs
COLORS Fawn with mask or traces of black overlay, black

Europe has four varieties of Chien de Berger Belge or Belgian Shepherd Dog: Groenendael, Malinois, Tervueren, and Lakenois. In North America, the first of these is called the Belgian Sheepdog.

BLACK   CREAM   RED/TAN   BLACK AND TAN

BREED ORIGINS

Across the world, herding dogs tend to have developed from local varieties without formal breeding, partly because they were the working dogs of the people, not high-status hunting dogs. At the end of the 19th century, breeders in Belgium set out to produce a small range of ideal types that could be recognized nationally: initial lists included as many as eight different types. In 1891 Professor Adolphe Reul of the Cureghem Veterinary Medical School organized a gathering of 117 representatives of the many diverse herding dogs from across the nation. The best were chosen, and the newly formed Belgian Shepherd Dog Club began some very close interbreeding involving a few stud dogs, working to a breed standard with three coat varieties, a fourth being recognized in 1897. However, the Lakenois remains unrecognized in the United States. The question of coat colors and types has remained a cause of lively debate, but the type has always been fairly settled.

MALINOIS This variety has short hair over most of its body, very short on the head and lower legs. There is more fullness around the neck and on the back of the thighs and the tail. It is fawn overlaid with black.

LAKENOIS This variety has a rough, dry, tousled coat, never long enough for the tail to look like a plume. It is fawn, overlaid on the muzzle and the tail with traces of black.

BREED QUALITIES

All of the Belgian Shepherd types are trainable, reliable characters, making good guard dogs as long as they are not left alone too much. They are often used in police work, with the Tervueren also employed as a sniffer dog. Surprisingly well suited to apartment living, they are relatively inactive indoors, but this does not mean outdoor pursuits can be skimped; the Tervueren is perhaps the most active, but all working dogs thrive on interesting exercise.

Of the four, the Groenendael is the most popular, followed by the Tervueren. These two have a reputation for being slightly snappy, perhaps due to breeding for use in security work, and are less suitable as family pets than the others. The lighter, short-haired Malinois is less often seen, and the curly-coated Lakenois is quite rare. All are fairly healthy, although skin allergies, eye problems, and dysplasia are seen.

TERVUEREN Sporting a rich fawn coat overlaid with black, this type and the Malinois have a dark mask. Six areas must be black: the two ears, the two upper eyelids, and the two lips.

GROENENDAEL This type is a uniform shade of black. It has a long, smooth coat over the body, forming a ruff at the throat and a "jabot" or apron over the chest.

Bergamasco

ORIGIN Italy

HEIGHT 22–24 in (56–61 cm)

WEIGHT 57–84 lb (26.0–38.0 kg)

EXERCISE LEVEL

COAT CARE

REGISTERED KC, AKCs

COLORS Solid or patched shades of gray, black, or fawn; some white patches allowed

Similar to the Briard in France, this breed fulfills the Roman criteria of a good herding dog: fearless in pursuit, and somewhere between the speed of a hound and the power of a guard dog.

BREED ORIGINS

This solid, compact dog from northern Italy represents an ancient type, thought to be at least 2,000 years old, and developed as a herd guardian in the Alps. It makes a protective watchdog, and is good with children, but can be dominant with other dogs. The long coat makes this a breed suited to cold climates, and it does not relish city life. Once "flocked," it needs occasional bathing.

YOUTHFUL LOOKS The soft puppy coat will "flock" into distinctive long dreadlocks, including a protective "sun visor" fringe.

Berger des Pyrénées

ORIGIN France

HEIGHT 15–22 in (38–55 cm)

WEIGHT 18–33 lb (8.0–15.0 kg)

EXERCISE LEVEL

COAT CARE

REGISTERED KC, FCI

COLORS Fawn, black-shaded fawn, gray, blue flecked with black, brindle, black

This compact bundle of energy has an alert air and lively way of moving. It comes in two varieties: the longhair is shaggy all over; the smooth-faced is sleeker, although still longhaired.

BLACK

CREAM

GRAY

BLUE

BLACK BRINDLE

SMOOTH-FACED TYPE Although it is less well insulated than the long-haired, this is still not a dog that will be happy in a hot climate.

BREED ORIGINS

This breed was not recognized until the early 20th century. The thicker coat of the longhair made it better suited to working in the higher mountains. The smooth-faced type was found mostly in the foothills, working as a cattle dog. This is an intelligent, trainable breed, good with children. It copes with apartment life if there are plenty of long, interesting walks.

VARIABLE LOOKS There were originally many local types of Berger, with each valley having its own look and its own coat.

Border Collie

ORIGIN United Kingdom

HEIGHT 18–21 in (46–54 cm)

WEIGHT 31–49 lb (14.0–22.0 kg)

EXERCISE LEVEL

COAT CARE

REGISTERED KC, FCI, AKCs

COLORS Any solid or mixed colors, white never predominating

This intensely intelligent and boundlessly energetic breed can be hugely rewarding to own. With an active, attentive owner, it is a superb dog; with an inactive or absent owner, it is a problem.

BLACK   CREAM   GRAY   BLUE

BREED ORIGINS

Developed in the borders of England and Scotland as a working sheepdog, today this remains the most popular herding breed. Although the breed was known since the 18th century, it was only recognized by its present name in 1915.

Centuries of breeding for ability rather than looks have created a supremely intelligent, fast, and responsive dog of great stamina. This is the ultimate breed for anyone who wants to compete in agility trials, or for an active family with older children who enjoy daily games with a canine companion. It is a perfectionist and will do almost anything for praise, so is highly trainable. The only difficulty is likely to be feeding its voracious appetite for activity, so couch-potatoes need not apply. If left alone for long stretches of the working day, Border Collies will become bored,

miserable, and destructive, and the negligent owner may find that they are snappily herded around their own home.

COLLIE LOOKS Although any color is allowed, and there is a smooth-haired variety, the Border Collie is most often seen as a classic black-and-white dog with a long, insulating coat—although this is shorter in puppies.

Dog trials

Border Collies can perform outstandingly in this alternative to the "beauty contest" dog show. There are classes devoted to tunnels, gates, jumps, and slaloms, as well as obedience classes, and herding trials for working lines. To a Collie, this is not a chore, but what it lives for. Anyone considering a Border Collie should visit a dog trial and ask themselves honestly if they could keep up.

Bouvier des Ardennes

ORIGIN Belgium
HEIGHT 22–25 in (56–64 cm)
WEIGHT 40–59 lb (18.0–27.0 kg)
EXERCISE LEVEL
COAT CARE
REGISTERED FCI
COLORS All colors except white; often a mixture of gray, black, and fawn

BLACK   GRAY

Also known as the Ardennes Cattle Dog, this lively, no-nonsense breed has a tousled, wiry coat and looks that its breed standard calls "forbidding." This is a dog lover's dog, never a fashion item.

BREED ORIGINS

This dog has been selected for its abilities and was known for centuries as the drover's dog of the Belgian Ardennes. It almost disappeared following changes in farming practices, but in the 1990s, breeders and drovers brought it back from a few surviving dogs. It is similar to the Border Collie: full of energy, an ideal working dog that craves activity.

WORKING CLOTHES A traditional herder of cattle and pigs, by the end of the 19th century this was described as a large sheepdog with a harsh coat.

HARDY BREED Muscular and sturdy, this compact breed has a heavy bone structure and powerful head. Its looks have been formed by hard work, difficult terrain, and a harsh climate.

Bouvier des Flandres

ORIGIN Belgium
HEIGHT 23–27 in (58–68 cm)
WEIGHT 59–88 lb (27.0–40.0 kg)
EXERCISE LEVEL
COAT CARE
REGISTERED KC, FCI, AKCs
COLORS Range of solid colors

CREAM   GRAY   RED/TAN

Also called the Flanders Cattle Dog or Vlaamse Koehond, this is the best-known Belgian cattle-droving breed. Nearly destroyed by World War I and supplanted by cattle trucks, breeders saved it.

BREED ORIGINS

The origins of this breed are unclear but it has been known since the 17th century. It was used as a rescue dog and message carrier in World War I. Now a popular household companion, it is also used as a police and guide dog. Generally calm and good with children, it can be dominant and needs firm training.

BURLY BREED This is the broadest and most powerful of the bouviers. Its rough double coat and beard need regular clipping.

Briard

ORIGIN France
HEIGHT 23–27 in (58–69 cm)
WEIGHT 75–76 lb (34.0–34.5 kg)
EXERCISE LEVEL
COAT CARE
REGISTERED KC, FCI, AKCs
COLORS Fawn, gray, or black

The other famous product associated with the French province of Brie, this breed has proved a popular export. It was once called the "goat-haired" variety of another French herder, the Beauceron.

 CREAM
 GRAY
 GOLD

BREED ORIGINS
Known as a shepherd's dog for centuries, this may be a cross of two other French breeds, the Beauceron and the longhaired Barbet: Both were used to improve the Briard's looks in the mid-19th century, when it became popular. It was used by the French army in World War I to carry messages, stand guard, and search for the wounded. Returning American soldiers took it along, and today it is a popular companion breed at home and abroad, while still serving in both herding and in police and rescue work.

BREED QUALITIES
Breeders have worked to make the Briard more of a household dog, and a well-socialized dog is a good guard or lively family dog for older children. Left alone too much, they can become dominant and territorial.

BIG BUILD The size and weight of this breed have both social and health implications. It can overwhelm small children, and it is prone to hip dysplasia.

OUTDOOR TYPE Although it is not overly active indoors, this breed needs plenty of varied exercise to keep its mind and body in good condition.

Catahoula Leopard Dog

ORIGIN United States

HEIGHT 20–26 in (50–66 cm)

WEIGHT 40–100 lb (18.0–45.0 kg)

EXERCISE LEVEL

COAT CARE

REGISTERED AKCs

COLORS Black, tan, chocolate, blue and red merle, yellow, white; patched and/or brindled

Also called the Louisiana Catahoula Leopard Dog, Catahoula Hog Dog, and Catahoula Cur, this rare breed is named after Catahoula, Louisiana. It is a dual-purpose livestock-guarding and hunting dog.

BLUE

BLACK AND TAN

MERLE EYES This patched blue merle has a blue eye, known as a "glass" eye in this breed. As in other breeds, the pattern carries implications for hearing.

SOMEONE TO LOOK UP TO The Catahoula is described as "a lot of dog," and needs a strong, experienced owner who provides plenty of attention and joint activity. Without assertive leadership, it can become aggressive.

BREED ORIGINS

Historical records trace these dogs back to mastiffs and greyhounds brought to Louisiana by Hernando de Soto in the 16th century, but archeological finds in Louisiana indicate there may have been domesticated dogs there up to 7,000 years ago. Settlers' hounds and herding breeds such as the Beauceron also contributed. Historically, the "Cat" was used in teams to round up feral pigs and cattle, and it is also competent and persistent in treeing raccoons. Today it remains rare, but an enthusiastic band of breeders organizes shows and trials in obedience, treeing, and herding.

BREED QUALITIES

This is not an easygoing domestic breed for an urban setting or family life. Intelligent but stubborn, it remains to its core a working dog, happiest ranging freely over a fairly large secure area. It can guard, but should not be left alone too much.

Catalan Sheepdog

ORIGIN Spain
HEIGHT 18–22 in (45–55 cm)
WEIGHT 39–42 lb (17.5–19.0 kg)
EXERCISE LEVEL
COAT CARE
REGISTERED FCI
COLORS Mix of fawn, reddish-brown, gray, black and white; no solid white or black spots

This lively individual originates in the northeastern province of Catalonia. It is called the Gos d'Atura Català in the Catalan tongue, and known as the Perro de Pastor Catalán in the rest of Spain.

BLACK

CREAM

RED/TAN

BLACK BRINDLE

BREED ORIGINS

First developed to herd and guard sheep in the Pyrenees, this breed spread through the rest of Catalonia by the 18th century, but has not become well known internationally. It is an intelligent dog, and learns fast, but also shows initiative and an independent spirit, so needs plenty of planned activity. Given this, it makes a loyal family companion, even settling well into apartment life. Some lines are prone to hip dysplasia, but it is a generally healthy and long-lived breed.

CLIMATE DOG The long, rough coat makes this a hardy breed. The front parts molt before the hindquarters, briefly giving an intriguing "half-and-half" look.

Caucasian Sheepdog

ORIGIN Russia
HEIGHT 25–30 in (64–75 cm)
WEIGHT 99–154 lb (45.0–70.0 kg)
EXERCISE LEVEL
COAT CARE
REGISTERED KC, FCI, AKCs
COLORS Banded shades of gray, buff, white, reddish-brown, brindle or patched

There are many variants of this breed's name, but its standard lists it as the Kavkazskaïa Ovtcharka, and it is often called the Caucasian Ovtcharka. It is still popular in former Soviet countries.

CREAM

GRAY

RED/TAN

BLACK BRINDLE

BREED ORIGINS

Known for six centuries in the Caucasus, this imposing, robust breed has enormous stamina, an assertive nature, and is suspicious of strangers. At home in its natural guarding role, it is gradually moving away from its working past, although it is not suited to urban or family life or living with other pets. It is generally healthy and long lived, but hip dysplasia, obesity, and heart problems do occur.

TWO TYPES Mountain Ovtcharkas are muscular and longhaired, plains dogs lighter and short-haired. The ears were traditionally cropped, but this practice is diminishing.

Central Asian Shepherd Dog

ORIGIN Asian Russia and Central Asia
HEIGHT 24–28 in (60–70 cm)
WEIGHT 79–110 lb (36.0–50.0 kg)
EXERCISE LEVEL
COAT CARE
REGISTERED FCI, AKCs
COLORS White, black, gray, gray-brown, rust, straw, may be brindled, patched, or speckled

This is recognized as a nominally Russian breed and called the Sredneasiatskaïa Ovtcharka. Its origins really lie over a wider spread of Central Asian nations with names ending in "-stan."

 BLACK
 CREAM
 GRAY
 BLACK AND WHITE
BLACK BRINDLE

BREED ORIGINS

These powerfully built herd guardians have existed for many centuries, and possibly much longer. They are close to the ancient Asian mastiff types that gave rise to many of the similar breeds in Europe, and related to the better-known Caucasian Sheepdog. Staunch in conflict, wary of strangers, they do not suit urban or family life, and the breed is in decline.

BUILT FOR COMBAT A massive build gives these dogs a heavy, shortened gait. Tails were docked and ears cropped to avoid injury in work or combat.

Croatian Sheepdog

ORIGIN Croatia
HEIGHT 16–20 in (40–50 cm)
WEIGHT 29–35 lb (13.0–16.0 kg)
EXERCISE LEVEL
COAT CARE
REGISTERED KC, FCI, AKCs
COLORS Black, with or without white markings

Known as the Hrvaski Ovcar in its homeland, this naturally developed breed is found principally in the northeastern regions bordering Hungary. It is related to the larger Hungarian Mudi.

 BLACK
 BLACK AND WHITE

BREED ORIGINS

This breed was described in 1374 by the Bishop of Djakovo, near Vukovar, as *"Canis pastoralis croaticus,"* a dog with pricked ears and a black, curly coat. Its ancestors may have arrived from Greece or Turkey centuries before. Healthy and superbly adapted for an active life, it can be destructive, snappish with children and strangers, and too noisy for urban living.

CURLY COAT This small to medium-sized, alert-looking breed is mostly distinguished by its coat. This is short on the head and the legs, but long, soft, and wavy or curly elsewhere.

Dutch Shepherd Dog

ORIGIN Netherlands

HEIGHT 22–25 in (55–63 cm)

WEIGHT 65–66 lb (29.5–30.0 kg)

EXERCISE LEVEL

COAT CARE

REGISTERED KC, FCI, AKCs

COLORS More or less pronounced brown or gray brindle, with a black mask preferred

Called the Hollandse Herdershond in its homeland, this breed should not be confused with the Schapendoes, sometimes also called the Dutch Sheepdog. This type is from the southern Netherlands, geographically and genetically closer to the Belgian Shepherd.

BREED ORIGINS

This energetic breed has been known since the early 19th century, although it was only divided into the short-, long-, and rough-coated varieties when showing began in the early 20th century. Although classed as a shepherd, it was an all-purpose farm dog also guarding, and even pulling small carts. Today it makes a fine working dog, used in police and security work, and a loyal, playful family companion for active households, but is rare even at home and almost unknown elsewhere.

VARIABLE COAT The three coat varieties may be one reason why this breed lacks a clear popular image; this is the shorthair. All three coats are hard and weatherproof, and grooming them is fairly easy.

Entelbuch Cattle Dog

ORIGIN Switzerland

HEIGHT 19–20 in (48–50 cm)

WEIGHT 55–66 lb (25.0–30.0 kg)

EXERCISE LEVEL

COAT CARE

REGISTERED FCI, AKCs

COLORS Tricolor

There are four cattle dogs or Sennenhund breeds in Switzerland: this, the Appenzell, the Bernese, and the Great Swiss. They vary in size, with the Entelbucher Sennenhund being the smallest, but all bear this striking tricolor coat pattern.

BREED ORIGINS

The Swiss farming breeds were not recorded before the 19th century, so their origins remain a matter of conjecture, but by type they appear to be descended from Roman mastiffs. Saved from extinction by dedicated breeders, the Entelbuch has increased in popularity at home, though it is still rare abroad. A good-natured, healthy, and energetic breed, it is not ideal for urban living.

DISTINCTIVE TAIL At first, this breed, from a valley near Lucerne, was one with the larger Appenzell, from further east; they were split in part because the Entelbuch is often bobtailed.

Finnish Reindeer Herder

ORIGIN Finland

HEIGHT 17–21 in (43–54 cm)

WEIGHT 59–66 lb (27.0–30.0 kg)

EXERCISE LEVEL

COAT CARE

REGISTERED FCI, AKCs

COLORS Black or dark grayish or brown, white markings on neck, chest, and legs

Known in its homeland as the Lapinporokoira, this is also called the Lapponian Herder and Lapland Reindeer Dog, pinning its origins to the northern province of Lapland where it was used by the Sami.

 BLACK

 DARK BROWN

 GRAY

 TAN AND WHITE

BREED ORIGINS

Dogs like this were used for herding reindeer for centuries, and the 18th-century naturalist Linnaeus commented on how essential they were, saying that without them the reindeer "would scatter in all directions." Until the 20th century, this was considered one with the longhaired Finnish Lapphund. Today, it is a rare relic of the past, and facing increasing unemployment as reindeer herding declines and snowmobiles come into wider use.

These herders were family dogs to their nomadic owners as well, however, and they adapt to domestic life well. They are enthusiastic barkers, so not suited to dense urban living, but in the country they make energetic companions and watchdogs.

EAGER PUPIL This breed is noted for its biddable nature. It learns fast, remembers well, and virtually lives to please.

LAPP LOOKS This medium-sized spitz has an elongated build, and while it is well muscled and strongly built, it is never heavy. The coat is adapted for the arctic climate, with a long, full, hard topcoat and fine dense undercoat.

German Shepherd Dog

ORIGIN Germany

HEIGHT 22–26 in (55–65 cm)

WEIGHT 49–88 lb (22.0–40.0 kg)

EXERCISE LEVEL

COAT CARE

REGISTERED KC, FCI, AKCs

COLORS Black, gray, black with reddish-brown, brown; yellow to light gray markings

The Deutscher Schäferhund, also once called Alsatian, has served in wars, achieved Hollywood fame, and spawned two offshoot breeds, the Shiloh Shepherd and the White Swiss Shepherd Dog.

BLACK

GREY

DARK BROWN

BLACK AND TAN

CHANGING LOOKS Breed standards have shifted over the decades, emphasizing smaller dogs with shorter, darker coats.

Security work

The German Shepherd was used as a military dog in World War I, and taken home by soldiers returning to the United Kingdom and the United States. Since then it has proved itself unparalleled in intelligence and trainability, and "police dog" became a synonym for the breed.

EVER READY The large pricked ears and clean-cut, tapering head mean that even at rest these dogs look alert and primed to spring into action.

BREED ORIGINS

The "wolf-like dog of the country around the Rhine" was noted by Roman historian Tacitus nearly 2,000 years ago, but the German Shepherd is usually dated to the 1890s and credited largely to Max von Stephanitz. He owned Horand von Grafrath, the founding male, reputed to have a recent wolf cross in his parentage. Thuringian dogs gave the upright ears and wolf-like appearance, while Württemburger dogs were used for their temperament and speed.

BREED QUALITIES

Today, North American dogs have a very sloping stance, quite distinct from the more level European lines. Dogs from the old East Germany are said to resemble the original most closely, and working dogs are largely drawn from east European lines. Hip and digestive disorders remain a problem despite the best efforts of good breeders, and while some individuals make excellent family dogs, caution is advisable.

GERMAN SHEPHERD DOG The temperament of these pups depends not only on their early socialization, but also on what breed lines they are from: some have suffered from indiscriminate breeding to meet demand.

Huntaway

ORIGIN New Zealand
HEIGHT 20–24 in (50–60 cm)
WEIGHT 55–79 lb (25.0–36.0 kg)
EXERCISE LEVEL
COAT CARE
REGISTERED None
COLORS Any color

This breed, also known as the New Zealand Huntaway, has an unusual trait: It uses its voice to herd sheep. New Zealand has some 45 million sheep, more per head of human population than any other nation, so a good sheepdog is a vital asset.

BLACK   BLACK BRINDLE

TEAM WORKER An average sheep or cattle station has five Huntaways. They can work all day, as much as a 1 mile (1.6 km) from the shepherd and guided by whistle and hand signals.

BREED ORIGINS

Most of the sheepdogs that were transported from the United Kingdom to New Zealand worked the sheep in traditional silence, but an occasional dog would use its voice. This trait intrigued the shepherds, who began to breed from the more vocal dogs in the early 20th century. Black Labradors, Border Collies, and German Shepherd Dogs were among the breeds that went into this melting pot. Eventually two types of dog were used: those that drove the sheep forward, and those that headed them off and turned them back. The latter were called, naturally enough, headers, and the former huntaways, which is also the name for the trials in which they demonstrate their skills.

BREED QUALITIES

These dogs are rarely seen outside New Zealand, and are not currently recognized by any kennel clubs, even in their homeland. It is usually too noisy to be a good household dog, and easily bored with a life of leisure.

BRAINS BEFORE BEAUTY Huntaways vary greatly in coat type and color, and even to some extent in conformation. They are bred true only for health and working ability.

Icelandic Sheepdog

ORIGIN Iceland

HEIGHT 12–16 in (31–41 cm)

WEIGHT 53–57 lb (24.0–26.0 kg)

EXERCISE LEVEL

COAT CARE

REGISTERED FCI, AKCs

COLORS White with shades from tan to red, chocolate, gray, or black

This energetic little spitz is Iceland's only native breed. Its varied names include Icelandic Dog, Iceland Spitz, Islandsk Farehond, and Friaar Dog, but is officially recognized as the Islenkur Fjárhundur.

LIVER

BLACK AND WHITE

TAN AND WHITE

BREED ORIGINS

The ancestors of this breed arrived in Iceland over 1,000 years ago with the first Viking settlers, and the breed resembles the Norwegian Buhund. They swiftly became indispensable to the farmers in their struggle for survival in the harsh conditions, and in 1650 it was recorded that "a type of dog resembling a fox" from Iceland was sometimes imported and popular with British shepherds. In the late 19th century distemper took a terrible toll on the breed, and imports of foreign dogs were banned. The breed was close to extinction again by the late 20th century, but it is now considered stable, although these dogs remain rare.

LOCAL ADAPTATIONS There are two types of coat, long and short, both of which are thick and extremely weatherproof. Double dew claws on the hind legs are desirable in the breed standard.

HARD WORKER Bred to be agile and tough enough for the terrain, this spitz has a confident attitude and will work livestock alone. It often uses its voice to assist this, and is too noisy for city life.

Karst Shepherd

ORIGIN Slovenia
HEIGHT 21–26 in (54–65 cm)
WEIGHT 55–92 lb (25.0–42.0 kg)
EXERCISE LEVEL
COAT CARE
REGISTERED FCI
COLORS Gray or sandy, with a dark mask and gray, sandy, or pale fawn on the head

Recognized as the Krasky Ovcar, and also called the Krasevec and the Istrian Shepherd, this cold-weather breed is from the Karst or Kras plateau of southwestern Slovenia.

BREED ORIGINS

These massive herd guardians, descended from Asian mastiffs, have existed in southeastern Europe for centuries. The type and its standard were officially recognized in the 20th century as the Illyrian Shepherd, but in 1968 this was split to recognize the Karst Shepherd and the Sarplanina as distinct historical breeds. The Karst has experienced something of a revival in recent years, and is now sometimes seen at European shows. Its vigilant nature, distrust of strangers, and strong inclination to defend its home against all comers rule it out as an ideal family or urban companion, but it makes an excellent guard dog for an experienced owner.

KARST LOOKS These dogs are harmonious and robust, with a proud carriage. They have a well-coordinated, elastic trot, but the gallop with long strides is slightly ungainly.

Komondor

ORIGIN Hungary
HEIGHT 26–36 in (65–90 cm)
WEIGHT 88–132 lb (40.0–60.0 kg)
EXERCISE LEVEL
COAT CARE
REGISTERED KC, FCI, AKCs
COLORS Ivory white

Perhaps thanks to its original looks, this is the largest and possibly the best known of all the Hungarian herding breeds, the only one to be recognized by national registries in the United Kingdom and United States.

BREED ORIGINS

Established for many centuries, and descended from mastiffs brought to the region over 1,000 years ago, this herder is large, powerfully built, and dignified in demeanor. The coat is shaggy, tending toward matting, or long and fully corded, and needs regular attention to keep the cords from uniting into large matts. It makes a better rural companion than urban family dog.

BUILT-IN SUN VISOR While it might be seen as a disadvantage, obscuring the vision, the fringe of this breed in fact serves as a visor, filtering the light that reaches the eyes.

Lancashire Heeler

ORIGIN United Kingdom
HEIGHT 10–12 in (25–30 cm)
WEIGHT 6–13 lb (3.0–6.0 kg)
EXERCISE LEVEL
COAT CARE
REGISTERED KC, FCI, AKCs
COLORS Black and tan, liver and tan

This breed is sometimes also called, with exacting geographical accuracy, the Ormskirk Heeler. A heeler was not a dog that walked tidily to heel, but a cattle-droving dog that worked by persistently nipping the heels of its charges.

BREED ORIGINS

Before motorized transportation, there were many working heeler breeds across the United Kingdom. Almost all died out in the 20th century, including the Lancashire heeler. Today's breed, still rare, is a recreation using Corgis for type and Manchester Terriers for the color. It has never been used in its historic role, and has more of a feisty terrier temperament. While it makes a frisky companion and alert, noisy guard, it is not the most trainable of breeds and is too much inclined to snappish behavior to be trusted around small children.

LANCASHIRE LOOKS This breed is small but sturdily built. It has an alert, energetic appearance, with a high-set tail carried over the back in a curve and a smart, brisk gait.

Maremma Sheepdog

ORIGIN Italy
HEIGHT 24–29 in (60–73 cm)
WEIGHT 66–99 lb (30.0–45.0 kg)
EXERCISE LEVEL
COAT CARE
REGISTERED KC, FCI, AKCs
COLORS White

Called the Cane da Pastore Maremmano-Abruzzese at home, this breed originates in central Italy, from southern Tuscany through Lazio to Abruzzo. There may once have been two breeds, a long-coated Abruzzese and short-haired Maremma, but they have been one for 50 years.

BREED ORIGINS

This breed belongs to a group of white herders stretching from the Kuvasc in Hungary to the Pyrenean Mountain Dog. All are descended from the Asian herders that arrived in eastern Europe some 1,000 years ago and gradually spread west; the Maremma is one of the smaller examples of the type. Although established beyond its homeland, it remains a minority breed.

True to its shepherd dog nature, it is steadfast and vigilant, making a fine guard dog, but it can be independent in spirit. Breeders in the United Kingdom have worked hard, with success, to produce a temperament more suited to a companion breed.

MOUNTAIN COAT The coat is long and abundant with a hard, weatherproof texture and a dense undercoat in winter. Slight shadings of ivory, lemon, or pale orange are tolerated.

Mudi

ORIGIN Hungary
HEIGHT 14–20 in (36–51 cm)
WEIGHT 18–29 lb (8.0–13.0 kg)
EXERCISE LEVEL
COAT CARE
REGISTERED FCI, AKCs
COLORS Black, blue merle, gray, fawn, brown

This Hungarian dog is rare even in its homeland, overshadowed by more distinctive national breeds such as the Puli, Komondor, and Pumi. Lively but trainable, it deserves a wider audience.

BLACK GRAY

BREED ORIGINS

The type of the Mudi probably emerged in the 18th or 19th century as a result of crosses between Hungarian herding dogs and German breeds. Planned breeding does not seem to feature in its development, and conformation only stabilized in the early 20th century. As everyday working animals, herding dogs in Hungary were all classed together until the 1930s, when Dr. Dezso Fenyesi separated the Mudi from the Puli and Pumi.

MUDI LOOKS The pointed face and pricked ears are thought to show a fairly recent influence from spitz-type German dogs, and the slightly oblique eyes are said to give a daredevil expression. The breed has a short-paced gait, described in the standard as "mincing."

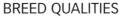

BREED QUALITIES

This is an all-purpose rural breed, lively, highly intelligent, and keen to learn. It has been used for herding sheep and cows, guarding flocks and homes, hunting, keeping down vermin, and in Finland for search-and-rescue work. Perhaps because of this broad curriculum, it adapts to family life better than many herders, although it can be enthusiastically noisy and does need plenty of interesting activity to occupy both body and brain. It is said that there is no such thing as a moody Mudi. No-frills looks and the lack of a noble history may be all that keep this breed from greater appreciation.

Norwegian Buhund

ORIGIN Norway
HEIGHT 16–18 in (41–46 cm)
WEIGHT 53–57 lb (24.0–26.0 kg)
EXERCISE LEVEL
COAT CARE
REGISTERED KC, FCI, AKCs
COLORS Wheaten, red, black

This brisk-looking breed is also called the Norwegian Sheepdog, although Norsk Buhund means something closer to "homestead dog," and it also guarded the home and served in the hunt.

BLACK

RED/TAN

GOLD

BREED ORIGINS

The name buhund has existed for many centuries—Viking burials have been found to include dogs, essential helpers for the afterlife—and exactly when the present type emerged is not clear. They were largely overlooked until the early 20th century, when the first ever Buhund show was held at Jaeren in the 1920s. The most beautiful, refined look of buhund was considered to have developed into in this southwestern, coastal region, and the best of the dogs became the foundation of the breed.

The Buhund has become popular abroad, perhaps most surprisingly in the very different climate of Australia; very adaptable to heat, it works tirelessly as a herding dog. It is also used in police work and as an assistance dog.

BREED QUALITIES

This cheerful and affectionate dog is one of the most trainable of the spitz-type breeds. Its intelligence means it is occasionally stubborn, but it can be left alone for a while. It makes a vocal but not aggressive guard, and is an excellent family dog. It is generally healthy and lives into its teens, but inherited eye and hip problems sometimes appear.

BUHUND LOOKS This compact and lightly built breed is a typical spitz, with pricked ears, an alert expression, small neat paws, and a high-set tail carried curled over the back. The coat is weatherproof, with a hard, smooth outer coat and a soft, wooly undercoat.

Old English Sheepdog

ORIGIN United Kingdom
HEIGHT 22–24 in (56–60 cm)
WEIGHT 65–66 lb (29.5–30.0 kg)
EXERCISE LEVEL
COAT CARE
REGISTERED KC, FCI, AKCs
COLORS Gray, blue, with limited white markings

Famous in much of the world as the "Dulux dog," this profusely shaggy breed has a personality to match its cuddly looks. This is a loyal and adaptable companion.

GRAY   BLUE

BREED ORIGINS
First bred selectively in the 19th century, mostly in southwestern England, the Old English may be descended from continental breeds such as the Briard, or even the Polish Lowland Sheepdog. Usually docked, it was also called the Bobtail. It was originally an aggressive and snappish character, but careful breeding has rendered it a biddable family dog, although it still makes a good guard.

SHAGGY DOG Square and thick-set, this is a sturdy breed with a rolling gait. A monthly clipping helps to keep it tidy.

Polish Lowland Sheepdog

ORIGIN Poland
HEIGHT 16–20 in (41–51 cm)
WEIGHT 31–35 lb (14.0–16.0 kg)
EXERCISE LEVEL
COAT CARE
REGISTERED KC, FCI, AKCs
COLORS Any color

Known in its homeland as the Polski Owczarek Nizinny, this muscular breed may be an antecedent of the Schaependoes, the Old English Sheepdog, and the Bearded Collie.

BLACK   CREAM   GRAY   BLUE   BLACK AND WHITE

BREED ORIGINS
This breed dates back at least to the Middle Ages, and is thought to be descended from Asian breeds with corded coats brought West over 1,000 years ago. Almost extinct after World War II, it is now a popular breed in Poland and Europe. It makes a good companion, although like most herding breeds it needs plenty of activity to keep it healthy and happy.

POLISH LOOKS The thick double coat is arresting when well groomed, unsightly when neglected. It is also highly insulating, and this is a true cold-climate breed, unhappy in the heat. Everything about the build, from nose to tail, is strong, compact, and blunt.

Puli

ORIGIN Hungary

HEIGHT 14–18 in (36–45 cm)

WEIGHT 22–33 lb (10.0–15.0 kg)

EXERCISE LEVEL

COAT CARE

REGISTERED KC, FCI, AKCs

COLORS Black, black with rust or gray shadings, fawn with black mask, white

This lively and intelligent little dog, originally a herder, is the best-known of the Hungarian breeds. Aided by its eye-catching coat, it has successfully made the shift to family companion.

BLACK   CREAM   GOLD

BREED ORIGINS

This breed's ancestors were probably large stock-guarding dogs that came to Hungary with the Magyars around 1,000 years ago. Black dogs were preferred, probably because they are easy to spot among sheep. The smaller Puli emerged as an agile herder, while the larger Komondor was used for guarding. Today the Puli makes an adaptable companion and guard dog, and does well in obedience trials.

CORDED COAT
Once it is worked into pencil-thick cords, the coat needs no daily grooming but regular bathing and drying. The Puli is remarkably adaptable to a wide range of climates, and enjoys swimming—it is also known as the Hungarian Water Dog.

Pumi

ORIGIN Hungary

HEIGHT 13–19 in (33–48 cm)

WEIGHT 22–33 lb (10.0–15.0 kg)

EXERCISE LEVEL

COAT CARE

REGISTERED FCI, AKCs

COLORS Black, shades of gray, brown, white

With its curled tail and pompom ears, the Pumi has a unique, jaunty look, and an alert, feisty personality to match. It is established in many countries but remains low in numbers.

BLACK   GRAY   DARK BROWN

BREED ORIGINS

The Pumi was first recorded in 1815, and probably descended from the Puli and German spitz-type dogs, as well as terriers. The result is an energetic cattle-droving dog, with the stubborn persistence the job requires. A noisy, restless breed, it makes a good guard and adapts surprisingly well to city life, but is not for those seeking a restful companion.

PUMI LOOKS This lively, expressive breed attracts attention wherever it goes. The curly, medium-length coat does not mat easily.

OLD ENGLISH SHEEPDOG (*see* p. 292) Young or old, this dog can be something of a couch potato in the home, although active once it gets outside. The Old English retains a playful character throughout much of its adult life.

Romanian Carpathian Shepherd Dog

ORIGIN Romania
HEIGHT 23–29 in (59–73 cm)
WEIGHT 80–110 lb (36.0–50.0 kg)
EXERCISE LEVEL
COAT CARE
REGISTERED FCI, AKCs
COLORS Pale fawn overlaid with black, with or without some white marks

The Romanian Shepherd Dog is a recently emerged breed. It is recognized by FCI under the name Ciobanesc Romanesc, with two types; a third, the Bukovina type, is still being considered.

GOLD

GOLD AND WHITE

BREED ORIGINS

The Carpatin or Carpathian type of Romanian Shepherd, once also called Zavod, arose naturally in the Carpathian mountains above the Danube, in southern Romania. Like many herding types, it was overlooked until the 20th century. In 1931 the National Zoological and Veterinary Institute in Bucharest set about finding the most representative Romanian sheepdog and promoting it as a national breed. Following extensive study, they settled on the flock guardians typical of much of eastern Europe and descended from dogs brought from the east. Herders from Rucar in Arges county were described in 1934 as "a sort of archaic gray Carpatin sheepdog," and set the standard for this type for decades.

A poorly written standard saw the dilution of the breed into a range of colors in the later 20th century, but breeders have worked hard to bring it back to its roots, and by 2002 a much tighter breed standard, based

CARPATHIAN LOOKS This breed is being developed to have a "lupoid" or wolfish build and head, which is based on the original 1930s description. For much of the 20th century, the breed tended toward a heavier, mastiff type.

on the original description, was back in place. Breeders are working to improve the consistency of the type, using dogs from the original area, but for now this remains a rare breed.

BREED QUALITIES

Although large, this breed is agile and vigorous. It makes a courageous and loyal guard dog, but is calm and stable enough to be a good household and family companion, and is becoming a popular urban dog in its homeland.

Romanian Mioritic Shepherd Dog

ORIGIN Romania
HEIGHT 26–30 in (65–75 cm)
WEIGHT 100–144 lb (45.0–65.0 kg)
EXERCISE LEVEL
COAT CARE
REGISTERED KC, FCI, AKCs
COLORS White, gray, white and black, white and gray

Recognized by FCI as Ciobanesc Romanesc Mioritic, this type was previously also known as Barac and is also sometimes simply called the Mioritic Sheepdog.

GRAY

BLACK AND WHITE

BREED ORIGINS

Exactly when dogs of this type first appeared in Romania is not known: some claim that they accompanied the Celts in their westward migrations at least 2,000 years ago. More certainly, they were used by Turkic peoples 1,000 years ago, and this breed bears a strong resemblance to others such as the Polish Lowland Sheepdog and Russian Ovtcharka types. In the rugged Carpathian mountains of Romania, well stocked with wolves, bears, and lynx, such a herd guardian was invaluable. Large, muscular but never unduly heavy, it developed naturally into the type we see today.

BREED QUALITIES

Described in the breed standard as "vigorous and spectacular," the striking looks of this breed undoubtedly contribute to its growing popularity at home and abroad. Renowned as an excellent herding dog and "incorruptible" flock guardian for centuries, this is a loyal and courageous breed. Generally calm and stable, it can make a good companion and family dog, but it was bred to be an efficient fighter, and remains wary of strangers. Exercise and coat care are likely to be fairly time-consuming commitments.

MIORITIC LOOKS The breed standard defines many apects of this dog as "muscular": as in all the Romanian Shepherd types, the males are taller and more heavily built than the females. The coat is long, thick, and flowing from head to tail.

Rough Collie

ORIGIN United Kingdom

HEIGHT 20–24 in (50–60 cm)

WEIGHT 40–66 lb (18.0–30.0 kg)

EXERCISE LEVEL

COAT CARE

REGISTERED KC, FCI, AKCs

COLORS Sable, sable and white, blue merle, tricolor

One of the world's most popular breeds, this looks too elegant for herding work, although it retains its original abilities. First made fashionable at home by Queen Victoria, in the 20th century it became familiar to a wider audience as "Lassie."

BLUE

BLACK, WHITE AND TAN

BREED ORIGINS

For centuries, this was an obscure Scottish herding dog, producing both long- and occasional shorthaired dogs. It was somewhat smaller than it is today, with a less luxuriant coat and shorter nose. Then it was crossed with Borzois, giving a taller, leaner build and an aristocratic face, and has been at home in the show ring ever since.

BREED QUALITIES

Intelligent enough to work as a rescue and guide dog, this amiable breed makes a good family dog, but occasional snappish individuals do occur. Its popularity makes it essential to buy a pup screened for eye defects and hip problems from a reputable breeder.

COLLIE COAT This is an active breed that needs plenty of free running, but the spectacular coat is the greatest commitment. Daily grooming is needed, with more thorough attention weekly. In Europe the Rough and Smooth Collies are recognized as separate breeds; in North America one breed with two coat lengths is recognized.

Sarplaninac

ORIGIN Balkan region

HEIGHT 22–24 in (56–60 cm)

WEIGHT 55–80 lb (25.0–36.0 kg)

EXERCISE LEVEL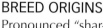

COAT CARE

REGISTERED FCI, AKCs

COLORS Black, gray, tan, or white; solid or blended

Names included on the FCI standard are Jugoslovenski Ovcarski Pas and Yugoslavian Shepherd Dog-Sharplanina. Others claim it as Macedonian or Serbian, or, historically, the Illyrian Sheepdog.

BLACK

GRAY

RED/TAN

BLACK, WHITE, AND TAN

BREED ORIGINS

Pronounced "shar-plan-ee-natz," this breed takes its present name from the Shar Planina mountains. It is thought to be an older breed than the Karst Shepherd. Military turmoil has reduced its numbers at home, but it is also established in North America, where it is valued as a hard-working herder and guardian. This is a working breed, conscientious and serious, not an urban or a family dog.

OUTDOOR TYPE The heavy, insulating coat and sturdy "molosser" type of this breed insure that it is well suited to a life outdoors. It makes a vigilant guard dog that will investigate and unhesitatingly confront any trespasser, regardless of the odds.

Schapendoes

ORIGIN Netherlands
HEIGHT 16–20 in (40–50 cm)
WEIGHT 32–34 lb (14.5–15.5 kg)
EXERCISE LEVEL
COAT CARE
REGISTERED FCI
COLORS Any color

Officially called the Nederlandse Schapendoes, the Dutch Sheepdog or Sheep Poodle is a lightly built dog full of bounce and spirit. Traditionally a herding breed, it is now mostly kept as a companion.

BLACK

GRAY

BLUE

BLACK AND WHITE

BREED ORIGINS

The emergence of this breed is not recorded, but herding dogs were common at the turn of the 20th century wherever there were sheep or cattle across the flat pastures and heathlands of the Netherlands. It is thought that the Schapendoes is related to the extinct German Schafpudel and other longhaired breeds such as the Briard, Polish Lowland Sheepdog, Bergamasco, and Old English Sheepdog.

During World War II, Dutch breeder P.M.C. Toepoel gathered remaining examples of the vanishing type. A breed club was founded after the war, and the breed was stable and healthy enough for the books to be closed to any further outcrosses by the 1970s. Despite its admirable character and good health, it remains a rare breed even in its homeland.

BREED QUALITIES

The breed standard describes this dog as "jolly," with a loyal and optimistic personality that makes it an excellent family dog, good with other dogs and children. Like most herding breeds, it needs a good deal of interesting activity to keep it happy: it runs with great stamina and is a remarkable jumper, clearing obstacles apparently without effort. However, given such daily activity it will settle into urban life well. The other major commitment is the long coat, which will need daily attention to keep it in good condition.

DECEPTIVE LOOKS This is a fairly small dog in a big coat: The shaggy hair gives it the appearance of being larger and in particular broader than it is. This misleading bulk makes the tireless speed and agility of the Schapendoes appear startling at first.

Shetland Sheepdog

ORIGIN United Kingdom
HEIGHT 14–15 in (35–37 cm)
WEIGHT 13–15 lb (6.0–7.0 kg)
EXERCISE LEVEL
COAT CARE
REGISTERED KC, FCI, AKCs
COLORS Sable, black and white, black and tan, tricolor, blue merle

Popularly known as the Sheltie, this is a favorite breed in both its homeland and North America, giving the looks of the Rough Collie in a smaller package.

 BLACK

 BLACK AND WHITE

 BLACK AND TAN

 BLACK, WHITE AND TAN

BREED ORIGINS

Although once called the Dwarf Scotch Shepherd, this is a true miniature, not simply short legged. The similarity to the Rough Collie makes it most likely that this breed is descended from Collies crossed with smaller dogs. One possible cross is the now-vanished Icelandic Yakkin, brought to the Shetlands by fishermen. The Sheltie was established by the 18th century, and was used to round up and guard the equally compact and hardy Shetland sheep. It remained a herding dog until the 20th century, when it attracted the attention of breeders and was officially recognized. It spread to mainland Scotland and beyond, being recognized in the United States just two years after it was in the United Kingdom.

BREED QUALITIES

Good with children and friendly with other dogs, this is a genial companion and a good city dog. However, elegant looks conceal a keen mind and hungry spirit. This highly trainable dog can herd, track, and guard, and remains among the top performing breeds in obedience trials. At home it needs varied activity to prevent it becoming bored and destructive. Generally healthy, but buy puppies screened for eye problems from a reputable breeder.

COAT CARE Regular brushing is important: It is often helpful to mist the coat lightly before brushing. The dense, insulating undercoat is shed twice a year, and at these times even more frequent brushing is essential.

Shiloh Shepherd Dog

ORIGIN United States
HEIGHT 28–32 in (70–80 cm)
WEIGHT 79–130 lb (36.0–59.0 kg)
EXERCISE LEVEL
COAT CARE
REGISTERED None
COLORS Black or dark shades and cream to red shades, solid or patched; white

This offshoot of the German Shepherd Dog was created to return to the wolf-like roots of the breed. It has a short but highly eventful history, and remains rare even in the United States.

 BLACK
 CREAM
 DARK BROWN

BREED ORIGINS

In the 1970s, German Shepherd breeder Tina Barber set about breeding dogs to conform to the breed's earliest standards: large, dark eyed, intelligent, healthy, and even-tempered. By 1990 she and her "satellite" breeders had a separate standard in place and called the dogs Shiloh Shepherds, after her kennel. Since then, there have been numerous splits and rival associations, in part because this is a lucrative "spin-off" from a hugely popular breed. Barber's requirements for Shiloh Shepherds are very stringent, and she feels major registries would dilute them; buyers should do plenty of research beforehand to be sure of exactly what they are getting.

WOLF-LIKE DOGS The parentage of the German Shepherd is vague, but seems to have included wolf hybrids. Shilohs aim for wolf traits by other means.

Slovakian Chuvach

ORIGIN Slovakia
HEIGHT 22–28 in (55–70 cm)
WEIGHT 66–99 lb (30–45 kg)
EXERCISE LEVEL
COAT CARE
REGISTERED FCI
COLORS White

A typical mountain dog from the Tatra uplands, this breed is called the Slovensky Cuvac in its homeland and also known as the Tatra Chuvach. Its name may be related to the Slovak word "cuvat," to hear, a guide to its vigilant nature.

LOCAL BOYS The strong-boned, muscular frame and thick white coat of this breed were essential in the harsh conditions of the central European mountains. They give it an impressive appearance, in many respects similar to the Hungarian Kuvasz.

BREED ORIGINS

An essential part of the rural economy of the Tatra mountains, this lively, hardy, and fearless breed has served as a guard, guide, and herding and droving dog since at least the 17th century. It was almost extinct after World War II, but revived through the efforts of Dr. Antonin Hruza. It still makes a fine working dog, but is not really suited to family or city life.

Smooth Collie

ORIGIN United Kingdom
HEIGHT 20–24 in (50–60 cm)
WEIGHT 40–66 lb (18.0–30.0 kg)
EXERCISE LEVEL
COAT CARE
REGISTERED KC, FCI, AKCs
COLORS Sable, sable and white, blue merle, tricolor

The Smooth Collie was once regarded as a variant of the Rough Collie, and in North America the two are still classed together simply as the Collie. In its homeland and the rest of Europe, however, the two are separate breeds.

CREAM

BLUE

BLACK, WHITE, AND TAN

BREED ORIGINS
When the Rough Collie breed came to prominence in the 1860s, occasional shorthaired puppies appeared in litters. Then in 1873 a smooth-coated, tricolored male named Trefoil was born, and while there are Rough Collies in all smooth lines and vice versa, the breeding lines diverged and this dog is seen as the main father of today's Smooth Collie.

In the 1950s Solo of Sheil, a beautiful Smooth Collie imported into the United States became one of the most influential dogs, appearing on the pedigrees of most American Smooth Collies, as well as many others around the world.

BREED QUALITIES
Smooth Collies show the same loyalty, intelligence, and vigor as

their rough-coated counterparts. As the breed lines have diverged, so have some aspects of the personality, and there is a greater tendency toward shy and potentially snappy individuals in the smooth-coated type. Although not bred in such numbers as the rough type, it is still advisable to buy a puppy that has been screened for eye and hip problems.

HISTORIC LOOKS Early show lines of Collies were crossed with Borzois, and diverged from the working dogs. Since then, the Smooth Collie has remained close to the 19th-century look, while the coat of the Rough has become ever more luxuriant.

South Russian Shepherd Dog

ORIGIN Russia
HEIGHT 25–36 in (63–90 cm)
WEIGHT 110–165 lb (50.0–75.0 kg)
EXERCISE LEVEL
COAT CARE
REGISTERED KC, FCI, AKCs
COLORS White, white and yellow, straw color, gray, white and gray, gray speckled

This breed is called Ioujnorousskaïa Ovtcharka in its homeland. It is a self-contained and determined breed, favoured as a shepherd and guard dog for centuries, a role it is still happiest fulfilling today.

BREED ORIGINS

Some believe this breed to be descended from bearded dogs living in the area in prehistory; others hold that European herding dogs imported with merino sheep in the 18th century were bred with sighthounds and Tatar shepherds similar to the Caucasian Sheepdogs to improve their ability to deal with large predators. The result is a large, cold-hardy, aggressive country dog.

CLOSE TO ITS ROOTS Other shaggy herding breeds from western Europe have been bred for decades to achieve a calmer temperament. The Russian looks similar to many, but remains close to its herding past: tenacious, suspicious, territorial, and highly active.

Swedish Lapphund

ORIGIN Sweden
HEIGHT 18–20 in (45–51 cm)
WEIGHT 43–45 lb (19.5–20.5 kg)
EXERCISE LEVEL
COAT CARE
REGISTERED KC, FCI
COLORS Black, brown, sometimes with limited white

This lively, cheerful, and intelligent little dog is known in its homeland as the Svensk Lapphund, and also called the Lapplandska Spets or Lapland Spitz.

BLACK   DARK BROWN

BREED ORIGINS

This breed has existed for many centuries as the herding dog of the Lapps, now more widely called the Sami; It was used to herd reindeer in the northern reaches of Sweden, and also has some skill in treeing game. The breed faded away with the changes in Sami lifestyles in the 20th century, but was revived in the 1960s. Today it is popular as a companion breed both at home and abroad.

LAPPHUND LOOKS Almost always black, this typical outdoor-loving spitz has the thick, weather-resistant coat of a cold climate breed.

Swedish Vallhund

ORIGIN Sweden

HEIGHT 12–14 in (30–35 cm)

WEIGHT 24–33 lb (11.0–15.0 kg)

EXERCISE LEVEL

COAT CARE

REGISTERED KC, FCI, AKCs

COLORS Gray and brown with darker overlay and lighter or white markings

This breed's Swedish name of Västgötaspets locates it more precisely in the southwest of the country. Vallhund means simply herding dog, but it is also called the Swedish Cattle Dog.

GRAY

DARK BROWN

TAN AND WHITE

BLACK AND TAN

BREED ORIGINS

This breed dates back to the Middle Ages, and seems to be related to the Corgis, although it is uncertain which came first. These dwarfed droving breeds may both ultimately derive from the short-legged bassets of continental Europe.

Like other cattle-herding breeds, the Vallhund was driven into redundancy by the coming of motorized livestock transportation, and by the end of World War II numbers were low. Two dedicated breeders brought it back from the brink, but it is still rare.

BREED QUALITIES

Cattle-droving dogs are bred to run back and forth behind the herd, nipping their heels to keep them moving, and avoiding any resulting kicks. As a result, they are fast, tough, determined dogs. Excellent as a working dog for experienced owners, this is likely to be a problem if kept as a family or city companion.

CONCENTRATED PERSONALITY This is one of those small breeds with the attitude of a large dog crammed into a concentrated package.

Tatra Shepherd Dog

ORIGIN Poland
HEIGHT 24–32 in (60–80 cm)
WEIGHT 80–130 lb (36.0–59.0 kg)
EXERCISE LEVEL
COAT CARE
REGISTERED FCI, AKCs
COLORS White

Known in its homeland as the Polski Owczarek Podhalanski, this is the mountain counterpart of the Polish Lowland Sheepdog: bigger, more heavily muscled, and better equipped to deal with mountain predators.

BREED ORIGINS

Known since the Middle Ages, this breed is typical of the white-coated herd guardians found across eastern Europe; further south, the Anatolian Shepherd has the same type. All are descended from Asian mastiff types that arrived over 1,000 years ago.

Like many working breeds, its numbers declined in the 20th century and it was almost extinct by the end of World War II. It was brought back by the Polish Kennel Club, and spread to the United States in the 1980s, but remains rare outside its homeland.

BREED QUALITIES

This hardy breed is happiest with a job to do. An excellent guard, it patrols, barks noisily at anything out of the ordinary, and defends its territory if challenged. These qualities make it unsuitable for urban living. It gets on with older children, but is not a family dog, needing a strong owner who will give it plenty of time and firm, fair, consistent training.

TATRA COAT This active and agile breed loves to run and needs its exercise. Fortunately the white coat sheds dirt fairly easily, but it does need daily attention. The insulating undercoat is shed profusely twice a year, when extra grooming is needed; dogs kept indoors will shed all year.

Tornjak

ORIGIN Former Yugoslavia
HEIGHT 24–28 in (60–70 cm)
WEIGHT 80–110 lb (37.0–50.0 kg)
EXERCISE LEVEL
COAT CARE
REGISTERED FCI
COLORS White with black, tricolor

This breed has a range of conflicting national names, including Bosnian-Herzegovinian Sheepdog and Hrvatski Pas Planinac or Croatian Mountain Dog. The neutral Tornjak may be more helpful.

BLACK AND WHITE

BLACK, WHITE. AND TAN

BREED ORIGINS

Mountains dogs such as this were described as long ago as the 11th century, probably derived from Asian mastiff types. Scholars called them *Canis montanus* or mountain dog, but the locals called them Tornjaks, from "tor" or sheep pen. With a long, dense coat and a robust build, these dogs were already perfectly suited to guarding flocks in high mountain pastures, and so survived unchanged over the centuries. Similar to the as yet-unrecognized Bukovina type of Romanian Shepherd, they represent a distinctive type that is most often seen in southeastern Europe.

The breed was largely overlooked outside its homeland until very recently, but a new breed standard in FCI was recorded in 2007, and a handful of dogs are now being bred in the United States.

BREED QUALITIES

Calm and dignified, this breed is a courageous, resolute guardian that is naturally suspicious of strangers. As an adult it does not readily interact with anyone beyond its family, so early socialization is vital. It is intelligent and enthusiastic, learning fast and remembering well. Unlikely to make a good urban companion, it is happiest as a rural working dog.

CONCEALING COAT Although this is a large and powerful dog, it is still fast and agile. The long, thick coat, which provides such effective insulation makes it appear more heavily built than it really is, especially in winter. The coat sheds dirt readily, but grooming is a major commitment.

Welsh Corgis

ORIGIN United Kingdom
HEIGHT 10–13 in (25–32 cm)
WEIGHT 20–26 lb (9.0–12.0 kg)
EXERCISE LEVEL
COAT CARE
REGISTERED KC, FCI
COLORS Red, sable, fawn, black and tan, white allowed (Pembroke); all colors (Cardigan)

Although the Pembroke and the Welsh Corgi remain distinct breeds with their own standards, they are very similar, a result of crossbreeding between them until the 20th century.

BLACK RED/TAN BLACK AND WHITE BLACK, WHITE, AND TAN BLACK BRINDLE

BREED ORIGINS
Romantics claim that Corgis arrived with the Celts over 2,000 years ago. Others believe they are descended from Swedish Vallhund stock arriving with the Vikings a little over 1,000 years ago, although it may be that the Vallhund is descended from Welsh dogs. The name corgi is recorded in *A Dictionary in Englyshe and Welshe* published in 1574, as "Korgi ne gostoc, Corgi or curre dogge," meaning working or guarding dog.

This was primarily a cattle-droving breed or "heeler," left unemployed by transportation developments in the 20th century. Only when the future

Queen Elizabeth acquired her first Corgis did the breed come back to popularity, this time as a companion breed.

BREED QUALITIES
Heelers had to be bold enough to run behind the feet of the cattle and nip their heels, low and robust enough to roll away from the resulting kicks, and determined enough to go back for more. These qualities make them lively companions, but too stubborn and snappish to be good family dogs.

CARDIGAN CORGI The ears of the Cardigan type are large and the nose less pointed than that of the Pembroke, although never blunt. The coat is hard and short or medium in length.

PEMBROKE CORGI Sturdily built but smaller than the Cardigan type, the Pembroke has a foxy, pointed face and a medium length coat. Pembroke Corgis often have naturally short tails; those with long tails were traditionally docked.

White Swiss Shepherd Dog

ORIGIN Switzerland
HEIGHT 22–26 in (55–66 cm)
WEIGHT 55–88 lb (25.0–40.0 kg)
EXERCISE LEVEL
COAT CARE
REGISTERED FCI
COLORS White

Although provisionally recognized as a Swiss breed, the Weisser Schweizer Schäferhund or Berger Blanc Suisse has international origins. It is descended from the white lines of German Shepherd Dogs that have been developed as "White Shepherds" in North America.

BREED ORIGINS

The recessive gene that produced occasional white coats was present in the German Shepherd breed from the start in the 19th and early 20th century. In Nazi Germany, breeding was politically significant, and the white coat became a disqualifying fault. After World War II, overseas registries adopted this standard, with lighter-colored dogs being either disqualified or "highly undesirable."

The pendulum began to swing when American breeders started to produce white dogs intentionally in the 1970s: one group has petitioned for recognition in American Kennel Club, while another has achieved it in United Kennel Club. In the same decade, dogs from American and Canadian lines were imported into Switzerland. Since 1991 they have been registered as a separate breed there, and today there are reasonable numbers scattered across Europe. The breed was provisionally accepted by FCI in 2001.

BREED QUALITIES

This breed resembles the German Shepherd in almost all respects. It has the same strengths—intelligence, loyalty, and courage—and the same weaknesses—joint and gastrointestinal problems, and a tendency toward fearful or aggressive individuals.

STRIKING Dark skin is preferred on the nose and rims of the eyes, making this a dramatic breed and helping to protect it from sunburn. The dense double coat is medium length and close lying, with a hard, straight topcoat.

WORKING DOGS

The classification of dog breeds is fairly fluid around the world: A dog that sits in one group in one registry might easily find itself in another elsewhere. At one time or another, the majority of all historical breeds have been working dogs of some kind or another, but this term generally covers guarding and rescue breeds, and includes sled-pulling dogs where there is a strong tradition of these breeds. Here, it includes some breeds that began as one thing but became another, such as the Lagotto Romagnolo, originally a hunting retriever but later the only recognized breed of truffle hunter.

ALASKAN MALAMUTE (*see* p. 313) One of the most ancient of all working breeds, the Malamute has the typical wolf-like spitz looks of a sled-pulling breed. Bred to the work for thousands of years, these dogs have boundless energy.

Aidi

ORIGIN Morocco
HEIGHT 21–24 in (53–60 cm)
WEIGHT 50–77 lb (23.0–35.0 kg)
EXERCISE LEVEL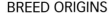
COAT CARE
REGISTERED KC, FCI, AKCs
COLORS White, red, black, black and white

Also called the Chien de Montagne de l'Atlas or Atlas Mountain Dog, this North African mastiff breed is primarily a livestock guardian, but also serves as a household guard dog and a hunting tracker.

BLACK   CREAM   RED/TAN   BLACK AND WHITE

BREED ORIGINS
Known since the Middle Ages, this dog is similar to other white livestock-guarding breeds found across southern Europe, and probably distantly related to them, originating in mastiffs from Asia. It is thought to be close to the Akbash. Traveling with nomadic herders, it has protected encampments and livestock for centuries. It was also used together with the Sloughi for hunting: The Aidi would track the quarry by scent, and at the last the Sloughi would pursue and bring it down. Protective and fearless, it makes a better guard than a family dog and does best in country homes.

COAT FOR ALL SEASONS The long, light-colored coat is an effective protection from bites in a fight. It provides insulation from freezing desert nights, but the Aidi can also tolerate baking sun.

Akbash

ORIGIN Turkey
HEIGHT 28–34 in (70–85 cm)
WEIGHT 90–121 lb (41.0–55.0 kg)
EXERCISE LEVEL
COAT CARE
REGISTERED AKCs
COLORS Creamy white

Also called the Coban Kopegi and the Akbas, this rare breed is from western Turkey. It is probably related to other white mastiff types, from the Anatolian in eastern Turkey to the Pyrenean mountain breeds of France and Spain.

BREED ORIGINS
Dating back to antiquity, this breed may be among the earliest guardians, but different strains have also been used as household guard dogs in their homeland. All types will bark at anything out of place, patrol conscientiously, and tend to behave aggressively to other dogs. They are not suitable for families or inexperienced owners, and do not suit city living.

WHITER SHADE OF PALE White has been a popular color from the earliest times for herd guardians, which see off predators but do not herd or move flocks. Their color distinguishes them from wolves, for the benefit of their owners and charges.

Akita

ORIGIN Japan
HEIGHT 24–28 in (60–70 cm)
WEIGHT 75–110 lb (34.0–50.0 kg)
EXERCISE LEVEL
COAT CARE
REGISTERED KC, FCI, AKCs
COLORS White, white and red, fawn, or brindle; any color (United States)

The largest of the Japanese breeds, this originates in Akita prefecture on the island of Honshu. It has developed along quite different lines in Japan and Europe and in the United States.

GOLD AND WHITE

TAN AND WHITE

BLACK BRINDLE

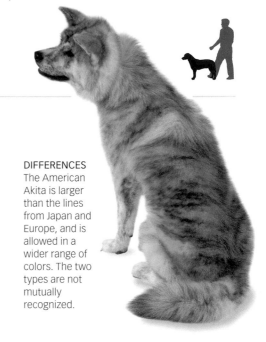

BREED ORIGINS

Used for hunting and fighting in the 19th century, after World War II, the Akita was low in numbers and included German Shepherd crosses. In Japan, breeders worked to restore the old breed, but hybrid dogs were taken home by American soldiers. The breed is now a Natural Monument in its homeland. All Akitas are staunch, fearless fighters that need experienced owners.

DIFFERENCES
The American Akita is larger than the lines from Japan and Europe, and is allowed in a wider range of colors. The two types are not mutually recognized.

Alaskan Malamute

ORIGIN United States
HEIGHT 23–26 in (58–65 cm)
WEIGHT 75–86 lb (34.0–39.0 kg)
EXERCISE LEVEL
COAT CARE
REGISTERED KC, FCI, AKCs
COLORS White with shades of gray or red

This was the preferred sled dog of North America for thousands of years. Its name comes from the Mahlemuts, the Alaskan tribe that kept it. Packs have been used in many polar expeditions.

BLACK AND WHITE

TAN AND WHITE

BREED ORIGINS

Recent genetic research confirmed that this is one of the world's oldest dog breeds. It is an intelligent and tireless pack dog. Loyal, affectionate, and gentle, Malamutes need plenty of work if they are not to become bored and destructive.

PRACTICAL STANDARDS Malamutes' sizes can vary widely, but the breed standards are healthy sizes ideal for pulling work in a matched team.

American Eskimo (Standard)

ORIGIN United States
HEIGHT Over 15 in (38 cm)
WEIGHT 20–35 lb (9.1–16.0 kg)
EXERCISE LEVEL
COAT CARE
REGISTERED AKCs
COLORS White

Not to be confused with the larger white Canadian Eskimo Dog recognized in the United Kingdom, this spirited spitz comes in Standard, Miniature, and Toy sizes (*see* p. 106), packing all the punch of a typical sled-puller in a compact parcel.

BREED ORIGINS

Despite its name, this breed is not actually descended from Eskimo or Inuit dogs, but white spitz dogs brought by European settlers and descended from the German Spitz; anti-German feelings during World War I led to a swift change of identity. Despite its diminutive appearance, this dog has earned its keep: It won popularity performing in the Barnum and Bailey circus, and does well in obedience and agility classes. It makes a noisy watchdog, but may not be appreciated by close neighbours. Some individuals are shy or overly aggressive, but in general this is a good family dog.

SNOW DOG This is a healthy and long-lived little dog that lasts into its teens. The thick double coat is fairly easy to groom, but there is a tendency to brown tear staining on the face.

Appenzell Cattle Dog

ORIGIN Switzerland
HEIGHT 19–23 in (48–58 cm)
WEIGHT 55–70 lb (25.0–32.0 kg)
EXERCISE LEVEL
COAT CARE
REGISTERED KC, FCI, AKCs
COLORS Tricolor

Scarcely seen outside Switzerland, and rare even in its homeland, the Appenzeller Sennenhund or Appenzell Cattle Dog comes from the mountainous northeast of the country. It is one of a quartet of tricolored Swiss farm dogs rescued from extinction in the 20th century.

BREED ORIGINS

The burly looks of the Appenzell suggest it descends from Roman mastiffs, but the quirky tail suggests a more northerly, spitz influence in its ancestry. First described in 1853, it was described as "used partly to guard the homestead, partly to herd cattle"; it was also put to work pulling small carts. Today it is still best suited to a role as a working or guard dog.

FAMILY LIKENESS The Appenzeller is related to the Entelbuch, Bernese, and Great Swiss Mountain breeds: all sharing the tricolor coat, they vary considerably in size, build, and the exact nature of their working history.

Argentinian Mastiff

ORIGIN Argntina
HEIGHT 24–27 in (60–68 cm)
WEIGHT 77–100 lb (35.0–45.0 kg)
EXERCISE LEVEL
COAT CARE
REGISTERED KC, FCI, AKCs
COLORS White

Tight skin shows off the muscle of this vigorous, powerful mastiff, giving it a particularly athletic look. Bred as a hunter, but used as a fighter, the Dogo Argentino has gained some following abroad but remains rare.

BREED ORIGINS

Argentina's first national breed was created in Cordoba, in central Argentina, in the 1930s. Dr. Antonio Nores Martinez crossed local fighting dogs descended from mastiffs, bulldogs, and bull terriers with recognized breeds including the Great Dane and Boxer. Although he used the dogs for hunting large and dangerous game, they were instantly popular in dog fights, a popular activity then and now in the region. Over time, this has also proved itself a formidable guard dog, but its dominance and tenacity require an experienced, firm owner and rule it out as a family or urban companion.

FIGHTING LOOKS The Argentinian Mastiff is often seen with cropped ears where these are legal. This reduces the risk of injury in fights, and gives the dog a more aggressive look.

DANGEROUS DOG? This breed is one expressly restricted to leash and muzzle in British legislation. Well handled, it can be a fine dog, but its image can attract dangerous owners.

Australian Cattle Dog

ORIGIN Australia

HEIGHT 17–20 in (43–51 cm)

WEIGHT 35–44 lb (16.0–20.0 kg)

EXERCISE LEVEL

COAT CARE

REGISTERED KC, AKCs

COLORS Blue or blue speckled, with tan or black markings, red speckled

A tough dog for tough conditions, this breed has also been called the Australian Heeler, Queensland Heeler, Blue Heeler, and Hall's Heeler. It was primarily a cattle drover, but is also a vigilant guard.

RED/TAN   BLUE MOTTLED WITH TAN

BREED ORIGINS

Dogs taken from temperate Europe in the early 19th century wilted in Australia's heat. Legend has it that Thomas Smith Hall of Queensland crossed heat tolerant dingoes with British breeds including Smooth Collies and a droving dog known as the Smithfield, after the London meat market. In another version, a drover named Timmins in New South Wales made the crosses. The resulting breed has boundless reserves of energy and stamina, and is intelligent, but wary of strangers; together these qualities make for a fine guard dog but a troublesome family companion, showing a tendency to snap.

ANCIENT HERITAGE The blue version came from the British breeds, the red from the dingo. The Smithfields had a bobbed tail, and FCI provisionally recognizes a "stumpy tailed" version.

Australian Kelpie

ORIGIN Australia

HEIGHT 17–20 in (43–51 cm)

WEIGHT 24–44 lb (11.0–20.0 kg)

EXERCISE LEVEL

COAT CARE

REGISTERED FCI, AKCs

COLORS Black, blue, red, fawn, chocolate, black and tan, red, red and tan

Australia's most popular working dog, this breed is known and shown around the world. In the United Kingdom it is only eligible for trials, but it excels in these, showing its collie heritage.

BLACK   BLUE   RED/TAN   DARK BROWN   BLACK AND TAN

BREED ORIGINS

There have always been tales that the Kelpie contains dingo blood, and dingo crosses might have been made but not admitted; however, the breed's remarkable trainability makes this claim dubious. Collies from northern England provided much of its stock, with a black-and-tan bitch named Kelpie giving fresh genes and the breed name. Kelpies are tenacious, intelligent, and enthusiastic workers, described as workaholics. They might be regarded as Australia's Border Collie, and need a similar level of commitment to an active and interesting life if they are not to be bored, snappy, and destructive.

BEAUTY OR BRAINS? Today the Kelpie is split into working and show lines. Those who breed working Kelpies for their abilities have less regard for looks.

Austrian Pinscher

ORIGIN Austria
HEIGHT 14–20 in (36–51 cm)
WEIGHT 26–40 lb (12.0–18.0 kg)
EXERCISE LEVEL
COAT CARE
REGISTERED FCI, AKCs
COLORS Shades of yellow to red, black and tan, usually with white

This breed was known throughout the 20th century as the Österreichischer Kurzhaariger Pinscher or Austrian Shorthaired Pinscher. It is still only found in a short but thick and double coat.

GOLD

BLACK AND TAN

BREED ORIGINS

This "biter," related to the German Pinscher, dates back at least to the 18th century. A versatile farm breed, it was kept as a ratter and guard dog, but declined in numbers despite breeders' efforts in the 20th century and is rarely seen today. Still a watchful and noisy guard, its suspicious nature and tendency to aggression prevent it from becoming a popular household dog.

LITTLE CHANGE This strongly built and lively breed is still almost indistinguishable from those found in 18th-century illustrations.

Azores Cattle Dog

ORIGIN Azores/Portugal
HEIGHT 19–24 in (48–60 cm)
WEIGHT 44–77 lb (20.0–35.0 kg)
EXERCISE LEVEL
COAT CARE
REGISTERED FCI, AKCs
COLORS Brindled gray, fawn, or fawn with black overlay

Also called the Cão de Fila de São Miguel or St Miguel Cattle Dog, this dog is a mixture of natural development due to its isolated island home and highly controlled breeding with imported stock.

GRAY

BLACK BRINDLE

BREED ORIGINS

When first discovered in 1429, the Azores lacked large mammals. Cattle were left to breed in the wild, and settlers needed hardy, intelligent dogs to control them. Working dogs from Spain developed into the fila de Terceira, which was crossed with mastiff types to produce this breed by the beginning of the 19th century. A typical cattle dog, this is a tenacious, wily breed and also proved itself capable as a household guard dog. It can have a distrustful attitude toward strangers, but makes a friendly companion if socialized and trained well when young.

LOOKS TOUGH The Azores Cattle Dog has traditionally been shown docked and with its ears cropped. Although carried out for practical purposes in working cattle dogs, this also enhanced guard dogs' aggressive appearance.

Beauceron

ORIGIN France

HEIGHT 24–28 in (60–70 cm)

WEIGHT 66–88 lb (30.0–40.0 kg)

EXERCISE LEVEL

COAT CARE

REGISTERED KC, FCI, AKCs

COLORS Black and tan; gray, black, and tan

Also called the Berger de Beauce or Beauce Shepherd, this breed has been used as a guard and for tracking, and police and military work. It proved unshakeable under fire, carrying messages and supplies and finding the wounded in both World Wars.

BREED ORIGINS

The earliest description of a dog similar to the Beauceron dates back to 1578, but it was not until the 19th century that the longhaired Briard and the shorthaired Beauceron were formally distinguished and described. The early Beauceron was an intrepid but somewhat snappy sheepdog, but careful breeding produced a more tractable character. Intelligent, reliable, and easy to train, it still performs well in agility and obedience classes and makes a good companion and watch dog. A healthy breed, it lives 10–12 years, although some lines are prone to dysplasia and bloat.

CHANGING LOOKS These dogs were also once known as Bas Rouge or Red Stockings, because the coat tends to be marked with tan on the paws and lower legs. The naturally soft ears are sometimes still cropped in some countries.

Bernese Mountain Dog

ORIGIN Switzerland
HEIGHT 23–28 in (58–70 cm)
WEIGHT 88–100 lb (40.0–45.0 kg)
EXERCISE LEVEL
COAT CARE
REGISTERED KC, FCI, AKCs
COLORS Tricolor

The Berner Sennenhund is the largest of the four tricolored Swiss mountain or cattle dogs, and the only one with a long coat. Historically used for herding and pulling carts, it is now a well-established companion breed.

BREED ORIGINS

The exact origins of these breeds are so far back that they are unknown, but Roman mastiffs are among the likely ancestors. The number of foreign dogs brought into Switzerland in the 19th century threatened the native breeds' survival: together with the Appenzell, Entelbuch, and Great Swiss, this breed was saved by the efforts of breeders led by Professor Albert Heim. It is a powerful but affectionate and reliable breed. Tragically, many die young through cancer; the average lifespan has fallen in recent years and is now somewhere around seven years.

BIG AND BOLD Despite its size and sturdy build, the Bernese has historically been a surprisingly agile and fast-moving breed. Like most large dogs, it is prone to hip dysplasia and can suffer from bloat if not fed carefully.

Black Norwegian Elkhound

ORIGIN Norway
HEIGHT 17–19 in (43–49 cm)
WEIGHT 37–40 lb (17.0–18.0 kg)
EXERCISE LEVEL
COAT CARE
REGISTERED FCI
COLORS Black

Smaller than the gray Norwegian Elkhound, the Norsk Elghund Sort is also slightly feistier and may be descended from a different parentage. It is a typical squarely built spitz with a close, short coat.

BREED ORIGINS

The Norwegian Elkhound was thought to be one of the oldest breeds in existence until genetic research showed it to be a recent "reconstruction." The same may be true of the Black breed, which was first distinguished as a separate breed in the late 19th century and is still not recognized in many registries. Traditionally a hunting dog that would stalk prey and then keep it at bay for the hunter, it also served as a guard dog. Today it is rarely seen abroad, but is still kept in its traditional roles in Scandinavia.

LEGGY LOOKS The black version of the Elkhound is longer in the leg than its gray counterpart and not so deep in the body. This lighter, rangier build makes it a more agile and swifter breed.

Black Russian Terrier

ORIGIN Russia
HEIGHT 26–30 in (66–77 cm)
WEIGHT 88–144 lb (40.0–65.0 kg)
EXERCISE LEVEL
COAT CARE
REGISTERED KC, FCI, AKCs
COLORS Black

Variously known in different registries as the Russian Terrier, Black Terrier, Tchiorny Terrier, this is a terrier in name only. Tailor-made as a military dog for the Red Army, it spread beyond its homeland with *glasnost*.

BREED ORIGINS

In the 1940s the Red Star Kennel in Moscow crossed breeds such as the Rottweiler, Airedale Terrier, and German Schnauzers to create a massive, robust, hardy dog of enormous spirit and adaptability. Although wider recognition means it is now bred for a more sedate temperament, it remains wary and quick to react, making it more of a guard than a household dog.

LATE BLOOMER In the early years of its development, this breed was selected purely for ability, health, and character, with little regard for looks. It is now more attractive and consistent, and other qualities have not as yet suffered for this shift in emphasis.

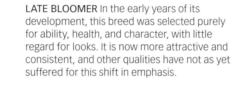

HIS FATHER'S NOSE The solid-looking, moderately broad head clearly shows the influence of Schnauzers and Airedales in the profuse hair, whiskers, and beard.

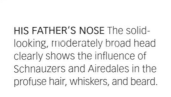

SMART TURN-OUT An imposing and strongly built dog, the Russian has a massive bone structure but should look balanced.

Boxer

ORIGIN Germany

HEIGHT 21–25 in (53–63 cm)

WEIGHT 53–70 lb (24.0–32.0 kg)

EXERCISE LEVEL

COAT CARE

REGISTERED KC, FCI, AKCs

COLORS Shades of fawn, brindle; solid or with white

More accurately known as the Deutscher Boxer, this breed is often seen with cropped ears in the United States. The natural look shows its playful, intelligent—if stubborn—nature far better.

 RED/TAN GOLD BLACK BRINDLE

BREED ORIGINS

The Brabant Bullenbeisser and similar hunting breeds are the immediate ancestors of the Boxer; their task was to seize large game and hold onto it until the huntsmen arrived; hence the broad, shortened muzzle. Bred by huntsmen, for their working qualities, they were variable in type. In the late 19th century, breeders created this physically consistent type for showing. Highly trainable and popular for military and police work, they are nonetheless clowns at heart, and make good family dogs.

TALL TAILS The Boxer was traditionally docked, but this has now changed in Europe. It was feared that the tail would prove variable, since it had never been a feature in breeding choices, but the standard for a high but not curled over tail of moderate thickness has now been set.

HIGH SPIRITS Many Boxers are great jumpers, and need firm, friendly training to keep them quite literally in their place.

Brazilian Mastiff

ORIGIN Brazil

HEIGHT 24–30 in (60–75 cm)

WEIGHT 88–110 lb (40.0–50.0 kg)

EXERCISE LEVEL

COAT CARE

REGISTERED FCI, AKCs

COLORS Any solid color; some white markings

Recognized as the Fila Brasileiro and also known as the Cao de Fila, this massive breed has a well-deserved reputation as a guard. It is prohibited in some countries, including the United Kingdom.

RED/TAN

GOLD

DARK BROWN

BLACK BRINDLE

BREED ORIGINS

This breed was developed in Brazil in the 19th century from Spanish and Portuguese mastiffs, combined with the Bloodhound. It was used to track big game and escaped slaves. It was at first largely a rural breed, but in the 20th century it was popularized by breeders such as Dr. Paulo Santos Cruz. Today this sole remaining Brazilian breed is split into differing bloodlines with differing registries in

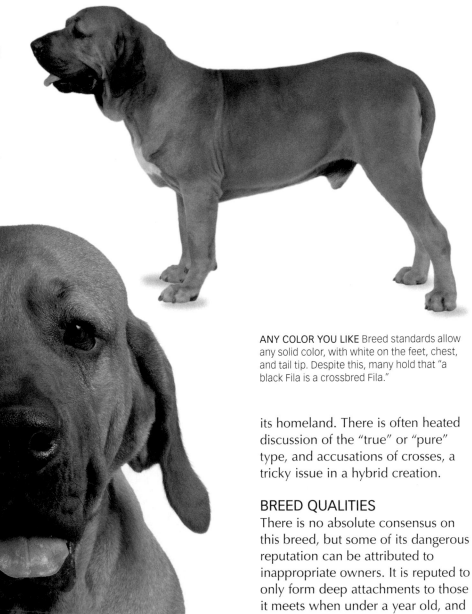

ANY COLOR YOU LIKE Breed standards allow any solid color, with white on the feet, chest, and tail tip. Despite this, many hold that "a black Fila is a crossbred Fila."

its homeland. There is often heated discussion of the "true" or "pure" type, and accusations of crosses, a tricky issue in a hybrid creation.

BREED QUALITIES

There is no absolute consensus on this breed, but some of its dangerous reputation can be attributed to inappropriate owners. It is reputed to only form deep attachments to those it meets when under a year old, and be standoffish after this age. It regards strangers with suspicion, and sees off any perceived threat.

British Bulldog

ORIGIN United Kingdom

HEIGHT 12–14 in (30–36 cm)

WEIGHT 51–55 lb (23.0–25.0 kg)

EXERCISE LEVEL

COAT CARE

REGISTERED KC, FCI, AKCs

COLORS Solid fawn, red, brindle, or with a black mask or white

TAN AND WHITE

BLACK BRINDLE

Recognized by registries simply as the Bulldog, this iconic breed is as British as the John Bull character that it so often accompanied in patriotic cartoons.

BREED ORIGINS

The name "bulldog" has been in use since the 17th century, but the term originally described crosses of bear-baiting mastiffs and tenacious terriers. Bred to hang on to a bull for all they were worth in a fight, they had the short, broad jaw also seen in German Bullenbeissers that performed the same role in the hunt. But these early dogs were lighter, more athletic examples than the breed we have today, with a true fighting dog temperament.

When bull baiting was banned in the 19th century, those who rescued the breed from oblivion created a new type of dog, not only much heavier set but utterly reformed in character.

BREED QUALITIES

Today's Bulldog is almost without exception tolerant and gentle. It might be said that it simply had no energy left for aggression: Breathing disorders and heart trouble plagued the breed. Of late, responsible breeders have begun to reject the extreme looks that exacerbated these conditions, and Bulldogs can now look forward to healthier and longer lives. Their characters are more lively, but still as sweet.

GOING TO EXTREMES The large heads of Bulldogs mean the breed has a high incidence of caesarian births, while the deep folds on the face need scrupulous care to keep skin problems at bay. But for their fans, there is nothing to beat the Bulldog breed.

BRITISH BULLDOG Their smiling faces, stout stature, and ponderous, almost waddling gait have endeared these affectionate dogs to many, insuring this is one of the most popular breeds in a host of countries.

Broholmer

ORIGIN Denmark
HEIGHT 28–30 in (70–75 cm)
WEIGHT 88–154 lb (40.0–70.0 kg)
EXERCISE LEVEL
COAT CARE
REGISTERED FCI
COLORS Yellow to golden red, black; limited white allowed

This large, powerful mastiff takes its name from the estate in Denmark where its champion, Niels Frederik Bernhard Sehested, was Master of the Royal Hunt.

 BLACK   RED/TAN   GOLD

BREED ORIGINS

This breed is descended from the Old Danish Dog, bred from the English Mastiff in the mid-16th century. By the 19th century this was on the verge of oblivion: Sehested re-established the type by the novel approach of giving dogs away but insisting that they be used to continue the breed. A practice favored by free software and "wiki" developers today, this was every bit as successful in the 19th century, and the Broholmer, as it came to be known, was soon widespread. A downturn in Denmark's fortunes in the early 20th century saw a similar decline in the breed, and after World War II it was virtually extinct.

In the 1970s, a group of breeders rebuilt the breed, crossing the best authenticated examples with mastiffs and mutts of the right type, and by the 1980s the results were recognized.

BREED QUALITIES

Today's Broholmer is a calm, confident breed, friendly enough to make a family dog but watchful enough for a guard, which was one of its original uses, alongside serving as a hunter's companion for pursuing stags. With only 1,000 or so registered, breeders still follow Sehested's rule that any dogs approved for breeding must be bred, to further the Broholmer's revival.

TRUE COLORS The original Broholmer was known in both tawny shades and a rich black, but the red was always more popular, perhaps because it was favored by the Danish royals. The revived breed lacked a black line until a carefully chosen black mastiff type was used in a cross in 1997.

Bullmastiff

ORIGIN United Kingdom
HEIGHT 24–27 in (61–69 cm)
WEIGHT 90–130 lb (41.0–59.0 kg)
EXERCISE LEVEL
COAT CARE
REGISTERED KC, FCI, AKCs
COLORS Fawn, gold, red, or brindle

Originally a gamekeeper's dog, bred to deter and detain poachers on nightly patrols, this imposing breed often works as a security or police dog, and is a popular guard breed in South Africa.

RED/TAN   GOLD   BLACK BRINDLE

BREED ORIGINS

The Bullmastiff was created at the end of the 18th century, from crosses of old-style Bulldogs and English Mastiffs. The combination of Bulldog tenacity and speed with Mastiff size and strength was ideal. It makes an effective guard, with a deep but sparingly used voice, and will implacably block intruders or knock them down rather than launch a frenzied attack. Training can be hard work, because it tends to be stubborn, but a well-socialized Bullmastiff is a loyal, even-tempered dog that loves company.

WORKING CLOTHES In gamekeepers' dogs, the camouflage-like brindle coat was common. The Bullmastiff is now usually found in clear red or gold.

Canaan Dog

ORIGIN Israel
HEIGHT 19–24 in (48–61 cm)
WEIGHT 35–55 lb (16.0–25.0 kg)
EXERCISE LEVEL
COAT CARE
REGISTERED KC, FCI, AKCs
COLORS White, sandy, brown, or black; solid or with white

Developed into a named breed in modern Israel, where it is the national dog, the Canaan is a distillation of the ancient pariah dogs that have lived in the Middle East for over 2,000 years.

BLACK   GOLD   DARK BROWN   BLACK AND WHITE

BREED ORIGINS

Archeological evidence and ancient texts show the long heritage of this breed. In the 1930s, Dr. Rudolphina Menzel, a dog trainer and breeder from Austria, was asked to create a breed for Jewish settlers in the Negev region of southern Israel, and the Canaan, drawn from the wild dogs, was the result. Loyal to those it knows, standoffish with others, it has been used as a herder, guard, and military dog.

ANCIENT TYPE The remains of several hundred dogs similar to the Canaan have been found in a Phoenician burial site in Ashkelon, and similar types are shown in a carving of Alexander the Great in Lebanon.

Canary Dog

ORIGIN Canary Islands
HEIGHT 22–26 in (55–65 cm)
WEIGHT 84–130 lb (38.0–59.0 kg)
EXERCISE LEVEL
COAT CARE
REGISTERED FCI, AKCs
COLORS Fawn, brindle shades

Called the Presa Canario or Perro de Presa Canario in Spain, this hunting, guarding, and fighting dog may be the same as the Dogo Canario provisionally recognized by FCI, but some dispute this.

GOLD

BLACK BRINDLE

BREED ORIGINS

This breed has existed on the Canaries, notably Gran Canaria, since at least the 18th century, although guard dogs of this general type are mentioned in documents from the previous two centuries. The Canary Dog is thought to have been created from crosses of the Perro de Bardino Majorero, a local farm breed, with the Mastiff and other foreign dogs brought by visitors and colonists, and was called the "perro de la tierra" or "dog of the land." Numbers decreased in the 20th century, and it faced extinction after dog fights were banned in the 1940s, but it was revived by breeders. Its character and future often raise heated arguments.

BREED QUALITIES

This imposing dog was bred for aggression, dominance, and a strong instinct to guard, so needs an experienced and strong owner to socialize it well. It may not share its home peaceably with other pets, and is not the first choice for a family.

MEAN LOOKER The Presa is powerful but still athletic. It often has its ears cropped, in countries where this is allowed, increasing the aggressive appearance of its distinctive, heavy head. This, and the training and use of the breed in illegal dog fights, have done nothing to help its cause.

Cane Corso Italiano

ORIGIN Italy

HEIGHT 24–27 in (60–68 cm)

WEIGHT 88–110 lb (40.0–50.0 kg)

EXERCISE LEVEL

COAT CARE

REGISTERED FCI, AKCs

COLORS Black, shades of gray or fawn, brindle

Also used for herding and hunting, this breed is primarily a guard. Its name translates approximately as Italian guard dog; it is also called the Cane di Macellaio, Sicilian Branchiero, and Italian Mastiff.

BLACK   GRAY   GOLD   BLACK BRINDLE

BREED ORIGINS

The ultimate ancestor of the Corso is the Roman mastiff. The lighter examples of this type were used not only as military attack dogs but in large game hunting. A natural continuation, the Corso has been kept throughout Italian history and across the country, although in most recent times the highest numbers have been found in southern Italy. A quiet, intelligent breed that is loyal and protective of its home and family, the Corso needs sound training to insure that it is not overly suspicious around strangers.

ROBUST BUILD Traditionally docked and often seen with cropped ears, the breed now sports a more natural look in Europe. It does suffer the same health concerns as other large breeds, particularly with regard to joints.

Carolina Dog

ORIGIN United States
HEIGHT 22 in (55 cm)
WEIGHT 30–40 lb (13.5–18.0 kg)
EXERCISE LEVEL
COAT CARE
REGISTERED AKCs
COLORS White with spots; shades of yellow, orange, fawn, and red

This dingo-like breed is rare, but has proved of interest to scientists because its behavior and DNA profile set it apart from most domesticated dogs. It is classed as a primitive or pariah breed.

RED/TAN   GOLD

BREED ORIGINS

Wild dogs in the woods and swamps of Carolina caught the eye of Dr. I. Lehr Brisbin Jr., who was studying the origins of wild, ancient dogs like the dingo. DNA samples seem to place them far back on the evolutionary tree; these dogs may be closely descended from those that accompanied the first humans to North America. They have been kept locally for their strong herding and hunting drives. They are still semiwild, and are said to need careful, early socialization and remain shy but loyal to their immediate human pack.

PRIMITIVE LOOKS The strong build, pricked ears and short, dense coat are close to wild features, and the curved "fish hook" tail is characteristic. The famous "Old Yeller" character may have been this type of dog.

Chinook

ORIGIN United States
HEIGHT 21–24 in (53–61 cm)
WEIGHT 65–90 lb (29.5–41.0 kg)
EXERCISE LEVEL
COAT CARE
REGISTERED AKCs
COLORS Golden

This rare breed was created to pull sleds, and suffered a decline in numbers as the need for its strength and determination at its task diminished. American breeders have worked hard to bring it back from extinction.

BREED ORIGINS

After working with dog teams in the Klondike, Arthur Treadwell Walden set out to create a powerful but gentle breed in the early 20th century. The breed founder, Chinook, named after an Eskimo dog that had impressed Walden, was bred to Belgian and German Shepherds and possibly huskies. Early Chinooks broke records, but by the 1980s the breed was virtually extinct. Crossbreeding has reduced its working drive to more manageable levels, but this is still a dog that likes a lot to do. They love sledding, skijoring, and carting and work well in harness.

UNUSUAL LOOKS Although Chinook's dam was descended from Admiral Peary's sled dog Polaris, his sire was a crossing of a yellow mongrel or mastiff type, giving this breed a type quite distinct from most sled dogs.

Chow Chow

ORIGIN China
HEIGHT 18–22 in (45–56 cm)
WEIGHT 44–70 lb (20.0–32.0 kg)
EXERCISE LEVEL
COAT CARE
REGISTERED KC, FCI, AKCs
COLORS White, cream, fawn, red, blue, black

Whether smooth or rough coated, the Chow Chow looks like no other breed. It is one of the most ancient of all breeds, and has a varied history covering every role from working dog to dinner.

BLACK

CREAM

RED/TAN

BREED ORIGINS

Genetic research confirms the Chow as an ancient type. In Asia it was used for hunting, sled pulling, herding, and guarding, while its fur was valued and its flesh was eaten. It came to the West from China in the 19th century and was named "chow chow"—a pidgin English term for miscellaneous cargo.

BREED QUALITIES

This breed is still more than capable of fulfilling its historic guarding role, although it has not found favor as a herding or hunting dog in the West. Although breeders have been working to produce a Chow with more of a laid-back, family dog temperament, it remains mostly an independent, stubborn, and slightly suspicious breed. Early socialization and a strong owner are vital.

CONSTANT CARE The Chow is prone to a range of joint problems and can suffer eyelid entropion. The coat is also a serious commitment, since it sheds heavily all year round.

PAINT IT BLACK One very distinctive feature of the Chow Chow is its completely black tongue. The trait appears to be dominant, because crossbreed offspring also show this feature.

Corded Poodle

ORIGIN Germany
HEIGHT 9–24 in (24–60 cm)
WEIGHT 45–70 lb (20.5–32.0 kg)
EXERCISE LEVEL
COAT CARE
REGISTERED KC, FCI, AKCs
COLORS Any solid color

Some dispute that this is a breed at all, since all Poodle coats form cords if allowed, and the coat of a Corded Poodle could be brushed out. But the types have been distinct for a century.

CREAM   GOLD   DARK BROWN

BREED ORIGINS

Although in general form, this is virtually identical to the more fluffy, pom-pom poodle, the differences do go a little deeper than a hairstyle choice. The coat of a Corded is finer in texture, and this type is said to be descended more from hunting than herding lines. In the 19th century the corded look was popular but probably a torment for the dogs, with greased dreadlocks trailing on the ground. The curly, clipped look eventually won more favor, and the corded looks and lines diminished. Some breed clubs, such as FCI (which calls this Caniche) and AKC, still include a section within the Poodle breed standard for all sizes of the Corded, but today it is a rarity and usually seen in the larger Standard Poodle size.

CORD COAT The coat is encouraged into narrow cords, splitting any broader matts. Leave-in conditioner is now used instead of oil or grease, which turned rancid. If shampooed, dogs should be rinsed well and blow dried very thoroughly after.

BREED QUALITIES

This is an intelligent, good-natured dog that trains easily, being equally at home in the family or guarding the home; the larger size in which this type is seen is the calmest. Like all poodles, they love energetic games, especially those involving water. Although long lived, there are hereditary health issues, such as thyroid problems and hip displasia.

Czechoslovakian Wolfdog

ORIGIN Czech Republic and Slovakia

HEIGHT 24–30 in (60–75 cm)

WEIGHT 44–77 lb (20.0–35.0 kg)

EXERCISE LEVEL

COAT CARE

REGISTERED FCI

COLORS Yellowish- to silver-gray with light mask, neck, and forechest

Recognized as the Ceskoslovensky Vlciak, this breed is not simply a dog that resembles an ancestral wolf but the result of crossing dogs back to wolves. This hairpin bend in canine evolution has both good and bad consequences.

BREED ORIGINS

The history of this breed begin in 1955, with the experimental crossing of a German Shepherd to a Carpathian wolf. These crosses, based on the reported occasional breedings between Eskimo dogs with these wolves, established that crosses with sire or dam of either type produced fertile offspring. From 1965 crosses were planned to improve the working abilities of the German Shepherd, which is genetically closer to Mastiffs, Boxers, and other guarding breeds than to herding dogs. The Wolfdog was officially recognized as a national breed in the USSR in 1982, and in 1999 by the FCI.

BREED QUALITIES

Wild pets have always had a certain glamor, but need special licences; hybrids are a legal gray area. They are also variably successful: With those wild looks come less desirable wild traits. The Wolfdog is lively, fearless, and courageous, but it is also very independent, not at all easy to train, and not recommended for city life, family homes, or frequent meetings with unfamiliar dogs—which can make it a challenge to own and exercise. Early and thorough socialization is vital.

WILD WAYS This breed doesn't just look like a wolf, it behaves like one, with a strong pack instinct and a reduced inclination to bark. It is easily bored and needs imaginative, structured training.

Dalmatian

ORIGIN Croatia or India
HEIGHT 21–24 in (54–61 cm)
WEIGHT 55–66 lb (25.0–30.0 kg)
EXERCISE LEVEL
COAT CARE
REGISTERED KC, FCI, AKCs
COLORS White with black or liver spots

Instantly recognizable, famous for one hundred and one reasons, the Dalmatian or Dalmatinac has in its time been a hunting dog, a herder, a ratter, and a carriage dog.

BREED ORIGINS

Dogs like this have been known in Dalmatia, now Croatia, for 4,000 years. But the Bengal Pointer, a similar dog from India, was known in the United Kingdom in 1700: Which is the ancestor of the breed we know today is not certain. Deafness and urinary stones are health issues, and males especially can be aggressive—early training is vital, as well as a long daily run.

LOOK DEEPER The smart coat and fame of the breed attract many owners, but some are just not prepared for the time and energy demanded, particularly by a young dog.

Danish Farm Dog

ORIGIN Denmark/Sweden
HEIGHT 12–16 in (30–40 cm)
WEIGHT 26–31 lb (12.0–14.0 kg)
EXERCISE LEVEL
COAT CARE
REGISTERED AKCs
COLORS White and red, white and black, tricolor

In Denmark and Sweden this is known as the Dansk/Svensk Gaardhund or Gardhund, but it served as a ratter, herder, and family dog as well as a watchdog. Today it is a cheerful companion.

BLACK   TAN AND WHITE   CREAM   RED/TAN   BLACK AND WHITE

BREED ORIGINS

Once, all-purpose farm dogs like this were found across Europe, declining as small farms gave way to larger, more industrial enterprises. Almost lost, it was revived in the late 20th century through the joint efforts of Swedish and Danish breeders, and recognized with dual nationality. It is still not often seen, and recognition beyond its homeland is only through a few rare breed societies so far.

Lively, curious, and playful, they learn quickly and love games such as hide-and-seek. They are friendly dogs, and never shy about asking for attention.

NATURALLY TRIM This breed can be gangly in youth, taking up to three years to develop its compact adult shape. The tail is naturally anything from full length to absent but is not docked, a practice illegal in its homeland.

Dobermann

ORIGIN Germany

HEIGHT 24–28 in (60–70 cm)

WEIGHT 66–88 lb (30.0–40.0 kg)

EXERCISE LEVEL

COAT CARE

REGISTERED KC, FCI, AKCs

COLORS Black, brown, blue, or fawn, with tan

More often called the Doberman Pinscher in North America, this breed bears the name of its original creator. It has been tremendously popular as a guarding breed and won notoriety as much as fame, not all of it deserved.

BREED ORIGINS

German tax collector Louis Dobermann created this dog in the 19th century as a bodyguard. He may have used the best of the dogs that came through his care as a part-time dog catcher, including some of the breeds used to create the German Shepherd; the Dobermann has also been used in police and security work.

A macho image and unscrupulous over-breeding have caused problems.

Some lines became aggressive or prone to fear biting, so check the breeder's history. Although this is not suitable as a family dog, it should not be left entirely alone as a guard dog either: It needs plenty of interaction from an experienced owner. Health problems include cervical spondylitis, Von Willebrands disease, bloat, hip dysplasia, and congenital heart disorders, so a veterinary check is essential before buying.

DOBERMANN STYLES Weimaraners, Manchester Terriers, Rottweilers, and German Pinscher may have influenced Dobermann looks. European dogs are now seen in their natural state, with long tails and soft ears, while American dogs are still usually docked and have ears cropped to points.

Dogue de Bordeaux

ORIGIN France
HEIGHT 23–27 in (58–68 cm)
WEIGHT 100–121 lb (45.0–55.0 kg)
EXERCISE LEVEL
COAT CARE
REGISTERED KC, FCI, AKCs
COLORS Shades of fawn

Also called the French Mastiff and Bordeaux Bulldog, this is the survivor of three historical types: the Toulouse, the Paris, and the Bordeaux. It won fame beyond its homeland slobbering over Tom Hanks in the 1989 film *Turner and Hooch*.

BREED ORIGINS

One of the most ancient French breeds, this is probably decended from Asian mastiffs, maybe crossed with English and Spanish types. Found in southwestern France, it was close to extinction after World War II, but revived in the 1960s. Still a formidable guard, and aggressive with other dogs, breeding has softened its temperament to make a loyal, calm companion.

RAW POWER All parts of this typical mastiff, from the broad head to the hock length tail, are thickset and powerful. The short soft coat should always show a mask on the face that is black or red, noticeably darker than the main color.

East Siberian Laika

ORIGIN Siberia
HEIGHT 22–25 in (56–64 cm)
WEIGHT 40–50 lb (10.0–20.0 kg)
EXERCISE LEVEL
COAT CARE
REGISTERED FCI
COLORS Solid, patched, or ticked white, gray, black, red, and brown

Known in its homeland as the Vostotchno-Sibirskaïa Laïka, this working dog is rarely seen elsewhere, but is an intriguing example of a breed that survived isolation, cut off from outside influences.

BLACK GRAY DARK BROWN BLACK BRINDLE

BREED ORIGINS

Siberia had a natural stock of spitz-type dogs close to the wolf, bred for hunting and pulling in the 19th century. In the mid-20th century, biologist K.G. Abramov was studying wildlife in an area now a UNESCO biosphere, and also wrote a breed standard for these dogs. Essentially a rural hunting and guarding breed, it does not adapt to other lifestyles easily. The dense double coat requires some care with grooming.

SIBERIAN STRENGTH This is a large, powerful breed, but does vary, including lighter pulling dogs and more powerful hunting types. The latter will bring game to bay and await the arrival of the hunter, barking all the time.

English Mastiff

ORIGIN United Kingdom
HEIGHT 28–30 in (70–75 cm)
WEIGHT 165–187 lb (75.0–85.0 kg)
EXERCISE LEVEL
COAT CARE
REGISTERED KC, FCI, AKCs
COLORS Shades of fawn

This is often recognized simply as the Mastiff, but because the term mastiff describes a whole group of dogs, it is helpful to acknowledge its national roots. The name itself may come from the Anglo-Saxon "masty," for powerful, an apt description.

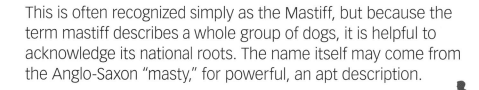

BREED ORIGINS
This large breed has existed in the British Isles for at least 2,000 years. It may have arrived with Mediterranean traders; the Romans took it home as a fighting dog. It is rare today, not least because it needs a generously proportioned home and takes a great deal of feeding, and its sheer size makes it unwise to keep around small children. It is prone to bloat and joint problems, and lives about ten years.

BIG LAYABOUT
Despite the formidable appearance, this breed is a gentle giant if well socialized and trained. It is inclined to be lazy, but ought to take plenty of exercise to avoid obesity.

Estrela Mountain Dog

ORIGIN Portugal
HEIGHT 24–28 in (62–72 cm)
WEIGHT 66–110 lb (30.0–50.0 kg)
EXERCISE LEVEL
COAT CARE
REGISTERED KC, FCI
COLORS Fawn, yellow, wolf-gray; may be with white

This is called the Cão da Serra da Estrela in its homeland, and known as a fierce and watchful herd guardian. It has become popular elsewhere in Europe, but is less so further afield.

GRAY   BLUE

BREED ORIGINS
This is the best known and oldest of all Portuguese breeds. For centuries, it moved from the lowlands to the high mountain ranges with the flocks, defending them from wolves. Developments in farming and the elimination of wolves have left it seeking new employment as a companion. Given firm training and plenty of activity, it makes a good rural companion and guard.

RUGGED TYPE The heavy coat of this breed provided protection from the cold and when fighting, but this dog came down the mountains in winter and can be comfortable in warm climates. Like other large breeds, it can suffer hip dysplasia.

Eurasier

ORIGIN Germany
HEIGHT 19–24 in (48–60 cm)
WEIGHT 40–70 lb (18.0–32.0 kg)
EXERCISE LEVEL
COAT CARE
REGISTERED KC, FCI
COLORS Any color except white and liver

Still a rarity outside Germany, this luxuriantly coated breed has the typical spitz-type looks of an energetic sledge-pulling dog, but in fact is something of a stay-at-home.

GRAY

BLUE

GOLD

DARK BROWN

BLACK BRINDLE

BREED ORIGINS
Although it resembles sledge dogs that have been known for centuries, this breed is in fact a recent concoction of older breeds. It was created in the 1960s by German breeder Julius Wipfel, beginning with a cross of the Chow Chow and the Wolfspitz or Keeshond. This crossbreed was first called, rather unimaginatively, a Wolf-Chow. It was in turn crossed with the Samoyed to bring in new genetic material, and was renamed the Eurasier.

BREED QUALITIES
Although intelligent, this breed can be stubborn and so not one of the most trainable. It responds well to a consistent, fair owner, but tends to bond strongly to that one person, and ignore all others. Reserve can border on timidity, and this is a quiet dog that rarely barks.

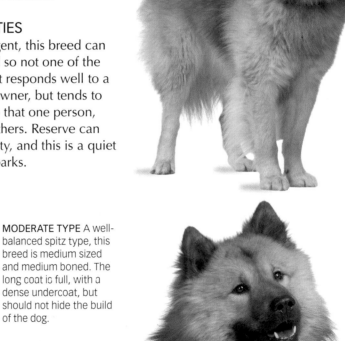

MODERATE TYPE A well-balanced spitz type, this breed is medium sized and medium boned. The long coat is full, with a dense undercoat, but should not hide the build of the dog.

Finnish Spitz

ORIGIN Finland
HEIGHT 15–20 in (38–50 cm)
WEIGHT 31–35 lb (14.0–16.0 kg)
EXERCISE LEVEL
COAT CARE
REGISTERED KC, FCI, AKCs
COLORS Fawn shades

This is the national dog of Finland, where it is called the Suomenpystykorva; it is also known as the Finsk Spets. A lively little spitz, it has become a popular companion at home and abroad.

BREED ORIGINS

The exact ancestors of this breed are unknown, but probably arrived in Finland with the original settlers. Dogs of this type have been used for hunting for centuries all over Finland, and it is still a popular gundog. When registration started in the 19th century, most were from the eastern and northern regions; when parts of Finnish Karelia were ceded to the Soviet Union, the dogs there became Karelo-Finnish Laikas. It makes a good companion for an active owner, but is rather independent in spirit and not the ideal choice for a family, and can be too noisy for close urban living.

OUTDOOR BREED Happiest when out and about, this active breed is still close to its hunting past, when it was used for treeing small game and barking until the hunter arrived.

Giant Schnauzer

ORIGIN Germany
HEIGHT 24–28 in (60–70 cm)
WEIGHT 70–77 lb (32.0–35.0 kg)
EXERCISE LEVEL
COAT CARE
REGISTERED KC, FCI, AKCs
COLORS Black, salt and pepper

Known as the Riesenschnauzer in Germany, this breed makes a set with the smaller Schnauzer and Miniature or Zwergschnauzer. A powerful breed with a dominant tendency, it is said by its devotees to be worth taking time and trouble over.

BREED ORIGINS

This was originally a herding dog, and common on farms across southern Germany as far back as the Middle Ages, although when it was first shown it was under the name Russian Bear Schnauzer. The costs of feeding such a large breed meant it eventually gave way to smaller breeds, but it enjoyed a revival of popularity in the late 19th century working to control livestock as a butcher's dog.

This breed is too territorial and dominant to be recommended as a family companion, and can be spectacularly destructive if neglected or bored. Given an active, involved, and experienced owner, a Schnauzer can excel as a guard or sporting dog. Giants are prone to cancer, bloat, epilepsy, and hip dysplasia.

BORN TO BE BOSS Everything about the Schnauzer, from its stocky build to its strongly boned face, is designed to inspire respect. It was traditionally docked, but European dogs now have a natural tail; American dogs may be docked and have ears cropped to points.

Great Dane

ORIGIN Germany
HEIGHT 31–36 in (79–92 cm)
WEIGHT 110–176 lb (50.0–80.0 kg)
EXERCISE LEVEL
COAT CARE
REGISTERED KC, FCI, AKCs
COLORS Fawn, brindle, blue, black, white with black or blue

German Mastiff is a better translation of this breed's other name, Deutsche Dogge: This breed has nothing to do with Denmark. Once a hunting dog, war dog, and guard, it is now mostly a companion.

 BLACK
 BLUE
 BLACK BRINDLE

BREED ORIGINS

The origins of this breed are obscure; it is probably descended from Alaunts, mastiffs brought to Europe by the Alans in the 5th century. A match for wild boar, bears, and wolves, these were crossed with Greyhounds to create more powerful but agile dogs called "Dogge" in Germany. The Deutsche Dogge was born out of an amalgamation of the various types in the late 19th century.

BREED QUALITIES

Today's breed is a gentle giant, relaxed around children and other dogs, quiet and relatively inactive indoors, which is fortunate given its size: A cluttered home is not recommended. Although adults are relaxed and dignified dogs, the energy and ungainliness of young Great Danes is legendary. This breed is also renowned as a champion drooler.

SIZE MATTERS The great size of this breed makes it particularly prone to joint problems, tail injuries, bone cancers, and heart disease. Bloat is also a danger if it is not carefully fed. This is not a long-lived breed, usually lasting no longer than a decade.

Great Swiss Mountain Dog

ORIGIN Switzerland
HEIGHT 24–28 in (60–72 cm)
WEIGHT 130–135 lb (59.0–61.0 kg)
EXERCISE LEVEL
COAT CARE
REGISTERED FCI
COLORS Tricolor

Also called the Great Swiss Cattle Dog, which is a more accurate translation of Grosser Schweizer Sennenhund, this is a very typical Swiss mountain breed and the largest of the four surviving cattle-droving breeds.

BREED ORIGINS

The various strains of Swiss cattle dog, probably descended from Roman mastiffs, were all in danger of dying out at the end of the 19th century. One of the people responsible for saving them was Professor Alber Heim. When presented with a "shorthaired Bernese Mountain Dog" in 1909, he recognized it as a separate strain of large Mountain Dog or butcher's dog, and found

enough remaining individuals to keep the breed going. Today they are bred across Europe and in North America, and make calm household companions, although they can be territorial and suspicious of strangers.

BIG BUT NOT CLUMSY Although large, these dogs are still agile, and appreciate plenty of activity. Bloat and joint problems are an issue. One unusual feature is that some grow too many eyelashes; this may need surgical correction.

Greenland Dog

ORIGIN Greenland (Denmark)
HEIGHT 22–25 in (56–64 cm)
WEIGHT 66–70 lb (30.0–32.0 kg)
EXERCISE LEVEL
COAT CARE
REGISTERED KC, FCI, AKCs
COLORS Any color

Also called the Greenland Husky or Grønlandshund, this robust and vigorous dog likes nothing better than to be on the move. Despite its friendly, "smiling" face, it is something of a one-person dog.

CREAM   DARK BROWN   GOLD AND WHITE   TAN AND WHITE

BREED ORIGINS

This is thought to be among the world's oldest breeds, developed in relative isolation from ancestors that arrived some 12,000 years ago. It was used for hunting and sled pulling, and its numbers diminished as lifestyle changes and motorized transportation rendered it less important. It is not naturally suited to life as a family dog, because it tends to be aloof with people other than the owner it

sees as pack leader, and it demands a great deal of activity if it is not to become bored. For some owners, however, these make it the perfect companion, and its popularity is growing among enthusiastic hikers.

PERFECT DESIGN This dog is designed to survive bitter cold. The coat is long, thick, and bristling to retain air, and has a dense wooly undercoat, while the small ears are unlikely to become frostbitten.

Hovawart

ORIGIN Germany
HEIGHT 23–28 in (58–70 cm)
WEIGHT 55–90 lb (25.0–41.0 kg)
EXERCISE LEVEL
COAT CARE
REGISTERED KC, FCI, AKCs
COLORS Gold, black, black and gold

This breed's name comes from Middle High German, and means yard or farm guard, describing what dogs like this did centuries ago. Today's breed is kept across Europe, with some in North America.

BLACK

GOLD

BLACK AND TAN

BREED ORIGINS

The "Hofwarth" was first recorded in the 13th century, but this ancient breed died out. In the early 20th century it was recreated using farm dogs from northern and southern Germany, and possibly other breeds including the German Shepherd, all chosen for type. Reserved, with a tendency to become very attached to one person, this elegant breed lives up to its historic role.

HEALTHY HIPS
Although this is quite a large and heavy dog, strict breeding practices have reduced the incidence of hip dysplasia to low levels in some lines, so it is important to choose healthy stock.

Kai

ORIGIN Japan
HEIGHT 18–22 in (45–55 cm)
WEIGHT 35–40 lb (16.0–18.0 kg)
EXERCISE LEVEL
COAT CARE
REGISTERED KC, FCI, AKCs
COLORS Black brindle, red brindle, and brindle

Like several other indigenous breeds, the Kai is designated a Natural Monument in its homeland. It is also known as the Kai Inu, Tora Inu, and Kai Tora-ken: *Inu* means "dog" and *tora* means "tiger."

BREED ORIGINS

Japan only came to classify and appreciate its native dogs in the 1930s, largely thanks to the research of breeder Haruo Isogai. The Kai takes its name from the isolated, mountainous region of Yamanashi Prefecture where it developed. Still rare even in Japan, it is distinguished by its brindled coat. It tends to attach itself to one person, and can be reserved with strangers.

WATCHFUL HUNTER
A well-balanced, sturdily built mountain dog, the Kai was an all-purpose country dog, used for guarding and hunting among other duties. This is an intelligent and brave breed.

Karelian Bear Dog

ORIGIN Finland/Russia
HEIGHT 19–23 in (48–58 cm)
WEIGHT 44–50 lb (20.0–23.0 kg)
EXERCISE LEVEL
COAT CARE
REGISTERED KC, FCI, AKCs
COLORS Black, usually with white

Also called the Karjalankarhukoira or Karelsk Bjornhund, this tough, powerful breed originates in the province of Karelia, largely ceded to the Soviet Union in the 20th century.

BLACK

BLACK AND WHITE

BREED ORIGINS

The exact origins of the breed are not known, although it is related to the lesser-known Russo-European Laika. but dogs of approximately this type accompanied the first settlers to Finland thousands of years ago. Surviving as hunters, these settlers valued dogs big and bold enough to tackle predators like bears, wolves, and lynx, as well as take down elk. Although a popular dog right into the 20th century, the breed was drastically reduced in World War II, and all Karelians today are said to be traceable back to just 40 individuals. Today it is once more bred across Europe and Scandinavia and even in North America. Fearless and stubborn, it is not a good city or family dog, but is an excellent rural companion.

ALWAYS KEEN A favored companion of hunters throughout Finland, Sweden, and Norway, where it is used mainly to pursue large game such as elk, this breed is a compulsive and even obsessive hunter.

REGIONAL SPECIALITY In many ways, this is an absolutely typical Scandinavian spitz. Only the black-and-white coat is unusual, distinguishing it from other breeds such as the Finnish Spitz.

Keeshond

ORIGIN Germany

HEIGHT 17–18 in (43–45 cm)

WEIGHT 55–66 lb (25.0–30.0 kg)

EXERCISE LEVEL

COAT CARE

REGISTERED KC, FCI, AKCs

COLORS Mix of gray, black, and cream

Although recognized in many registries as the Keeshond, this is known within FCI by its German name of Wolfspitz, and classed as a subcategory of the Deutscher Spitz or German Spitz, an umbrella breed that also includes the powde puff Pomeranian.

BREED ORIGINS

All the spitz dogs of Germany are descendants of the ancient Torfhund or "peat dog"; devotees claim them to be the oldest breed in Central Europe, and progenitors of other spitz breeds. They worked as guards, ratters, and barge dogs in Germany and the southern Netherlands, and the name Keeshond is Dutch, coming from the dog owned by the 18th-century rebel

Cornelis or Kees de Gyselaer. Calm and amiable enough to be a good family dog, alert enough to be a guard, they remain a popular breed today, although they are spirited dogs and need firm, consistent training.

CROWNING GLORY Various shades of coat were once linked with different regions, but today the thick coat is more uniform. Daily grooming is a must, especially during the twice-yearly molts.

Korean Jindo Dog

ORIGIN Korea

HEIGHT 16–23 in (41–58 cm)

WEIGHT 22–44 lb (10.0–20.0 kg)

EXERCISE LEVEL

COAT CARE

REGISTERED None

COLORS Red or black, solid or with white, black and tan, white

Similar to the Japanese breed the Shiba Inu, this dog is designated a National Monument in its homeland, and export is restricted.

BLACK   RED/TAN   BLACK AND WHITE   TAN AND WHITE   BLACK AND TAN

BREED ORIGINS

This compact, lively, and healthy spitz of primitive type developed naturally in isolation on Jindo Island. Its defining qualities are intelligence, independent spirit, and loyalty—legends of Jindo Dogs returning home even when sold to distant new owners abound in Korea. While not ideal for family or city life, it can be rewarding for an experienced owner, and, although not recognized abroad, many expatriate Koreans take these dogs with them.

TRUE COLORS In Korea only white Jindos and red or tan Jindos are currently recognized, so these are the most frequently seen colors. Historically, black, black-and-tan, and red-and-white Jindo Dogs have also been valued.

Labradoodle

ORIGIN Australia
HEIGHT 13–26 in (33–65 cm)
WEIGHT 22–88 lb (10.0–40.0 kg)
EXERCISE LEVEL
COAT CARE
REGISTERED None
COLORS Wide range of solid colors

This is the standard-bearer for today's fashionable crossbreeds. In Australia, the Labradoodle has a breed standard with three sizes and is on the way to being regarded as a "purebred."

BLACK

CREAM

BLUE

GOLD

DARK BROWN

BREED ORIGINS
In the 1990s, breeder Wally Conron began crossing Labradors and Poodles, aiming to create a nonshedding guide dog suitable for allergy sufferers. This is a work in progress, but Australian breeders hope to achieve a reliable coat while retaining a broad gene pool and an intelligent, biddable nature from the parent breeds. Elsewhere, Labradoodles are often first-generation crosses and highly variable.

CRUCIAL COAT The nonshedding coat is not fixed in early generation Labradoodles. To meet the breed standard in Australia the coat must be single.

Lagotto Romagnolo

ORIGIN Italy
HEIGHT 14–19 in (35–48 cm)
WEIGHT 24–35 lb (11.0–16.0 kg)
EXERCISE LEVEL
COAT CARE
REGISTERED KC, FCI, AKCs
COLORS White, brown, orange, white with brown or orange

Although it is by no means a numerous or widespread breed, the Romagna Water Dog has two distinct strains: Some are bred for their working qualities, while others are bred for family life.

DARK BROWN

TAN AND WHITE

BREED ORIGINS
This is an ancient breed, developed to retrieve game in the marshes of Ravenna and Comacchio. When these marshes were drained, it found new employment as a truffle-hound in the open country and hills of Romagna, and a good truffle hunter is still a valuable dog. It makes a healthy, long-lived, energetic, and affectionate family dog, although it does not suit city life.

CARING FOR CURLS Some hold that the Lagotto coat should simply be clipped twice a year and then left, but it can become matted and regular combing is advisable. Brushing will make the coat frizzy and poodle-like, destroying the characteristic ringlets.

Landseer

ORIGIN Canada/Germany/Switzerland
HEIGHT 26–28 in (66–71 cm)
WEIGHT 110–150 lb (50.0–68.0 kg)
EXERCISE LEVEL
COAT CARE
REGISTERED KC, FCI, AKCs
COLORS Black and white

In most registries, this name means simply a Newfoundland in a piebald coat. FCI, however, recognizes a separate Landseer breed or "European Continental type," named after painter Sir Edwin Landseer, who frequently depicted this type.

BREED ORIGINS

Dogs in Newfoundland developed from a complex mix of ancient arrivals with water dogs and mastiffs brought by fishermen. Most famous is the sturdily built Newfoundland, but some breeders continued to produce a leggier type close to the original Greater St John's Dog, and this has become the Landseer. A true gentle giant, it makes calm and biddable family dog.

ARTISTIC CHOICE
As well as appearing in famous Landseer paintings, this dog was the original canine nursemaid, Nana, in *Peter Pan*— although she has also been depicted as a St. Bernard and an Old English Sheepdog.

Leonberger

ORIGIN Germany
HEIGHT 26–32 in (65–80 cm)
WEIGHT 100–165 lb (45.0–75.0 kg)
EXERCISE LEVEL
COAT CARE
REGISTERED KC, FCI, AKCs
COLORS Cream to red with a dark mask

This dog takes its name from the town of Leonberg in Baden-Württemburg, where it was created as a hybrid from established breeds. Despite outrage from other breeders, skilled marketing by its creator saw the Leonberger become a status symbol.

BREED ORIGINS

In the early 19th century, a local politician Heinrich Essig created this majestic breed from a Newfoundland and a St. Bernard. Its strength, calmness, loyalty, and obedience insured its eventual acceptance. Reduced in numbers by two World Wars, it is a much-loved family dog today, although it is sadly short lived; cancer is a common cause of death, as in some other giant breeds.

LEONINE LOOKS The Leonburger is said to have been inspired by the town's heraldic emblem, the lion, but early dogs were black and white since they were bred from a Landseer-type Newfoundland.

LEONBERGER Like many modern crossbreeds, this mix of older breeds was at first dismissed as a novelty, but it has become established and is growing in popularity. However, it is not easy to breed and remains relatively rare.

Neapolitan Mastiff

ORIGIN Italy
HEIGHT 24–30 in (60–75 cm)
WEIGHT 110–165 lb (50.0–75.0 kg)
EXERCISE LEVEL
COAT CARE
REGISTERED KC, FCI, AKCs
COLORS Solid black, blue, gray, solid or brindled fawn to red

The ancestor of many mastiff breeds, the Mastino Napoletano is distinguished by its loose, drooping skin, a relic from its distant past as a fighting dog.

 BLACK
 GRAY
 BLUE
 RED/TAN
 BLACK BRINDLE

BREED ORIGINS

This is probably the most direct descendant of the great Roman Mastiff, described in the first century by Columella as a perfect house guard. On the verge of extinction after World War II, it was saved through the efforts of Dr. Pierro Scanziani and Mario Querci. Instinctively protective and dominant, it makes a good guard if given early and thorough obedience training and socialization.

INNER BEAUTY Messy eaters and champion droolers, these are not for the houseproud. Cropped ears and docked tails have given way to natural looks in Europe.

New Guinea Singing Dog

ORIGIN New Guinea
HEIGHT 14–15 in (35–38 cm)
WEIGHT 18–31 lb (8.0–14.0 kg)
EXERCISE LEVEL
COAT CARE
REGISTERED AKCs
COLORS Shades of red with or without white markings, black and tan

Named for their unique modulated howling, this breed is just one small step away from its time in the wild. Thought to be close to the Dingo, it is a true curiosity of the canine world.

 RED/TAN
 BLACK AND TAN

BREED ORIGINS

The Singing Dog was part of New Guinea's rich endemic fauna. One of the oldest dogs, it bred in isolation there for some 6,000 years, and is close to a living fossil of the early dog. It disappeared in the wild in the 20th century, but was saved by breeding in zoos. Still dangerously rare, it is intelligent, free-spirited, and not a breed that simply anyone eager or curious could take into their home.

CALL OF THE WILD These hardy dogs have a fox-like build and graceful movements. If socialized early they can be affectionate with their owners, but tend to be aloof and usually aggressive toward other dogs. They have a strong hunting drive, likely to overcome what training they do absorb.

Newfoundland

ORIGIN Canada
HEIGHT 26–28 in (66–71 cm)
WEIGHT 110–152 lb (50.0–69.0 kg)
EXERCISE LEVEL
COAT CARE
REGISTERED KC, FCI, AKCs
COLORS Black, brown, white with black

The ancient Molossus of the eastern Mediterranean gave us all the mastiff breeds we have today. They range from fighting dogs, through guardian breeds, to the gentle giant that is the Newfie.

DARK BROWN

BLACK AND WHITE

BREED ORIGINS

The Newfoundland's origins are uncertain enough to attract romantic legends. Nomadic Indian dogs, Viking bear dogs, and the Labrador are all cited as ancestors, as are crosses in the 18th century between local dogs and mastiffs owned by passing fishermen. Whatever its roots, the Newfie was invaluable to fishermen, pulling boats, carrying fishing lines to shore, and retrieving anything—or anyone— that fell overboard. Today, transportation and communications improvements have left the breed without an obvious working role, but it has easily made the transition to much loved family companion.

ABLE BODIED Many people have owed their lives to the Newfies' water rescue skills. Their weight-pulling abilites also saw them haul supplies through blizzards during World War II.

Nordic Spitz

ORIGIN Sweden
HEIGHT 16–19 in (40–47 cm)
WEIGHT 26–33 lb (12.0–15.0 kg)
EXERCISE LEVEL
COAT CARE
REGISTERED FCI, AKCs
COLORS Any color

Known in its its homeland as the Norbottenspets and in Finland as the Pohjanpystykorva, this breed is the Swedish equivalent of the Finnish Spitz.

RED/TAN

GOLD

GOLD AND WHITE

BLACK AND WHITE

TAN AND WHITE

BREED ORIGINS

This breed dates back to the 17th century, when it was used to hunt squirrels for their fur. It is smaller than most other Scandinavian spitz breeds, and may be close to the similarly diminutive Norwegian Buhund. Almost extinct after World War II, it enjoyed a comeback, but remains rare even in its homeland. This may be because as an active and strong-willed breed, it is not a restful companion. Essentially a hunting dog, it can also turn its skills to guarding and has even been used to pull small carts.

BRIGHT EYED AND BUSHY TAILED Daring, alert, and always on the move, this is a confident and intelligent dog that lives up to its perky appearance. The coat is short, but a dense undercoat insures that this is still a cold-hardy breed.

Norwegian Lundehund

ORIGIN Norway

HEIGHT 12–15 in (31–39 cm)

WEIGHT 12–14 lb (5.5–6.5 kg)

EXERCISE LEVEL

COAT CARE

REGISTERED KC, FCI, AKCs

COLORS White with black, gray, or fawn to red shades

Lunde is the Norwegian word for "puffin," and the Norsk Lundehund's original role was taking puffins from their nests on the precarious cliffs of Væroy in the Lofoten Islands.

BLACK AND WHITE

TAN AND WHITE

BREED ORIGINS

The Lundehund has hunted puffins since at least the 16th century. Breeding in isolation, it has developed some unique adaptations. Starting at the top, it has ears that can be held erect or folded shut to protect the ear canal. Moving down, the head can tilt back past the vertical on the flexible neck, while the forelegs can splay out sideways like human arms. At the ends of the legs, the paws have extra toes, jointed like thumbs. All these help the dogs to squeeze through tight spaces and stay on narrow cliff ledges.

BREED QUALITIES

This isolated breed only came to the attention of the outside world in the 1930s. When puffin hunters turned to using nets, it almost died out; despite the efforts of breeders and its export to new countries, it remains rare. A lively and engaging companion, it can suffer a digestive disorder that makes it less able to absorb nutrients.

NICE LITTLE EARNER A natural history of 1753 records:"Their catch enriches the farmer very often more than does his other work."

Perro de Pastor Mallorquín

ORIGIN Majorca
HEIGHT 24–29 in (62–73 cm)
WEIGHT 77–88 lb (35.0–40.0 kg)
EXERCISE LEVEL
COAT CARE
REGISTERED KC, FCI, AKCs
COLORS Black

This breed is officially recognized by its Catalan name of Ca de Bestiar, which roughly translates as "dog of the livestock." Also known as the Majorca Shepherd Dog, it is a rare breed, and almost unseen outside Spain.

BREED ORIGINS

This farm dog shares some of its original ancestry with the Perro de Presa, but developed along very different lines as a herd guardian and farm watchdog. It may be related to the similar Portuguese Cattle Dog or Cao de Castro Laboreiro, and has great tolerance for extreme heat. Working dogs like this, bred on farms, are not uncommon across Spain, but pedigree examples are far fewer.

It has been exported to South America and is bred as a guarding breed there. This is very much a working dog: Aggressive and territorial, it can try to dominate owners.

SHORT BACK AND SIDES This breed is officially recognized in a long- and a shorthaired version, but the longhaired type may very well be extinct.

Perro de Presa Mallorquín

ORIGIN Majorca
HEIGHT 20–23 in (52–58 cm)
WEIGHT 66–84 lb (30.0–38.0 kg)
EXERCISE LEVEL
COAT CARE
REGISTERED FCI, AKCs
COLORS Brindle, fawn, black

The Majorca Mastiff is also called the Ca de Bou, meaning "bulldog," and officially recognized as the Perro Dogo Mallorquín. A medium-sized mastiff, it makes a formidable guard.

GOLD   BLACK BRINDLE

BREED ORIGINS

This breed is descended from the old Spanish Mastiff, brought to the Balearic islands in the 13th century for hunting, herd guarding, and fighting. In the 18th century it may have been crossed with British or Spanish bulldogs to perform in the new sport of bull-baiting. The breed declined in the 20th century and was "re-created" in the 1980s. Today it is still rare: It has spread across Europe, but very thinly.

Less ferocious than the old type, today's Perro de Presa is still stubborn and hard to train: It is not for inexperienced owners, or multiple-dog households.

WORKING DESIGN This is a typical broad-chested mastiff. The massive head, particularly pronounced in males, has the shortened muzzle that allowed bull baiting dogs to hang on to their opponent.

Poodle (Standard)

ORIGIN Germany
HEIGHT 15–24 in (38–60 cm)
WEIGHT 45–70 lb (20.5–32.0 kg)
EXERCISE LEVEL
COAT CARE
REGISTERED KC, FCI, AKCs
COLORS Any solid color

This breed's origins are acknowledged in its name, from the old German word *pudeln*, "to splash"; it is called the Caniche, or duck dog, in France. This practical retriever can be a smart companion.

BLACK   CREAM   BLUE   GOLD   DARK BROWN

BREED ORIGINS
This breed can be traced back at least to the Middle Ages, and probably arose in Germany, eastern Europe, or even Asia. It is officially recognized as French, however, and in France it developed into the modern sizes of Standard and the smaller Miniature and Toy types (*see* p. 131). It worked in French circuses, its intelligence and trainability making it hugely popular, and as a truffle hound. This is a healthy, able, adaptable breed, and certainly no fluffy toy.

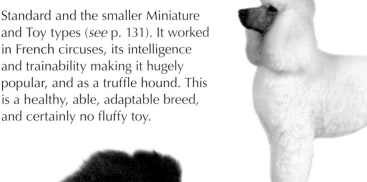

CONTINENTAL AND LION CLIPS Although these look ornamental, their original purpose was to reduce the resistance of the coat in the water but leave the chest and the leg joints insulated.

SHORT CLIPS All-over clips are now allowed for showing. This simpler look is far easier for most owners to maintain, and allows the breed a little more of its natural dignity in everyday life.

STANDARDS FOR STANDARDS The allowed sizes for the different Poodle classes vary among registries, with FCI starting at a threshhold 3 in (8 cm) taller than others.

Portuguese Water Dog

ORIGIN Portugal
HEIGHT 17–22 in (43–57 cm)
WEIGHT 35–55 lb (16.0–25.0 kg)
EXERCISE LEVEL
COAT CARE
REGISTERED KC, FCI, AKCs
COLORS Black, white, or brown; black or brown with white

Resembling some curly-coated gundog breeds, the Cão de Agua Português's working role was similar to that of the Newfie. Also called the Cão Pescador Português, this was a fisherman's dog.

BLACK

DARK BROWN

GOLD AND WHITE

BREED ORIGINS

The most ancient ancestors may be curly-coated Asian dogs; in Portugal this type can be traced back to the Middle Ages. An exceptional swimmer and diver, it was once employed all along the coast, retrieving broken nets, carrying messages from boat to shore, and even driving fish into the nets. Onshore, it was a capable guard for equipment and the landed catch. Changes in the fishing industry have seen numbers decline, and it is mostly found in the province of Algarve.

BREED QUALITIES

This is a spirited dog, but its desire to please and intelligence make it highly trainable. It has almost limitless stamina, and needs an active, involved owner if it is not to become bored and destructive. It can become an accomplished sneak-thief in the kitchen, and puppies are inveterate chewers. Puppies should be tested for GM-1 Storage Disease, a fatal nerve disease.

ROUGH AND READY The robust, well-proportioned build of this breed should convey its strength and spirit. It may be clothed in one of two coat types, either the curly type seen here, typically forming ringlets, or a longer, gently wavy coat. Both are dense and profuse but lack an undercoat.

Pyrenean Mastiff

ORIGIN Spain
HEIGHT 28–32 in (72–80 cm)
WEIGHT 121–165 lb (55.0–75.0 kg)
EXERCISE LEVEL
COAT CARE
REGISTERED FCI
COLORS White with gray, golden yellow, brown, black, silver, beige, sand, or marbled

A herd and farm guarding breed, the Mastin del Pireneo, sometimes called the Mastin d'Aragon, could take on bears and wolves. This robust, trainable breed makes a good guard for rural households.

GOLD AND WHITE

BLACK AND WHITE

TAN AND WHITE

BREED ORIGINS
Phoenician traders probably brought the first mastiffs to Spain from Asia thousands of years ago. This dog developed in the southeastern Pyrenees, and guarded both flocks and the home. A large breed with a deep voice, a strong protective instinct, and inherent reluctance to back down, it is not ideal for urban life. Sometimes aggressive toward other dogs, it controls its power.

UNDEREXPOSED BREED This is a solid, imposing dog but never gives the impression of being overly heavy or slow. It is one of the rarer mastiff breeds, perhaps overshadowed by—or confused with—the Pyrenean Mountain Dog.

Pyrenean Mountain Dog

ORIGIN France
HEIGHT 26–32 in (65–80 cm)
WEIGHT 121–165 lb (55.0–75.0 kg)
EXERCISE LEVEL
COAT CARE
REGISTERED KC, FCI, AKCs
COLORS White, white with very limited gray, pale yellow, or orange patches

Originating on the French side of the Pyrenees, this dauntless, intelligent breed is called the Chien de Montagne des Pyrénées in France and is also known as the Great Pyrenees in some registries.

GOLD AND WHITE

BIG AND BOLD The sheer size and weight of this breed make it unsuitable for city living. Like other large breeds, it is susceptible to joint problems, and it can develop skin problems in the heat.

BREED ORIGINS
Probably descended from ancient Asian mastiffs, this dog is recorded as a herd and home guarding breed by the Middle Ages, and was found at the French royal court in the 17th century. Nearly extinct in the early 20th century, it is now established across Europe and North America. Early examples were markedly wary, but breeding for companionship has mellowed the character.

Rhodesian Ridgeback

ORIGIN South Africa
HEIGHT 24–27 in (60–69 cm)
WEIGHT 70–80 lb (32.0–36.0 kg)
EXERCISE LEVEL
COAT CARE
REGISTERED KC, FCI, AKCs
COLORS Light wheaten to red wheaten

The only registered breed indigenous to southern Africa, the Rhodesian is characterized by the stripe of hair that grows forward along its spine that also gives the breed its name. It was believed unique in this trait until the discovery of the Thai Ridgeback.

BREED ORIGINS

Dogs with this characteristic ridge of hair, kept for hunting by the Hottentots, interbred with settlers' hounds and mastiffs in the 19th century. The resulting breed was used in pairs or trios to find lions for hunters, and an old name for the Ridgeback is the African Lion Hound. With changing attitudes to wildlife, the breed has moved into the home, and it makes a loyal guard dog or companion. It is a dignified breed that can be aloof with strangers, and it prefers to have its owners to itself, rather than sharing them with disruptive children or other dogs.

KEPT IN TRIM The first standard for the Ridgeback, written in the 1920s, was based on that of the Dalmatian. It placed the emphasis on agility and elegance, producing a breed of great endurance and speed.

Rottweiler

ORIGIN Germany

HEIGHT 23–27 in (58–69 cm)

WEIGHT 90–110 lb (41.0–50.0 kg)

EXERCISE LEVEL 🐎

COAT CARE 🖌️

REGISTERED KC, FCI, AKCs

COLORS Black and tan

Originally a cattle dog and hauler of carts, later a guard, military dog, and police dog, the Rottweiler was never, as is sometimes asserted, a fighting dog. This belief is just part of the sometimes unfavorable, often unfair, reputation this breed has gathered.

Dangerous dogs?

Rottweilers are intelligent and highly trainable, and a well-socialized Rottie in the hands of an experienced and sensible owner is a fine dog. However, there is no denying that they are protective, assertive, and can show a temper.

BREED ORIGINS

The Rottweiler's earliest ancestors were probably Roman mastiffs; an ancient military route ran through the town of Rottweil in southern Germany. They were popular on farms, and were also known as "Rottweil butchers' dogs" because of their usefulness in controlling animals at slaughter, pulling carts, and guard duties. Numbers declined greatly in the 19th century, but they were saved by proving their efficiency

CATCH THEM YOUNG How a breed like a Rottweiler is brought up has a great effect on its behavior. Puppies that are constantly exposed to human play, children, and other animals are very different from guard dogs kept outside.

when tested for their potential as police dogs. Now they are recognized as guards around the world, but seen with less favor as companions. Their size and weight alone make them a better choice as a guard than as a family dog around small children.

BIG AND BRAVE Powerful and impressive in build, the Rottweiler unfortunately suffers the dysplasia problems almost inevitable in larger breeds. The tail was customarily docked in the past, but is now left natural in Europe.

Russian-European Laika

ORIGIN Russia/Finland
HEIGHT 20–23 in (51–58 cm)
WEIGHT 46–50 lb (21.0–23.0 kg)
EXERCISE LEVEL
COAT CARE
REGISTERED FCI
COLORS Black, gray, white, pepper and salt, bicolor

Almost identical to the Karelian Bear Dog of Finland, the Russko-Evropeïskaïa Laïka owes its existence as a separate breed to the historically disputed status of its homeland, the region of Karelia.

 BLACK
 GRAY

BREED ORIGINS

Spitz dogs came to this region thousands of years ago and have been used ever since to hunt large game such as elk, and defend against predators like bears, wolves, and lynx. Karelia has been held by Sweden, Russia, and Finland, and when Russia took control of most of Finnish Karelia in World War II, the local dogs were split between two nations. Ignoring the existing Finnish breed, Russians declared the dogs Laikas, a name they insisted marked them out as uniquely Russian. Today this energetic, powerful hunting dog remains restricted to working use and rarely seen.

NOT ADAPTABLE This Laika, or "barker," has not shifted from its historical purpose and type. Immensely tough, powerful, and cold hardy, it is unsuited to the role of household companion.

Saarloos Wolfhound

ORIGIN Netherlands
HEIGHT 24–30 in (60–76 cm)
WEIGHT 80–90 lb (36.0–41.0 kg)
EXERCISE LEVEL
COAT CARE
REGISTERED FCI, AKCs
COLORS Shaded gray to black, light to dark brown, or white to cream

While many dog breeds have been crossed with wolves, most European breeds have played down the link. The Saarlooswolfhond was different: it proclaimed its heritage in its name.

 GRAY
GOLD

BREED ORIGINS

Leendert Saarloos began crossing German Shepherd Dogs to wolves in the 1920s, hoping for superior disease resistance and working abilities. Gradually it became clear that his European Wolfdog was closer to a wolf than a working dog. Recognized after Saarloos's death, it was renamed in his honor. It is more trainable than the Czech Wolfdog, and makes a good guard, but nevertheless it is not recommended as a family companion.

TRICKY CUSTOMER The appearance of the breed is strongly reminiscent of a wolf. Hybrids raise ethical questions not only about the keeping of part-wild animals as pets, but also accidentally contaminating the bloodlines of endangered wolf species.

St. Bernard

ORIGIN Switzerland

HEIGHT 26–36 in (65–90 cm)

WEIGHT 100–300 lb (45.0–136.0 kg)

EXERCISE LEVEL

COAT CARE

REGISTERED KC, FCI, AKCs

COLORS White with reddish-brown patches or mantle

Regarded as the Swiss national breed, these massive dogs are also called St. Bernhardshund or Bernhardiner, and have been known as Saint Dogs—still sometimes used in North America—Alpenmastiff, and Barry Dogs.

BREED ORIGINS

These dogs are descended from Swiss farm breeds, but their original ancestors were Roman mastiffs. They probably came via the most ancient pass through the Western Alps, the Great St. Bernard Pass. In 1049, monks founded a hospice there named after St. Bernard of Menthon, and since at least the 17th century, mastiffs lived there as companions and guards, hauling carts and creating paths through deep snow. They became legendary rescue dogs after Napoleon's army went through the pass in 1800.

BREED QUALITIES

These lugubrious-looking dogs are gentle, friendly, loyal, and obedient. Their size makes them unsuitable for many homes, but their ponderous movements mean they are unlikely to bowl children over. Like many large breeds, they are prone to bloat and joint problems.

START SLOW Big dogs like the St. Bernard take as much as 18 months to become fully physically mature. Exercise should be carefully monitored while their bones are still growing.

LESS IS MORE There are two coats: This shorthaired or *stockhaar* has a dense double coat and was more used for work in the snow. The medium-length, straight to slightly wavy coat of the longhair could gather icicles.

Samoyed

ORIGIN Northern Russia/Siberia
HEIGHT 18–22 in (46–56 cm)
WEIGHT 50–66 lb (23.0–30.0 kg)
EXERCISE LEVEL
COAT CARE
REGISTERED KC, FCI, AKCs
COLORS White, cream, white and biscuit

Called the Samoiedskaïa Sabaka in their native land, but affectionately known as the Sammy, these smiling dogs were the working companions of the nomadic, reindeer-herding Samoyed peoples. They were once generally called Bjelkier or Voinaika.

BREED ORIGINS

Samoyedic peoples have been in Siberia for some 2,000 years. Their dogs were essential to their lifestyle, just like the Malamute in Alaska or Lapphund in Finland. They would herd reindeer, sometimes pull sleds, and sleep alongside their owners for warmth. Over the centuries, they acquired an almost mythical reputation for their abilities and loyalty. Pioneering Norwegian explorer Fridtjof Nansen took a team of 28 over the polar ice in the 1890s, and his praise of the breed influenced other explorers to use it, including Amundsen when he reached the South Pole in 1911.

BREED QUALITIES

These dogs always lived close to their owners, and as a result thrive on human company, with a friendly greeting for all. Established as good-natured family dogs in many countries, they are full of energy and need an active life to keep them occupied. They can suffer an inherited kidney problem.

COLD PROOF The double coat is water repellant on top, impenetrably wooly beneath. Black skin resists snow glare, and the tail covers the nose when sleeping, warming the inhaled air.

MAN'S BEST FRIEND With a smiling face and a nature that "displays affection to all mankind," this is a companion, not a guard.

Schipperke

ORIGIN Belgium
HEIGHT 8–13 in (22–33 cm)
WEIGHT 6–18 lb (3.0–8.0 kg)
EXERCISE LEVEL
COAT CARE
REGISTERED KC, FCI, AKCs
COLORS Black

Small but tough, this energetic little spitz has an established image as a working breed of the people, but it was also made fashionable in the 19th century through the patronage of Queen Marie-Henriette of Belgium.

BREED ORIGINS

The beginnings and use of this breed are murky. It was once called simply the Spits or Spitzke, to distinguish it from the German Spitz. As the Schipperke, it was recorded mostly in hunting periodicals as a dog for small prey rather like some terriers. Today, there is some dispute over whether Schipperke means "little captain," a reference to a history as a barge dog, or "little shepherd,"

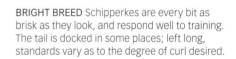

BRIGHT BREED Schipperkes are every bit as brisk as they look, and respond well to training. The tail is docked in some places; left long, standards vary as to the degree of curl desired.

giving it a common ancestor with the much larger Belgian Shepherd types.

BREED QUALITIES

This versatile dog makes any of these histories plausible. Its reputation as a boat dog makes it a popular companion for recreational as well as professional sailors. On barges one of its roles would have been to keep down vermin, and it is an accomplished ratter when given the chance. It also acted as a guard for cargo, and although small is a formidable barker and not to be challenged lightly; it can also be aggressive around other dogs.

Shar Pei

ORIGIN China
HEIGHT 18–20 in (45–50 cm)
WEIGHT 45–60 lb (20.5–27.5 kg)
EXERCISE LEVEL
COAT CARE
REGISTERED KC, FCI, AKCs
COLORS Any solid color except white

This breed is named in China for its harsh coat: Shar Pei means 'sand skin'. But when the breed became fashionable in the West in the 1980s, it was the wrinkles that caught the imagination.

BLACK   GRAY   BLUE   RED/TAN   GOLD

BREED ORIGINS
The Shar Pei may have existed for over 2,000 years, kept on farms for hunting and guarding. More recently it was used in fights, and it can be stubborn and aggressive. The communist regime nearly saw the demise of the dog, but exports from Hong Kong in the 1970s saved it. There are hereditary problems with skin allergies and ingrowing eyelashes: Choose breeders carefully.

FIGHTING COAT
There are two lengths of coat: the short horse coat seen here and the longer brush or bear. Loose skin and a prickly coat were good defences in dog fights, but some Shar Peis are more dramatically wrinkled than others.

Shiba Inu

ORIGIN Japan
HEIGHT 13–16 in (34–41 cm)
WEIGHT 15–24 lb (7.0–11.0 kg)
EXERCISE LEVEL
COAT CARE
REGISTERED KC, FCI, AKCs
COLORS Red, red overlaid with black, black and tan, white

This is the smallest of Japan's native breeds, and its name describes it in minimal terms: *Shiba* means "small," and *inu*—or sometimes *ken*, another reading of the same *kanji*—simply means "dog."

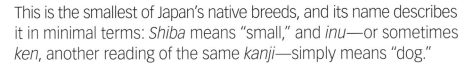
RED/TAN   BLACK AND TAN

BREED ORIGINS
Small dogs of this type have been present in Japan for millennia, and used to hunt small animals and birds. Pure specimens became scarce through crossing with imported English gundogs in the 19th century. In the 1920s, work to conserve them began, and in 1937 the breed was designated a Natural Monument. A quiet and loyal breed, they can be aloof with strangers.

ANCIENT PATTERN
In all colors, the Shiba Inu has a pattern called *urajiro* or "white beneath." The coat is light on the underparts and has light areas on the sides of the muzzle and the cheeks.

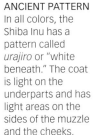

Shikoku

ORIGIN Japan
HEIGHT 17–22 in (43–55 cm)
WEIGHT 33–44 lb (15.0–20.0 kg)
EXERCISE LEVEL
COAT CARE
REGISTERED FCI
COLORS Mingled black and white or black and red

This breed is one of the Japanese *shika inu* or medium-sized dogs. Also called the Kochi-ken, it takes its name from the island of Shikoku, where it was chiefly found in Kochi province.

BREED ORIGINS

The Shikoku is an almost primitive type from the spitz family, which includes the other ancient Japanese breeds of Akita, Hokkaido, Japanese Spitz, Kai, Kishu, and Shiba Inu. It was used for many centuries to hunt large game, including deer and especially wild boar. By the 20th century the breed had almost died out, but it was brought back from the brink and was one of the breeds to be declared a Natural Monument in 1937. Historically, there were three regional variations within Kochi province: the Awa, the Hata, and the Hongawa. Of all of them, the Hongawa was the most isolated and was felt to have maintained the highest degree of purity when it came to rebuilding the breed numbers. Even in Japan, this is

SPLIT PERSONALITY This dog has sharper features than those of other Japanese dogs, and its alert, occasionally stubborn temperament matches its no-nonsense appearance. Although very energetic and active outside, they can be surprisingly peaceful indoors.

still a rare dog, and only a handful of breeders keep it beyond its homeland.

BREED QUALITIES

Owners claim the character of the Shikoku is still very closely tied to nature. Loyal and submissive to its owner, it may be friendly toward other people but is usually cautious; with other dogs it may be aggressive. It is intelligent, active, and playful, an ideal dog for very active people, relishing plenty of varied exercise. Shikokus are tenacious hunters, still sometimes used for hunting boar in Japan, and even with firm training from an early age they may be hard to call back from a trail.

Siberian Husky

ORIGIN Siberia
HEIGHT 20–24 in (50–60 cm)
WEIGHT 35–60 lb (16.0–27.5 kg)
EXERCISE LEVEL
COAT CARE
REGISTERED KC, FCI, AKCs
COLORS Any color

One of the lighter sled-pulling breeds, the Siberian Husky has become more famous as a breed in Alaska than in its original homeland. For a time it was the ultimate racing dog.

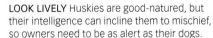

BLACK GRAY GOLD AND WHITE TAN AND WHITE

BREED ORIGINS

These dogs were used for centuries by the Chukchi people of Siberia for sled pulling and reindeer herding. DNA analysis has confirmed it as one of the oldest breeds in existence. It was brought to Alaska by fur traders for arctic races, and used by Peary in his trip to the North Pole in 1909, but won most publicity and popularity in the 1925 serum run to Nome, or Great Race of Mercy, when teams of sled dogs carried diphtheria antitoxin to the isolated town of Nome, traveling 674 miles (1,085 km) in a record-breaking five and a half days to halt an epidemic.

BREED QUALITIES

Lighter than most other sled-pulling breeds, the Husky is characterized by a seemingly effortless gait and enormous stamina. These qualities mean it is a breed for the active, and left alone they can be destructive. They are generally cheerful dogs, gentle and friendly.

LOOK LIVELY Huskies are good-natured, but their intelligence can incline them to mischief, so owners need to be as alert as their dogs.

SIBERIAN LOOKS The breed has a tendency to blue in one or both eyes, but this is by no means universal. The thick coat is fairly tangle free, but needs plenty of combing when it molts.

SLED DOGS Siberian Huskies have been replaced in arctic races by the faster Alaskan Husky, but are still excellent dogs for moderate loads over long distances. They are also popular for pulling skiers in the sport of skijoring.

Spanish Water Dog

ORIGIN Spain
HEIGHT 16–20 in (40–50 cm)
WEIGHT 31–49 lb (14.0–22.0 kg)
EXERCISE LEVEL
COAT CARE
REGISTERED KC, FCI, AKCs
COLORS White, black, chestnut, white and black, white and brown

The name this breed carries in Spain, Perro de Agua, is the latest in a long line including Perro Turco, Laneto, Perro de Lanas, Perro Patero, Perro Rizado, Churro, and Barbeta.

BLACK

DARK BROWN

BLACK AND WHITE

BREED ORIGINS

Wooly-coated dogs have been recorded in Spain since the 12th century: Theories suggest that they arrived with Turkish merchants or from North Africa. The breed was used for herding over long distances, hunting water fowl and game, and towing boats in ports, like the Portuguese Water Dog. Intelligent and adaptable, they like to be working, and can weary of children quickly.

RECENT DISCOVERY These dogs were used in Andalucia when other breeds became popular elsewhere, and were overlooked until the 1980s.

Thai Ridgeback

ORIGIN Thailand
HEIGHT 23–26 in (58–66 cm)
WEIGHT 50–75 lb (23.0–34.0 kg)
EXERCISE LEVEL
COAT CARE
REGISTERED FCI, AKCs
COLORS Black, blue, red, very light fawn

Recently discovered in Thailand, where it is called the Mah Thai Lang Ahn or simply Mah Thai, this primitive dog has a distinctive ridge of hair growing the "wrong" way up its spine.

BLUE

RED/TAN

GOLD

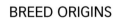

FAMILY LIKENESS It is likely that the Thai Ridgeback and the similarly tonsured Phu Quoc Dog of Vietnam are related.

BREED ORIGINS

This breed has been a hunting dog, companion, and house guard for centuries, and is in records dating back at least 300 years. It may owe its survival to poor transportation links into eastern Thailand, keeping it isolated from foreign breeds. Only recently recognized abroad, this lively, independent breed is protective of its home, sometimes aggressive to outsiders, and not for beginners.

Tibetan Kyi Apso

ORIGIN Tibet
HEIGHT 25–28 in (63–70 cm)
WEIGHT 70–90 lb (32.0–41.0 kg)
EXERCISE LEVEL
COAT CARE
REGISTERED None
COLORS Any color

Although it was briefly called the Tibetan Bearded Mastiff, this is one of the world's rarest breeds, hailing from Mount Kailash, a sacred place in the Hindu, Buddhist, Jain, and Bön faiths.

GRAY   GOLD   DARK BROWN   BLACK AND WHITE   BLACK AND TAN

BREED ORIGINS

In rural Tibet, Kyi Apsos have traditionally been guardians of flocks and homes. They were unknown to the outside world until the late 20th century, when keen and curious Westerners trekked across mountains to find them and even smuggled them out of Tibet. A deep, sonorous bark is as much a hallmark of the breed as its coarse double coat, and makes them unsuitable for urban life.

Energetic workers, they need plenty of attention and activity, and can be destructive left to themselves, although they like to relax with their owners when off duty. As a guarding breed, they are inherently distrustful of strangers.

TOP AND TAIL The Kyi Apso begins and ends with distinctive features. The profuse facial hair makes the head seem larger than it is, and the well-furnished tail forms a complete circle.

Tibetan Mastiff

ORIGIN Tibet
HEIGHT 24–28 in (61–71 cm)
WEIGHT 141–180 lb (64.0–82.0 kg)
EXERCISE LEVEL
COAT CARE
REGISTERED KC, FCI, AKCs
COLORS Black, black and tan, gray, gray and tan, golden

This massive breed is called Do-khyi in Tibetan, which means "tied dog" and indicates its guarding history. The Mandarin name is Zang'Ao, and in Nepal it is called Bhote Kukur, or Tibetan Dog.

BLACK   GRAY   GOLD   BLACK AND TAN

BREED ORIGINS

This ancient breed has been a flock guardian for nomadic herders, and a guard dog in fixed residences, notably monasteries. They existed as long ago as 1121BC, when one trained to hunt humans was given to the Chinese emperor. Dogs like this traveled west with migrating tribes to give rise to European mastiff breeds; the breed itself was brought to the West in the 19th century and

is widespread but not common. Protective, fearless, and distrustful of strangers, it is a fine guard, but too strong willed and massive to make a good family dog.

BIG VOICE The breed in Tibet is larger and more ferocious than Western examples. Marco Polo described them in the 13th century as "tall as a donkey with a voice as powerful as that of a lion."

Tosa

ORIGIN Japan
HEIGHT 22–26 in (55–65 cm)
WEIGHT 190–200 lb (86.0–90.0 kg)
EXERCISE LEVEL
COAT CARE
REGISTERED KC, FCI, AKCs
COLORS Red, fawn, apricot, black, brindle

Tosa Inu or Tosa Ken simply mean "dog of Tosa," the province where this breed originated. It is also called the Japanese Mastiff and the Japanese or Tosa Fighting Dog, or even Sumo Dog.

BLACK   RED/TAN   GOLD   BLACK BRINDLE

TREAT WITH CARE Massive, powerful, and relentless in a fight, this breed is not for families, homes with close neighbors, or any but the most experienced owners. Ownership is banned or restricted in several countries, including the United Kingdom.

BREED ORIGINS
Japan's history of dog fighting goes back to the 14th century, but the Tosa was created in the late 19th century. The local spitz-type Shikoku was crossed with Western mastiff and fighting breeds for greater stamina and fighting instinct. The breed was at its height in Japan in the 1920s; today, although it has spread to other countries, it is often not welcome.

West Siberian Laika

ORIGIN Siberia
HEIGHT 20–25 in (52–64 cm)
WEIGHT 40–50 lb (18.0–23.0 kg)
EXERCISE LEVEL
COAT CARE
REGISTERED KC, FCI, AKCs
COLORS White, pepper and salt, red shades, gray shades, black

The Zapadno-Sibirskaïa Laïka is the most popular of the Russian Laikas, both at home and abroad. It is an excellent hunting dog for treeing small quarry, and a powerful sled dog.

GREY   RED/TAN

BREED ORIGINS
The dog of the Siberian people for centuries, this originally had two strains, the powerful Hanti and rangy Mansi. When industrialization opened up the region, they almost died out, but a single breed was formed and recognized in 1947. Today, Russian hunters prefer prestige foreign breeds, but American hunters have taken to the dog. It is happier hunting or working than as a family companion.

TRUE COLORS Brown shades are unacceptable, and black or black and white are discouraged as too similar to the Russian-European Laika.

Wetterhoun

ORIGIN Netherlands

HEIGHT 22–23 in (55–59 cm)

WEIGHT 33–44 lb (15.0–20.0 kg)

EXERCISE LEVEL

COAT CARE

REGISTERED KC, FCI, AKCs

COLORS Solid black or brown/liver, black or brown with white

This breed's name is from the Frisian for "water dog," and it is also known as the Dutch Spaniel or Frisian Water Dog. It originally specialized in killing otters, and was occasionally called Otterhoun.

BLACK   DARK BROWN   BLACK AND WHITE

BREED ORIGINS

This breed is probably descended from the now extinct Old Water Dog, a type that was an ancestor of several modern spaniels. Along with the Stabyhoun, a pointing and retrieving breed with which the Wetterhound was crossbred in the past, it was developed in the province of Friesland in the Netherlands at least 400 years ago. Originally used to control otters that competed with fishermen, it later proved itself fearless in pursuit of small prey and vermin on land and as a guard dog on farms. Today, it is a popular rural dog in its homeland, but it is seldom seen elsewhere.

BREED QUALITIES

This rugged, capable breed is still used for flushing and retrieving on land and in water. It is intelligent but with a tendency to independence, so needs an experienced and firm owner and early training. A strong protective instinct makes it a brave, reliable guard dog. It is rarely seen in the city, and may not adapt well to the confinement or, given its suspicion of strangers, the crowds.

ALL-WEATHER DOG Curly hair covers the entire body except the head and legs, where the coat is shorter. For maximum waterproofing, this coarse coat is oily, never wooly, in texture.

USEFUL BOOKS AND REFERENCES

USEFUL BOOKS AND PAPERS

Alderton, David. *The Dog Interpreter.* Reader's Digest, 2007.

Alderton, David. *Top to Tail.* David & Charles, 2006.

Alderton, David. *Smithsonian Handbooks: Dogs.* Dorling Kindersley, 2002.

Alderton, David. *Hounds of the World.* Swan Hill Press, 2000.

Alderton, David. *Foxes, Wolves and Wild Dogs of the World.* Facts on File, 1998.

American Kennel Club, The. *The Complete Dog Book.* Ballantine Books, 2006.

American Kennel Club, The. *Dog Care and Training.* Howell Book House, 2002.

Bower, John and Caroline. *The Dog Owner's Problem Solver.* Reader's Digest, 1998.

Clutton-Brock, Juliet. *Eyewitness Books: Dog.* Dorling Kindersley, 1991.

Canadian Kennel Club, The. *The Canadian Kennel Club Book of Dogs.* Stoddard Publishing, 1988.

Combe, Iris. *Herding Dogs: Their Origins and Development in Britain.* Faber & Faber, 1987.

De Prisco, Andrew and James B Johnson. *Canine Lexicon.* TFH Publications, 1993.

Eldredge, Debra M., Carlson, Lisa D., Carlson, Delbert G., and James M. Giffin. *Dog Owner's Home Veterinary Handbook.* Howell Book House, 2007.

Fergus, Charles. *Gun Dog Breeds: A Guide to Spaniels, Retrievers and Sporting Dogs.* Lyons & Burford, 1992.

Fogle, Bruce. *The Dog's Mind.* Howell Book House, 1990.

Fogle, Bruce. *The Complete Dog Training Manual.* Dorling Kindersley, 1994.

Fogle, Bruce. *The New Encyclopedia of the Dog.* Dorling Kindersley, 2000.

Glover, Harry. *Toy Dogs.* David & Charles, 1977.

Jackson, Frank. *Dictionary of Canine Terms.* Crowood Press, 1995.

Kennel Club, The. *The Kennel Club's Illustrated Breed Standards.* Ebury Press, 1998.

Kern, Kerry. *The New Terrier Handbook.* Barron's, 1988.

Larkin, Peter and Mike Stockman. *The Complete Dog Book.* Lorenz Books, 1997.

Millan, Cesar and Melissa Jo Peltier. *Cesar's Way: The Natural, Everyday Guide to Understanding and Correcting Common Dog Problems.* Three Rivers Press, 2007.

Monks of New Skete, The. *How to be Your Dog's Best Friend: The Classic Training Manual for Dog Owners (Revised & Updated Edition).* Little, Brown and Company, 2002.

Monks of New Skete, The. *The Art of Raising a Puppy.* Little, Brown and Company, 1991.

Morris, Desmond. *Dogs: The Ultimate Dictionary of Over 1000 Dog Breeds.* Ebury Press, 2001.

Sanderson, Angela. *The Complete Australian Dogs.* The Currawong Press, 1981.

Thomas, Elizabeth Marshall. *The Hidden Life of Dogs.* Houghton Mifflin, 1993.

Wilcox, B. and C. Walkowicz. *The Atlas of Dog Breeds of the World.* TFH Publications, 1989

Yamazaki, Testsu. *Legacy of the Dog: The Ultimate Illustrated Guide to over 200 Breeds.* Chronicle Books, 1995.

USEFUL WEBSITES

http://www.aspca.org—The leading animal welfare organization in the United States.

http://www.dogstrust.org.uk—The UK's largest dog welfare charities, offering education and advice. Also has a active rehoming program, never destroying a healthy dog.

http://www.canismajor.com/dog/idx1.html—The Dog Owner's Guide. A resource covering all aspects of the care and breeding of dogs, with plenty of information about health care. Includes an easily searchable index of articles.

http://dogs.yellopet.com—A North American search engine, helping to locate all things canine in many different countries around the world, from dog rescue organizations to information on dogsledding, discussion groups, and traveling with your pet.

http://www.pethouseclub.com—David Alderton's new website, full of fun and advice about dogs and a host of other pets too, for surfers of all ages, with topical tips, advice, news updates, and much more.

http://www.wolf.org/wolves/index.asp—If you want to learn more about your dog's wild relatives, this site is a very useful place to start. There are opportunities to take part in trips to observe wolves in the wild, as well as watching wolf cams online.

BREED REGISTRIES

NORTH AMERICA

American Kennel Club
260 Madison Avenue
New York, NY 10016
United States
919 233 9767
http://www.akc.org

Canadian Kennel Club
89 Skyway Avenue
Suite 100, Etobicoke
Ontario, M9W 6R4
Canada
416 675 5511
http://www.ckc.ca

Continental Kennel Club
P.O. Box 1628
Walker
LA 70785
United States
800 952 3376
http://www.continentalkennelclub.
com

National Kennel Club
255 Indian Ridge Road
P.O. 331
Blaine, TN 37709
United States
865 932 9680
http:// www.nationalkennelclub.com

United Kennel Club
100 East Kilgore Road
Kalamazoo, MI 49002
United States
269 343 9020
http:// www.ukcdogs.com

Universal Kennel Club International
P.O. 574
Nanuet, NY 10954
United States
http://www.universalkennel.com

World Kennel Club (registered name)
P.O. 60771
Oklahoma City, OK 73146
United States
405 745 9520
http://www.worldkennelclub.com

World Wide Kennel Club
P.O. Box 62
Mount Vernon, NY 10552
United States
914 771 5219
http://www.worldwidekennel.qpg.
com

EUROPE, ASIA, AND AFRICA

Australian National Kennel Council
P.O. Box 285
Red Hill South, Victoria 3937
Australia
http://www.ankc.aust.com

Fédération Cynologique Internationale
Place Albert 1er
13 B-6530 Thuin
Belgium
+32 (0) 71 59 12 38
http://www.fci.be

Irish Kennel Club
Fottrell House
Harold's Cross Bridge
Dublin 6W

Republic of Ireland
+353 (1) 4533300
http://www.ikc.ie

The Kennel Club
1–5 Clarges Street
London, W1Y 8AB
United Kingdom
+44 (0) 870 606 6750
http://www.thekennelclub.org.uk

The Kennel Club of India
Old No.89, New No.28, AA-Block,
1st Street
Anna Nagar, Chennai-600040
India
+91 (0) 98400 43296
http://www.dogsindia.com/
registered_kennel_clubs_in_india.htm

The Kennel Union of Southern Africa
(formerly The South African Kennel
Club)
P.O. Box 2659
Cape Town 8000
South Africa
+27 (0) 21 423 9027
http://www.kusa.co.za/home.php

New Zealand Kennel Club
Prosser Street, Private Bag 50903
Porirua 6220
New Zealand
+64 (04) 237 4489
http://www.nzkc.org.nz

GLOSSARY

A

Allele Paired genes at a specific location on a chromosome controlling a particular trait, such as long hair.

Amino acids "Building blocks" that form animal proteins.

Apple-headed Domed-shape skull.

Awn Bristly undercoat hair. *See also* **Down**, **Guard hair**.

B

Back Typically defined as the part of the body extending from the withers down the vertebral column to the base of the tail.

Bad mouth A fault affecting the teeth—in some cases, especially with hairless breeds, there may be missing teeth in the mouth.

Barrel A term used to describe the shape of the chest.

Bat ears The shape of the ears seen in cases such as the French Bulldog, with the ears being erect, pointing forward and rounded at their tips.

Bay The howling calls made by scenthounds, helping pack members to keep in touch with each other.

Beard Thicker, longer hair extending off the chin.

BIS Abbreviation standing for "Best-in-Show" award.

Bicolor A dog with a combination of white as well as plain or patterned coloring.

Bird dog A dog trained to find birds.

Bitch A female dog.

Bite The relative positions of the upper and lower jaws to each other.

Blaze A stripe of white on the face.

Blue merle Color effect created by the presence of gray, blue, and white hair, associated with some breeds such as Shetland Sheepdogs.

Bobtail Term used for the Old English Sheepdog. A dog without a full-length tail.

Booster An annual vaccination to maintain immunity after an initial dose.

Bracelets The circles of longer hair left on the feet of a poodle in a show clip.

Break A change in direction from the brow to the nose in profile; less defined than a stop.

Breed A type of dog with distinctive features that reproduces to type reliably and whose breeding is controlled and recorded in a pedigree.

Breed club An organization devoted to the promotion of one breed, usually affiliated to a larger breed registry. There may be several clubs representing more popular breeds within one registry.

Breed registry A large organization that maintains pedigree information and controls the breed standards and shows for many breeds in a particular country or, sometimes, internationally.

Breed standard Written description of the ideal appearance of a breed, with a standard of points.

Breeder Someone who breeds dogs. Breeders are divided into the mainstream show breeders, who work within breed registries, and so-called "backyard breeders," who simply breed and sell dogs, not registering or exhibiting them.

Brindle The effect created from black hairs and hairs of a lighter color running together in the coat.

Brisket Area of the chest between the forelegs.

Broken-coated see **Wirehaired**.

Brush Tail with long fur, resembling that of a fox.

Burr Inner surface of the ear.

Button ears Semi-erect ears, with the tips hanging forward.

C

Canid A member of the dog family, Canidae.

Canines The long, pointed teeth set at all four corners of the mouth.

Castrate Neuter a male dog.

Ch An abbreviation for "Champion," written before a dog's show name.

Chest The area of the body encompassed by the ribs.

Chromosome Structure within a cell made up of DNA and carried in pairs (one from each parent).

Conformation see **Type**.

Clip The trimming of the coat, especially in poodles.

Congenital A trait, usually a health problem, present at birth and resulting from either genes or influences during pregnancy.

Crossbreeding The mating of dogs from two different breeds or a breed and a non-pedigree dog, with the resulting puppies often being called crossbreds.

D

Dilute Paler shades of coat colors, e.g. blue rather black.

DNA Deoxyribonucleic acid, a long, chain-like molecule containing the "instructions" used by all organisms to build new cells and function. Often described as the blueprints for an organism. *See also* **Chromosome**, **Gene**.

Double coat A dense layer of insulating underfur means that the coat is not sleek, with the guard hairs being raised. *See also* **Down**, **Guard hair**, **Single coat**.

Down Soft, shorter, insulating undercoat hair. *See also* **Awn**, **Guard hair**.

E

Entire Unneutered or unspayed dog, likely to still be capable of breeding.

F

Fault A significant departure from the breed standard. May result in a loss of points or disqualification.

Feral A domesticated species living independently, not in a domestic situation, reverting to a free living existence.

Flanks The sides of the body.

G

Gene A section of DNA within a chromosome carrying the instructions for a particular trait or process in the dog's body.

Genotype The genetic make-up of an organism.

Guard hair Long, relatively coarse hairs making up the top layer of the coat. *See also* **Awn, Down.**

H

Hackles The hair on the back of the dog's neck, which it may raise to make itself appear more threatening.

Handler Person accompanying the dog in the show ring, or at a field trial.

Hard-mouthed A dog which marks game with its teeth when carrying it.

Hare foot An elongated foot shape.

Harlequin Black or blue areas in the coat set against white, as associated with Great Danes.

Harsh coat Coat that has a stiff, wiry texture.

Haunch The area above the hips.

Haw The third eyelid or nictitating membrane, present at the corner of the eye but usually not conspicuous.

Heat The period, usually twice a year, when a bitch is reproductively active. Also known as "being in season."

Hock Hindleg joint between the stifle and pastern, equivalent to our heel joint.

I

Incisors The teeth present at the front of the dog's mouth.

Intact A dog that has not been neutered.

J

Jowls Fleshy areas of the lips that hang down in some breeds.

K

Knuckling over A weakness affecting the carpus (wristbone), causing the joint to be directed forward.

L

Litter Collective term for all the puppies born to a mother at one time.

Liver Reddish-brown coloration.

Loins Area of the body extending from the last ribs to the hindquarters.

Lurcher Crossbred hound.

M

Mane Area of long hair on the head, resembling the mane of a lion.

Milk teeth The first set of teeth that a puppy develops, ultimately replaced by the time it is six months old by the permanent teeth.

Miscellaneous Class A class for breeds that cannot be shown in other classes.

Molars Flattened teeth, present toward the rear of a dog's mouth. Also known as cheek teeth.

Molera A gap in the center of the skull, especially associated with the Chihuahua.

Mongrel Puppy resulting from the random mating of crossbred dogs.

Muzzle The area of the face in front of the eyes.

N

Nose The ability to track by scent.

O

Occiput The highest part of the skull, at the back.

Overshot The incisor teeth in the upper jaw protrude beyond those in the lower jaw when the jaw is closed.

P

Pack A group of hounds together.

Pad The seemingly tough covering on the base of the feet, which can nevertheless bleed easily.

Particolor Patched appearance.

Pastern Area extending from the carpus (wristbone) down to the toes.

Patella Knee cap.

Pedigree The ancestry of a particular individual, of particular concern in the case of purebred dogs.

Pigeon-toed The toes are not directed forward but point inward, to the midline.

Plume Fringe of hair seen on the underside of the tail in breeds such as setters.

Point The rigid posture adopted by pointers, revealing that they have detected quarry nearby.

Pompon The circular ball of hair at the end of the tail, associated with poodles.

Premolars Teeth that lie between the canines and molars.

Pricked ears Ears that are carried erect, with pointed tips.

Puppy A dog up to 12 months of age.

Q

Quality The rating of a dog's conformation and other features set out in the breed standard.

R

Ring The area where dogs are paraded in front of the judge.

Roached back A back that curves down toward the hindquarters.

Ruff Relatively long hair around the neck.

S

Sable A dark brown coat color.

Saddle Area of black over the back.

Season The bitch's period of reproductive activity.

Single coat The relative lack of undercoat means that the fur is comprised mainly of the guard hairs, which lie sleekly against the body. *See also* **Double coat**, **Down**, **Guard hair**.

Spay Surgical neutering of a bitch.

Stern The tail of a hound.

Stifle The joint between the thigh and second thigh.

Stop The area between the eyes where the skull and nasal bone meet.

Substance The development of the dog.

T

Texture Describes the feel of the coat, e.g. harsh.

Top knot The tuft of long hair seen on the head of some breeds.

Tricolor White, black, and tan coloring in the coat.

Tucked up The curve from the end of the chest to the stomach.

Type A summary of all the essential attributes of the breed.

U

Undershot The lower incisors protrude out beyond those in the upper jaw when the jaw is closed.

W

Wall eye The eye may have either whitish or blue coloration.

Wheaten Yellowish-fawn coloration.

Whelping The act of giving birth.

Wirehaired Rough-textured coat.

Wrinkles Folds of skin on the head.

INDEX

ACKNOWLEDGMENTS

Studio Cactus and the author would like to thank
Candida Frith-Macdonald for providing text for the breed
catalogue and for her invaluable contribution to the
project. In addition, thanks to Laura Watson for design
work; Sharon Cluett for original styling; Jennifer Close and
Jo Weeks for editorial work; Sharon Rudd for additional
design work; Adèle Linderholm for Americanizing;
Penelope Kent for indexing; Peter Bull for illustrations;
and Robert Walker for picture research. Special thanks to
Tracy Morgan from Tracy Morgan Animal Photography
for commissioned photography and to her assistants Stella
Carpenter and Sally Berge-Roose.

Studio Cactus and Tracy Morgan would like to thank
all the owners of the dogs whose photographs appear
in this book. In particular, thank you to all of the owners
at the Euro Dog Show 2007 in Zagreb, Croatia, who
gave permission for their dogs to be photographed
for this book.

PICTURE CREDITS

The publishers would like to thank the following for permission to reproduce copyright material:

Abbreviations: a = above, b = bottom, c = center, l = left, r = right, t = top

Jacqueline Abromeit 163 (tl); Jerri Adams 18 (t); alexan55 182 (t), 182 (bl); amrita 97 (b); David Anderson 39 (t); Animal Photography 190 (t), 190 (b), 191 (b), 196 (bl), 197, 220 (b), 221, 224 (br), 232 (t), 236 (t), 243 (b), 258 (bl), 263 (b), 287 (l), 287 (r), 288 (t); Utekhina Anna 81 (t), 82 (t), 87 (b); Annette 143 (tl); Anyka 37 (t); Yuri Arcurs 55 (b); Attsetski 22 (l); teresa Azevedo 36 (t); Galina Barskaya 49 (c); Charlene Bayerle 58 (t); Fred Bergeron 38 (b); bierchen 49 (b); Casey K Bishop 87 (t); Aleksander Bochenek 33 (t); Aleksander Bochenek 313 (br); Emmanuelle Bonzami 28 (t), 40–41, 151 (br), 329 (t); Jennie Book 58 (b); Kanwarjit Singh Boparai 73 (tl); Pavel Bortol 114 (t), 114 (b); Joy Brown 29 (b), 96 (b), 117 (t); ChipPix 96 (t); Lars Christensen 341 (l); Mary E Cioffi 49 (t), 69 (b), 78 (t); Stephen Coburn 39 (b); Stephanie Coia 12 (t); Matthew Collingwood 71 (b), 313 (bl); Corbis 183 (bl), 188 (t), 189 (t), 193 (tl), 193 (b), 208 (b), 223 (b), 229 (t), 242 (t), 242 (b), 243 (t), 257 (t), 274 (t), 303 (r); Jay Crihfield 142 (b); Diane Critelli 82 (tl); Jack Cronkhite 106 (b); Waldemar Dabrowski 11 (br), 60 (t), 127 (b), 146 (tr), 166, 202–203, 225 (b), 283 (b), 284–285, 333 (br); Jeff Dalton 61 (br), 240–241; Nicholas Peter Gavin Davies 123 (t); Lindsey Dean 20 (b); Julie DeGuia 264–265; Tad Denson 27 (tl), 73 (tr), 351 (tr); DK Images 191 (t), 196 (t), 200 (t), 211 (t), 216 (t), 217 (t), 217 (b), 257 (b), 259 (t), 302 (t), 319 (b), 330 (t), 335 (bl), 350 (b), 351 (b), 359 (t), 368 (br); Olga Drozdova 16 (t); Max Earey 310; Ecoprint 11 (cb); Ecoprint 17; Kondrashov Mlkhail Evgenevich 21 (t); Johannes Flex 62 (t); Sonja Foos 133 (t); Jean Frooms 22 (br), 32 (b), 90–91; Alex Galea 35 (t); Anna Galejeva 55 (c); Kirk Geisler 93 (b); Kirk Geisler 254 (bl); Getty Images 129 (t), 129 (b), 134 (b), 139 (t), 146 (tl), 163 (tr), 178 (b), 220 (t), 222 (b), 225 (t), 312 (t), 314 (t), 337 (tl), 342 (b); Joe Gough 33 (b), 63 (bl), 66–67; HANA 54 (t); Susan Harris 19 (t); Margo Harrison 80 (t); Jeanne Hatch 103 (tr); Jostein Hauge 31 (b); Nicholas James Homrich 52 (b); Nicholas James Homrich 363 (br); Cindy Hughes 73 (b); Sergey I 63 (r), 80 (b); Aleksey Ignatenko 298 (bl); ingret 115 (bl); iofoto 59 (cl), 59 (bl), 59 (br), 130 (t), 143 (tr), 154 (br); Eric Isselée 23 (all), 26 (tc), 29 (t), 35 (b); 38 (t), 74 (t), 79 (t), 81 (c), 81 (b), 82 (br), 117 (b), 139 (b), 151 (l), 174 (all), 178 (t), 275 (tl), 300 (t), 300 (b), 319 (t), 321 (bl), 321 (br), 323 (t), 334 (tl), 338 (all), 341 (r), 360 (t); istock 169 (t); JD 86 (t); JD 156 (b); Michael Johansson 106 (t); Verity Johnson 24–25; Neil Roy Johnson 89 (t); Glen Jones 26 (tr); Ingvald Kaldhussater 347 (b); Laila Kazakevica 22 (ar); Cynthia Kidwell 101; Rolf Klebsattel 283 (tl); James Klotz 195 (t); Abramova Kseniya 88 (b), 378; Erik Lam 115 (t), 254 (t), 314 (b), 342 (t), 350 (tl), 350 (tr); Vitalij Lang 46 (b); Carrieanne Larmore 119 (br); Jim Larson 124–125; Michael Ledray 108 (t); Laurie Lindstrom 181; Jaroslav Machacek 104; Sean MacLeay 176–177; MalibuBooks 74 (bl); Marc Henrie 140 (t), 153 (b), 155 (t), 209 (b), 212, 214 (b), 235, 279 (b), 329 (b), 337 (b), 339, 356 (t), 356 (b); Patrick McCall 102; Michelle D Milliman 44 (b); Pedro Jorge Henriques Monteiro 92; Joseph Moore 21 (b); Phil Morley 78 (b); Tom Nance 83 (b); Michal Napartowicz 165 (t); Michal Napartowicz 345 (t); N Joy Neish 97 (t); NHPA 2–3, 4–5, 8, 36 (b), 42, 70, 71 (t), 89 (b), 94 (t), 94 (b), 95, 121 (t), 123 (b), 136, 160–161, 226, 261 (b), 266, 336 (t);

Andrey Nikiforov 34; Niserin 79 (b); Iztok Noc 45 (b), 76, 93 (t), 275 (b), 366–367; Rhonda O'Donnell 83 (t), 131 (t), 358 (b); OgerCo 343 (t); OlgaLis 348–349; Jason X Pacheco 32 (t); Pavrita 57 (t); Steven Pepple 164 (t); Andrey Perminov 120 (t); Maxim Petrichuk 331 (bl); Petspicture 65 (t), 277 (r); Photos.com 111 (cl), 134 (t), 135 (t), 138 (t), 245 (b), 303 (t), 354 (br), 357 (b), 358 (c), 363 (t), 369 (b); pixshots 26 (b), 112–113, 173 (t), 251 (tl); plastique 45 (t); Kateryna Potrokhova 30 (bl); Glenda M Powers 12 (b), 27 (b); Rick's Photography 100; Robynrg 56 (b), 59 (t); Mike Rogal 312 (b); RTimages 54 (b); Robert Sarosiek 14–15; Emily Sartoski 255; David Scheuber 53 (t); Adriana Johanna Maria Schrauwen-Rommers 79 (c); Oskar Schuler 55 (t); Rebecca Schultz 358 (t); Alistair Scott 47 (t); Kristian Sekulic 68 (b), 247; Micha Shiyanov 74 (br); Shutterspeed Images 16 (b); Shutterstock.com 44 (t), 46 (t), 56 (t), 62 (b), 316 (t), 365 (t); Natalia Sinjushina & Evgeniy Meyke 230–231; Ljupco Smokovski 37 (b); Spauln 68 (t); Eline Spek 75, 253 (t), 253 (b), 324–325; Sklep Spozywczy 115 (br); Radovan Spurny 302 (b); Nikolay Starchenko 6; Debbie Steinhausser 11 (bl); Claudia Steininger 27 (r), 64 (l), 375; Vendla Stockdale 69 (t); Werner Stoffberg 86 (b); Gemmav D Stokes 158 (t); stoupa 254 (br); Kathleen Struckle 294–295; Studio Cactus 52 (t), 53 (cr), 53 (br), 57 (bl), 60 (b all), 61 (t), 61 (tc), 61 (c), 65 (bc), 65 (br), 120 (b), 126 (t), 141 (bl), 141 (br), 143 (b), 149 (b), 150 (t), 152 (t), 152 (b), 154 (t), 157 (bl), 157 (br), 158 (b), 162 (t), 162 (tr), 171 (t), 171 (b), 173 (b),175 (t), 175 (b), 179 (bl), 179 (br), 180 (all), 184 (t), 184 (b), 185 (bl), 185 (br), 188 (bl), 188 (br), 189 (b), 194 (bl), 194 (br), 198 (all), 199 (b), 204–205 (all), 206 (all), 210 (all), 215 (all), 234 (bl), 234 (br), 237 (b), 238 (t), 238 (b), 244 (t), 244 (b), 245 (tl), 245 (tr), 248–249 (all), 250, 251 (tr), 256, 260 (t), 260 (b), 261 (t), 262 (t), 263 (t), 268–269 (all), 271 (tr), 272–273, 274 (bl), 274 (br), 276 (b), 277 (l), 279 (b), 280–281 (all), 282 (l), 282 (r), 289 (b), 290–291 (all), 292 (b), 293 (bl), 293 (br), 296–297 (all), 299 (t), 304 (t), 305 (t), 305 (b), 306–307 (all), 309 (l), 309 (r), 313 (tl), 313 (tr), 315 (all), 318 (t), 320 (all), 322 (t), 322 (b), 323 (b), 326 (l), 326 (r), 328 (all), 340 (all), 347 (t), 351 (tl), 352 (all), 355 (l), 355 (r), 357 (t), 360 (t), 360 (r), 363 (bl), 368 (bl), 370 (bl), 370 (r); Lorraine Swanson 103 (b); Graham Taylor 64 (br); Albert H Teich 103 (tl); Cappi Thomson 11 (ca); Nikita Tiunov 383; Dragan Trifunovic 19 (b); Nikolai Tsvetkov 48 (t); Julie Turner 50–51; April Turner 56 (c); Hedser van Brug 88 (t), 195 (b), 218–219; Simone van der Berg 31 (t); Krissy VanAlstyne 63 (tl); Emily Veinglory 53 (bl); vnlit 138 (bl), 138 (br); Gert Johannes Jacobus Vrey 13; Jennifer A Walz 18 (b); Elliott Westacott 61 (bl), 72 (t); wheatley 65 (bl); Aaron Whitney 47 (b), 234 (tl); Andrew Williams 233 (t); Cindi Wilson 144–145; Wizdata Inc 130 (b); wojciechpusz 165 (b); Jun Xiao 384; Jeffrey Ong Guo Xiong 308 (bl); Lisa F Young 48 (b), 98–99; Lisa F Young 84–85; Ryhor M Zasinets 327 (t); Dusan Zidar 57 (br), 72 (b); zimmytws 262 (b); Artur Zinatullin 182 (br); Yan Zommer 30 (br) Zuzule 28 (b)
All other images © Tracy Morgan Animal Photography

COVER IMAGES: Front cover top from left to right: Claudia Steininger (1); Zuzule (2); Mary E Cioffi (3); Joy Brown (4). Front cover bottom from left to right: photos.com (1); Waldemar Dabrowski (2); Cindi Wilson (3); Jim Larson (4). Back cover top from left to right: Casey K Bishop (1); Johannes Flex (2); Alexan55 (3); Natalia Sinjushina & Evgeniy Meyke (4). Back cover bottom from left to right: Andrew Williams (1); Emily Sartoski (2); Laurie Lindstrom (3); NHPA (4)